EMANCIPATORY POLITICS:
A CRITIQUE

Edited by

STEPHAN FEUCHTWANG

AND ALPA SHAH

OPEN ANTHROPOLOGY COOPERATIVE PRESS

Open Anthropology Cooperative Press

Centre for Cosmopolitan Studies, 71 North Street, St Andrews,

Fife KY16 9AL Scotland, U.K.

http://openanthcoop.net/press/

First published in November 2015 by Open Anthropology
Cooperative Press

ISBN-10:1542490030

ISBN-13:978-1542490030

Cover illustration: "A Naxalite (Communist Party of India-
Maoist) camp in the forests of Jharkhand." Photograph by Alpa
Shah

CONTENTS

ACKNOWLEDGMENTS

This project emerged from a workshop on 'People's Movements: Strategy and Tactics' held in Oxford in June 2011. Unlike many such events, there was no ambition to publish; just a desire to learn from each other and from the movements we were discussing. But, over the two days we spent with each other, participants had the overwhelming feeling that we must publish some of the discussions. We are extremely grateful to our contributors for their enthusiasm and support of and to other participants in the workshop: David Gellner, Saroj Giri, Barbara Harriss-White, Feyzi Ismail, Steffen Jensen, George Kunnath, Savaldor Marti I Puig, Luisa Steur and Lewis Taylor. We are also grateful to George Kunnath for initially setting up the workshop; to Demeter Chanter in copy-editing the volume; and to Keith Hart's enthusiasm to publish this collection with the *Open Anthropology Cooperative Press*. Many thanks finally to Justin Shaffner of OAC Press for producing our text as an online publication. Funding was received from the Economic and Social Research Council of the UK.

Introduction

Chapter 1

EMANCIPATORY POLITICS: AN EMPIRICALLY GROUNDED CRITIQUE

Stephan Feuchtwang and Alpa Shah

We live in a world where capital has become ever more concentrated and predatory. A world of increasing inequality where a super-rich minority lives in shiny malls and gated communities with armed guards patrolling their borders incarcerating in reverse a vast mass of people living in slums on their doorsteps. Yet, the possibility of people coming together and mobilising to change the course of history to create a better future for all has come to seem almost implausible. In Euro-American debates, the demise of Soviet Russia in the 1990s and Maoist China's turn to capitalism have heralded a new era where organised change for a socialist future has been discredited as virtually dead. Instead, spaces of hope have been sought in the momentary euphoria of mass awakenings against state regimes, whether it is Occupy or the Arab Spring. In much of the world the critical lens of debate about emancipatory politics has turned away from class struggle and from organised change for a socialist future to social-media-fed mobilisations of ephemeral organisation, sometimes peaceful, occasionally violent.

This volume shows that organised emancipatory politics, in part or mainly reinforced by arms, is still very

1

much alive in a range of postcolonial states. By 'emancipatory politics' we mean political activities that aim to end exploitation and enhance participatory democracy through which leadership can be held to account on a daily as well as periodic basis, in the workplace and beyond. Whether it be India, Nepal, the Philippines, Peru or Columbia, long-standing armed movements aiming to seize and transform state power are still burning and working for a different future. In Euro-American debate it is easy to forget those movements – some of which have a more than forty-year history – of the Maoists in India or Nepal, FARC in Columbia, or the Communist Party of the Philippines. We focus here on movements which are still very much active as well as on movements of Marxist emancipatory change that achieved state power – the Mozambican case of Frelimo and the Sandinistas of Nicaragua – whose experiences shed an important critical light on those which are still in active struggle.

These cases have been chosen to illustrate a range of reasons for embarking on and sustaining armed struggle. Most are adaptations of Mao's Chinese revolutionary movement and its tenets, but others also refer to other revolutionary traditions. The selection is not meant to be comprehensive, but to focus on the reasons for armed emancipatory movements and the limitations that this mobilisation and its ties to Maoist teachings have placed on their emancipatory politics.

We take these emancipatory political movements seriously as forces of change in the contemporary world, but at the same time we also provide *critiques* of the tenets on which their politics are based, and the means they use to achieve their goals. We two are anthropologists; but our contributors are not all anthropologists – they come from a range of disciplinary backgrounds – yet they all share the basis of our aims in their analysis of the movements, and provide well-grounded critiques that do not denigrate these emancipatory projects. They take seriously their desire for a better world as not just a worthy, but also a sane cause.

Three inter-related themes emerge from this critical engagement.

The first theme is the challenging tension between mass organisation and the party in charge of an armed force. The involvement of people through mass organisations is crucial for the expansion of any movement. When faced with the necessity to take up arms in counter-violence against a repressive state, the party's organisation, leadership and discipline become important in maintaining the struggle. Further, the conduct of armed struggle opens its own territorial spaces of embryonic emancipation. The issue here is the two-way relation between army and party leadership, and the building of embryonic welfare and other 'state' organisations with people in their strongholds. The danger, which we see in varying degrees in all of these cases, is that the party (the leaders of the revolutionary struggle) substitutes itself for the base (the people who they live amidst and work for). A significant issue here is the extent to which inner party democracy allows for questioning and review of current strategy and tactics. Rethinking and critique too often stand the risk of being branded as revisionist, reformist or adventurist, of amounting to betrayal. Democratic centralism, crucial to unified leadership, can easily become an inflexible inability to accommodate different local conditions.

This tension between mass organisation and the party is a critical one and it raises the question of the relationship between democracy and emancipatory politics, our second theme. It is not just that too often autocracy replaces substantive democracy, that the party stops being accountable to the people it seeks to serve, but also the question of whether, and when, to participate in mainstream electoral politics and what the implications of doing this may be. The Indian Maoists, who boycott electoral politics, see their Nepali northern Maoist neighbours who have done so as having given up on emancipatory politics. Yet as shown by Anne de Sales in this volume, the Nepali Maoists at least succeeded – for some time – in leading previously marginalised groups who had never had a voice in the state into debates on the making of the new democratic Constitution. And, as argued by Dominique Caouette, selective participation in elections by the Communist Party of Philippines strengthened its movement.

Analysis of class, social issues and social forces is crucial to the aim of any movement of emancipatory politics as it determines the question of who is an enemy, who is a friend, and what kind of alliances are to be entertained in the struggle for emancipation. This is our third theme. As Bridget O'Laughlin points out in the context of Mozambique, it is not enough to take the 'poetry of the future' as the basis of emancipatory change because class relations shape the outcome of strategy, and understanding them is crucial to any politics of emancipation. When, as in the case of the Indian Maoists analysed in this volume by Bernard D'Mello, movements of emancipatory politics fail to undertake an adequate analysis, the risk is that they become isolated and outflanked by social forces they could not take into account. In these scenarios, revolutionary struggles fail to acknowledge conscious and unconscious aspirations, intentions, habits, and forms of association, organisation and joint action, all of them undergoing slow or faster change under transforming influences. This includes the changing means of forming ideas of a future, and their changing content, among those who are most exploited and oppressed. It includes their current modes of organisation – be they informal associations, or more formal organisations, of kinship, of ritual life, of electoral mobilisation, of work and of unions, and the communicative media they use and receive. It also includes their demands, whether they are for better social security and protection or for nationality and identity based claims. It is not just the 'poetry of the future,' but – as one of us has argued in relation to the Indian Maoists – 'the muck of the past' (Shah 2014) which matters to the shaping of new futures.

In sum, the following arguments run through every chapter. One is that emancipation from exploitation and for socialist democracy is a sane aim. Second is that armed defence against the most brutalising exploitation and state repression of protest is often a necessary strategy in pursuit of this aim but armed leadership has in many (but not all) instances become a politics of command removed from its bases and the organisation of the people upon whom the struggle relies and the leadership claims to represent. Third, reliance on models of class analysis and mobilisation from long gone conditions and other contexts has often led to inadequate appraisals of present conditions in particular contexts. Adequate class analysis must be the basis for the formation of alliances and assessment of conditions for working with organisations that are engaged in electoral politics, even though they may not share the same long-term aims.

This volume is entitled *Emancipatory Politics* because the movements examined in this book foreground the political at the expense of economic analysis. We turn to this lack of economic analysis later. But first we take up another problem that the chapters of the book address: incorporation into emancipatory politics of armed defence against extreme violence.

Violence and its Organisation

Politics is inextricably bound up with violence – whether politics is thought of as domination of people and territory or as resistance and efforts to end such domination. Any attempt to come to terms with the subject of emancipatory armed struggle must include the political programme of the armed struggle and how it aspires to form alliances that can transform state power into the capacity to emancipate the exploited and oppressed whose forces it leads, or professes to lead. Armed struggle usually starts from situations of exploitation and oppression that include the exertion of extreme violence, against which armed defence is thought to be a necessary if only a provisional and locally limited liberation.

The classic point of reference for a national as well as a class liberation are the writings of Mao on revolutionary guerrilla warfare and how it must turn into the capacity to wage a war of standing armies in order to seize state power. By the 1940s, the Chinese Communist Party, led by Mao, with its headquarters in its northern Chinese base in Yan'an consolidated the various analyses of the possibilities for a revolutionary movement of protracted war in China. It was a 'People's War' to set up a state with the power of what was called 'New Democracy'. This strategy has recently been summarised by Lin Chun:

> In the Chinese Marxist conception, this revolution, led by a communist party, is defined as 'new democratic' because its maximum programme contained a socialist ambition. It is thus categorically distinguished from the classical bourgeois revolutions which, while having a democratic aspect, only paved the way for capitalist development. The 'new democratic' revolution relied on a worker-peasant alliance as well as a 'united front' that also included the national bourgeoisie, the progressives and patriots from intermediate social groups, and even an 'enlightened' gentry. The united front was seen as one of the 'three magic weapons' of revolutionary success, along with party construction and armed struggle.

> A 'land revolution' in a 'semi-colonial, semi-feudal' society appears problematic to anyone who believes that a large proletariat is needed for any socialist transition. But they are mistaken, both empirically and conceptually, in relation to the Chinese case. In the first half of the twentieth century, China's relatively small working class was significantly larger in size and stronger in political capacity than the weak national bourgeoisie. This asymmetry is

explained by the substantial foreign presence in the Chinese economy: workers in foreign-controlled factories were a growing class, while domestic industrialists and merchants were a shrinking one, squeezed by foreign capital. The industrial working class became an independent and vital revolutionary force, taking such tremendously daring actions as the Hunan miners' movements (1922-25), the Guangzhou-Hong Kong general strikes (1925-26) and the three Shanghai workers' uprisings (1926-27). Even after the counterrevolutionary slaughter of 1927, despite their devastating losses, workers became the core of the red army and urban underground party work. In addition, as exemplified by the founders of Marxism themselves, the communist intellectuals were an organic component of the proletariat. 'Petty bourgeois' intellectuals drawn to the Chinese revolution had to temper themselves through guerrilla warfare and grassroots work. These locally specific class factors, the party, workers and sympathetic intellectuals, were what in turn made it possible to educate and organize the poor and middle peasants, who were crucial in enabling the revolution to recruit soldiers and constantly defend and expand its rural bases. (2015: 26-27)

The chapter by Bernard D'Mello takes up the application of this analysis in India, referring to the key texts of Mao. We cite Lin Chun here because of the key points she makes about the proletariat and the urban bases of the Chinese revolution. One is the counterpoint to the strategy of setting up rural bases and building from there an armed organisation that can surround the cities where, first the occupying power Japan had its centres of state power and then (after 1945) the Nationalist Guomindang government resumed its own counter-revolutionary bases. The ongoing work of underground urban organisation is vital both as a source of leaders and for the fermentation of forces that will welcome the revolutionary army. The other is the necessity of a united front, which is an alliance built to fight colonial and semi-colonial powers of capitalist concentration in the cities and in the extractive and processing industries. In other words, the Maoist rural base is part of an alliance of classes that are anti-imperialist in the two senses that Lenin had identified: the formation of monopoly and in particular finance capitalism and the support for its investments in the course of colonial expansion and the local subordination of formally independent states such as that of Tsarist Russia or, in the case of China, the Guomindang and its warlord allies responsible for the anti-socialist 'counter-revolutionary slaughter' of workers and their union leaders in Shanghai. The achievements of the Guomindang did include curbing but not eradication of imperialist powers, the setting up of secular government and some institutions of electoral democracy, as well as a degree of prosperity and growth for an indigenous capitalist class. But that was a limit beyond which the socialist new democracy sought to and did go, with state and collective ownership of land and the privileging of the working class and a peasantry turned into a rural working class in cooperative joint ownership of land, at least until the disaster of the Great Leap Forward and the famine in which some thirty-five million farmers died.

Following what they understand to be Mao's tenets on guerrilla warfare, as the chapters in this book show, the partisan – the guerrilla fighting for a particular political ideology – in many parts of the world became the soldier fighting the revolutionary war against the violent oppression of the states they were in. As Gautam Navlakha's chapter points out, Carl Schmitt (1964), had noticed that following the two World Wars, belligerent acts around the world began to assume a distinctly partisan character and that they were carried out by non-state actors. In contrast to battlefield war and regular armies, the partisan was characterised by irregular guerrilla warfare, intense political engagement, tactical versatility and speed, and was tied to an idea of homeland. Taking up this emancipatory, class-based warfare directly, Schmitt considered Mao's revolutionary war to be a key example.

Such revolutionary war – whether it is the Maoists in India or Frelimo in Mozambique – is fought against an absolute enemy, the international class enemy, and it is therefore a war of extinction, to destroy the old social order and establish the embryos of the revolutionary order. Schmitt's theory is based on his political theology, which is that the ultimate decision of a state, bearing the sovereignty of its laws, is the declaration of an enemy and of a state of 'exception' or emergency suspension of law to combat that enemy, which is either another state or a force both within and without its borders. For Schmitt, this is suspension of the normality of states which, when the Congress of Vienna (1815) ended the Napoleonic wars, had established laws of warfare – of battlefield war and civilian life in the war of regular armies in uniform – that upheld fiscal and national territorial sovereignty in Europe. In this context a new kind of war, partisan war, is necessary and legitimate if it is to overthrow a repressive dominant state order. Both sides declare the enemy within to be an object to be extinguished.

Partisans are not visible. They fight among civilians irregularly. State military strategists have, as Schmitt points out, classically declared that it is necessary to fight like a partisan to combat the partisan. Mao's writings develop partisan armed combat into a revolutionary war. To combat it, state forces become as absolute and ruthless as the partisans. The new warfare is absolute warfare.

Schmitt's theory, while decriminalising and legitimising the partisan war as a just war, has its limits. It does not allow us to see the problems inherent in partisan warfare. He does alert us to see the stakes: to create a new order demands the destruction of the old order and thenceforth to create conditions that eliminate the possibility of its return, which is also how Mao Zedong saw the necessity of war. Long after the partisan army and its Party had established their own state power in China it was still necessary to wage war against what he called 'revisionism,' an enemy within as well as without, just as the partisan was both of these for the previous state power.

Schmitt underplays the strategic calculation of revolutionary partisans and their leadership in deciding who, in any one situation, is the enemy and therefore among whom and with whom the partisan can move and form an alliance. This is one crucial element on which our book focuses. Schmitt's limited terms suggest that partisan strategy alternates between two possibilities. In one the partisan armed forces and their leadership, the party, seek to be recognised as a legal and legitimate army for a peace negotiation that is provisional from the point of view of absolute revolutionary aims and therefore itself provisionally recognises a state or parts of a state as legitimate. In the other, it recognises no such legality and demands of itself and its forces a sacrificial fight to the death. The first is what preoccupies us. Declarations of who is the enemy and therefore who are allies either enable or isolate the revolutionary party.

Armed struggle and its small-scale realms of normative violence are 'emancipatory' not only in relation to the state and the vigilante or other less formally organised violence, what we call for short 'gangs,' against which it erects a defence. It establishes a different peace, whose (violently sanctioned) norms include institutions of welfare that had not been available to those it has now released from state and gang violence, discrimination and entrapment. But they are small in scale compared to the necessary aims of these armed struggles, which are at least as territorially broad as the states against which they are set.

To bring to such situations an organisation of armed force and its ideology carries two risks. One risk is the treatment of the subjects of violent defence as passive, from whom there is nothing to be learned except how to turn them into revolutionary forces. This was the tendency sometimes condemned by the Chinese Communist Party as 'commandism' but at most times was enacted by it in rectification campaigns (Dutton 2005). The other risk is to bring down upon them renewed violence from state forces and private gangs.

What is unavoidable is that release from the perpetration of licensed extra violence does require establishing a new, differently organised realm of peace and the violence that sanctions it. That does not mean that armed force is the only way to establish such a realm of liberation. Each situation is specific and requires its own politics of liberation. But, at a more general level of theorising, we have to interrogate not just the adequacy of the political programmes of armed movements, but also whether armed struggle has its own political dynamic and consequences. Our answers are based on empirical examples, including those elaborated in this book.

Gautam Navlakha and Bernard D'Mello, in addressing the internal political dynamics of armed struggle in the case of the revolutionary struggle of the Communist Party of India (Maoist), show the dangers of the dynamic of violence turning into commandism and to a diminution of the Maoist mass line, which in theory but seldom in practice is to learn from the people that the Party purports to lead. Too often the slow and painful task of mass organisation and mass mobilisation is reduced to only the military needs of the war. The result can be brutal killing of men and women, on the assumption that they have become class enemies or informers, thereby undermining their mass base and alienating potential allies.

This diminution of defensive margins is the fate of all the armed struggles described here. The main question is what potential for extension and emancipation each retains, in alliance with other political forces.

Liberation or Self-determination and Democracy

One major force of alliance for all of the movements in this book is that of religious, linguistic or ethnic minorities, some of which are struggles for self-determination coalescing around ideas of national liberation. This, as the chapters here show, is another hornet's nest for emancipatory struggles.

Whereas in India the Maoist-inspired movement has in recent years retreated to the remote and impoverished forested hills of tribal areas, in Nepal the crucible of the movement was such territories. In both cases the revolutionary war based on class struggle meant setting up bases in impoverished areas where armed defence and its extension inevitably became involved in minority liberation struggles. The Nepali Maoists, as Ismail and Shah (2015) argue, have paid much greater attention to the relationship between class struggle and ethnicity in their struggle. Anne de Sales' chapter here analyzes this relationship and shows how the Maoists became ethnicised by a politics of nationality and successfully incorporated these minorities. She shows how, though it was their economic marginality and not their ethnic/cultural marginalisation that incited the Kham-Magars to join the Maoist movement, over time the latter's lack of attention to the cultural nuances of the Kham-Magars politicised their ethnic identities. After using these struggles for autonomy as a base for achieving the downfall of the monarchy, the Maoist party in Nepal entered government and established electoral politics, but then severely neglected their original mass (ethnic) base beyond acknowledging that it had already enabled their participation in national politics.

Meanwhile, the Indian Maoist-inspired emancipatory struggle lives on underground but has recently too often been turned into an ethnic movement. Another potential consequence of focussing on the military needs of their struggle above all else, as D'Mello and Shah (2013) have argued, in contrast to the Latin American revolutionary debates, is that not enough attention is being paid to the relationship between class struggle and ethnic politics, with the danger that the movement could be reduced to identity politics alone and can never expand beyond the hilly forests of tribal India.

Allying with wider forces to increase the scope of the emancipatory struggle is inextricably tied to the thorny issue of participation in electoral politics. While ensuring that inner party democracy will remain a key issue in such struggles, the degree of engagement in electoral politics is a bone of contention. Caouette describes the Philippino Maoists as having successfully immersed themselves in electoral party lists. Meanwhile, the Indian Maoists, fearing the consequences of a factionalism that strategic use of electoral politics could cause within the movement, moved participation in elections away from tactical considerations (that could vary according to context) to a strategy of avoiding it at all costs.

Perhaps they were right to do so. Party politics, to put it simply, corrupts. This is not only shown by how the Nepali Maoists were undermined once they engaged in democratic politics, but also in the case of the Sandinistas in Nicaragua. Partially inspired by Marx, Lenin and Mao but taking their primary inspiration from home-grown Latin American revolutionary traditions, after successfully taking state power in Nicaragua, the Sandanista Party found itself engaged in electoral politics. However, as Harry E. Vanden shows in his chapter here, participation in electoral politics entailed the Sandinistas losing touch with their original bases. The loss of revolutionary momentum associated with participation in electoral politics poses a real dilemma. But, as Vanden argues, mass mobilisation was as crucial as armed struggle in the overthrow of the dictatorial Somoza government, in particular through the fusion, more than just alliance, of Marxism and liberation theology and the popular church, fostering participatory democracy. Once in power the Sandinista government instituted local and class-based mass organisations of participatory democracy that made policy through a Council of State. But the Sandanista Party remained separate and kept a traditional form of democratic centralism. It ruled through a national junta in which the majority were Sandinistas. It had to maintain the organisation of armed force to fight the contras, backed by the USA. But the struggle was fatally compromised within the country when the Sandinistas, to placate Western democrats, eventually opted for a form of representative democracy in the 1984 and 1990 elections, at first winning and then losing against opposition parties. This electoral process excluded the mass organisations it had helped to foster. Thus the Sandanista Party became less revolutionary as it transformed a practice of substantive democracy and betrayed its progenitor Sandino's inspiration. But the initial example remains for future inspiration.

The Economy and its Organisation

One of the greatest failings of the emancipatory political struggles described in this book is the inadequacy of their economic analyses and of relations between their own and surrounding economies. These might have illuminated the constraints and possibilities of the new, less exploitative forms that they fostered.

'Socialism' is an over-simplified term to describe the aim and its approximation in base areas. How political and economic democracy could be promoted not only within the base areas but in the rest of India is beyond the Indian Maoists, as the chapters by Bernard D'Mello and Gautam Navlakha show. D'Mello in particular highlights the inadequacy of the Indian Maoists' economic analysis of their struggle. Despite recent sympathetic critiques that India is not semi-colonial – not even in the guerrilla zones – (see Basu and Das 2013; Shah 2013), these Maoists have stuck to the Mao-inspired Chinese formula that India is (still) semi-feudal and semi-colonial and so what is needed is a democratic revolution after a protracted revolutionary war. D'Mello argues that this analysis has disabled extension of their politics to wider parts of the country, which, as we have pointed out with the help of Lin Chun above, was always part of Chinese Communist Party practice under Mao.

There is a fascinating contrast between theory's inadequacy to generate strategic analysis and the elasticity of dogma to accommodate changing tactics without altering strategy. For example, as one of us has argued (Shah 2013), in the contemporary guerrilla zones of the Maoists in India, despite an overall analysis of India as semi-feudal, tactically the main war of the Maoists in these areas has not been against landlords but against the Indian state.

Similarly, in the Philippines extending the revolution beyond an officially declared semi-feudal, semi-colonial struggle is much more marked than in the Indian Maoists' case. Dominique Caouette's chapter shows the expansion of the Philippine Communist Party beyond the Maoist formulae, enabling it to make alliances and form powerful social movements outside its base areas. The Party's ideological leader is working from exile in Europe. This has enhanced the Philippino movement's international experience and skill in connecting with various anti-globalisation movements, making it possible, Caouette argues, for the revolution to appear quite contemporary and yet remain Maoist at its core. This movement has also been able to maintain solidarity with the Philippine diaspora that contributes financially and organisationally to its continuing persistence. Moreover, although there was internal criticism of exactly the kind made by D'Mello and Navlakha, rectification back towards the Maoist strategic line resulted in more coherent organisation *and*, crucially, effective participation in electoral politics. Maoist dogma was combined with a pragmatic strategy, despite the absence of an explicit political economic analysis derived from its strategic practice.

How economic democracy could be promoted within a country as a tactic within an electoral alliance in or out of government and how to reduce poverty there within a capitalist world economy is, however, a very tricky issue for most of the movements considered here. As Bridget

O'Laughlin puts it for Mozambique, Frelimo performed a dream of politics that should introduce the necessary economic magic, but instead destroyed the capacity to make economic strategy. She describes the complexity of agrarian class structures in the immediate pre- and post-independence periods, showing how Frelimo as a liberation movement addressed this complexity in its approach to production during the armed struggle and on assuming government. O'Laughlin traces various experiences in different rural areas that she engaged with, arguing that an increasingly repressive populist conception of a worker/peasant alliance looked at class relations purely as social groups that could be jurally redefined, particularly given the flight of so many settler farmers. Focusing on why state-farms under Frelimo were not able to recruit the workers they needed, this chapter provides a critical analysis of Frelimo's characterisation of Mozambique's political economy, showing how its agrarian projects were undermined by a lack of attention to the politics of production and especially by its inability to account for unproductive gendered labour. As she concludes, Frelimo 'had no strategy for addressing the ways that capitalist relations of production were embedded in the organisation of work, including non-commodified work. Its strategy for markets was to limit their functioning, not to reorganise the ways they continued to matter both for the state-farms and for the livelihood of rural people. Frelimo could not recognise ongoing class struggle in its planning processes and saw resistance as..."enemy action."' Here both political analysis and economic strategy reinforced each other in failure.

In contrast, the Revolutionary Armed Forces of Colombia-People's Army (FARC-EP) has maintained its base among small-holders including coca farmers and has expanded its struggle by maintaining a much more local interpretation of Marxism and Leninism. James Brittain reviews current accounts of its history and contemporary presence. He then provides his own analysis of their strategy, namely that they have gradually developed a separate power base and economy from that of the state and its capitalist economy, a situation that Lenin described as 'dual power,' or, in Gramsci's terms, a challenge to the hegemony of the ruling bloc. Based on his own visits, interviews and two recent documentary films, Brittain finds that, similarly to the Sendero areas in Peru, FARC, which raises taxes and controls processing and selling of coca, leads an economy of private small-holders, many still growing coca as their main crop, but also to some extent now diversifying into subsistence crops. He considers this to be successful preparation for eventual state power when the economy will be socialised.

How this might actually be realised in the greater economy of Columbia (or Peru) neither he nor FARC can say. But the new imperialism of financialised capitalism is an anti-political force, reducing rule to corporate executive standards and economies to the buying and selling of debt, including state finances. This new imperialism works through sub-contracting and creating dire poverty and super-exploitation on an unprecedented scale. All the more reason for emancipatory counter-violence. But this must include concerted action within a political process that extends capacities and competences for action. This places a premium on the courage to open and extend the space for thought, for listening, learning and judgement, for concerted action with others and not just fighting.

References

Basu, D. & D. Das 2013. The Maoist Movement in India: Some Political Economy Considerations. *Journal of Agrarian Change* 13: 3, 365-381.

D'Mello, B. & A. Shah 2013. Preface to *An Anthology of José Carlos Mariátegui* (trans. H. E. Vanden & M. Becker). Delhi: Cornerstone Publications.

Dutton, M. 2005. *Policing Chinese Politics: A History.*

Durham, NC and London: Duke University Press.

Ismail, F. & A. Shah 2015. Class Struggle, the Maoists and the Indigenous Question in Nepal and India. *Economic and Political Weekly.*

Lin, C. 2015. The Language of Class in China. *Socialist Register* 51, 24-53.

Schmitt, C. 2007 [1964]. *The Theory of the Partisan: Intermediate commentary on the concept of the political.* New York, NY: Telos Press Publishing.

Shah, A. 2010. *In the Shadows of the State: Indigenous Politics, Environmentalism and Insurgency in Jharkhand, India.* Durham NC, and London: Duke University Press.

_____ 2013a. The Agrarian Question in a Maoist Guerrilla Zone: Land, Labour and Capital in the forests and hills of Jharkhand, India. *Journal of Agrarian Change* 13: 3, 424-450.

_____ 2013b. The Muck of the Past: Revolution and Social Transformation in Maoist India. *Journal of Royal Anthropological Institute* 20: 2, 337-356.

Part 1

Armed Movements in India

Chapter 2

THE PEOPLE'S WILL TO CHANGE TO CHANGING THE WILL OF THE PEOPLE: REFLECTIONS ON THE INDIAN MAOIST STRUGGLE

Gautam Navlakha

Abstract *Based on a fresh look at Marx's and Engels' and some contemporary theoreticians' writings on war, on an intimate acquaintance with the history of the Indian Maoist movement, and on internal party documents, this chapter conducts a critical appraisal of the military philosophy and practices of the Indian Maoists. Armed struggle is a necessity in situations of extreme state violence where the Maoists have established themselves in defence and for the emancipation of the violated. The author shares his detailed knowledge of some of the Maoist guerrilla zones. Within this account his critical attention is drawn to the lack of judicial process whereby those accused of betrayal are summarily executed. This and other aspects of the movement's military strategy has alienated the leadership from its own base, in its strong areas and elsewhere, and has undermined developing mass organisations. 'It is people's will to change that must prevail over attempts to change the will of the people. This is the challenge posed to Maoists in India.'*

As the single biggest internal security threat, according to the Indian Government, the Communist Party of India (Maoist) is today placed at a crossroads. The Party owes its resurgence to the strategy of Protracted People's War (PPW). However, recent setbacks suffered by the Maoists also highlight the problems they face. Their success in war, but setbacks in mass mobilisation and mass struggle point towards a developing hiatus between armed struggle and mass struggle which now impacts their Protracted People's War. While mass mobilisation requires patient and painstaking work, armed conflict requires both mass struggle and territorial expansion. How prepared is the Party subjectively to confront the Indian State and to mobilise the masses in a context where reckless killing and the alienation of potential allies make it difficult to expand outside, as well as sustain itself inside, forested hill areas? I look here at the concept of Protracted People's War as it is practiced by the CPI(Maoist) and examine the challenges that arise out of the dialectical interplay between theory and practice.

> What has been called the "Marxist dialectical tradition" is the form of theoretical structuring which runs all through the evolution of Marxism, with Marx himself as its chief representative. At the heart and centre of this problematic lies the determining role of the dialectical method ... There can be no theory that is not also practice, and vice versa. The basis for Marxist methodology is praxis, practical work ... Practice is only a starting point. Dialectics is conceptual ... Concepts are no longer the phenomena, the separate aspects of, and the external relations of things; they grasp the essence, the totality and internal relations of things. (Lew 1975: 129-131)

There is a 'vein of political prudery' (Galle 1978: 67)[1] in Marxist scholarship where matters of war and its relevance for revolutionary transformation are concerned. Marxist scholars are reluctant to study wars or engage in analysis of military affairs and instead undermine Marxism by reducing class struggle to competitive electoral politics in pursuit of government power rather than seeking to replace one system of class rule with another through armed seizure of political power.

This 'prudery' is also linked to generalising the specific experience of the socialist movement in Western Europe, which eventually embraced class reconciliation and gave tacit support to colonialism.

Engels published more on military matters than on any other subject. Both Marx and Engels favoured some wars and opposed others. Wars which were seen as accelerating social change could play a progressive role. Armed members of the working class were held up as heroes. Engels, in particular, took Carl Von Clausewitz's work seriously and was attracted to the idea that war 'is not an activity of the will exerted upon inanimate matter ... but against a living and re-acting force' (Clausewitz cited in Galle 1978: 43).

With the triumph of Bismarck's militarism and the suppression of the Paris Commune, Marx and Engels turned their attention to preparation for war between European powers and worked to forestall the outbreak of a world war. For Engels, the prospect of a world war was deeply disturbing for he feared both the destruction it would bring about and the possibility that 'it would set jingoism going everywhere' (Engels cited in Galle 1978: 92).

Engels was no longer unequivocal in seeing opportunities for revolutionary transformation in the impending war. Marxism's ambiguity about war draws much on these anxieties and proposals of Engels which directly addressed the challenge posed to socialists in Europe towards the end of the 19th century.

Some of Lenin's and Mao's seminal contributions make their mark here. They found insights in Clausewitz's writings that helped to conceptualise revolutionary warfare. For Clausewitz, as for other reformers in his circle in early 19th century Germany, guerrilla warfare was pre-eminently a political matter in the highest sense, having an almost revolutionary character (Galle 1978). Creative application of Clausewitz's theory to the concrete reality of Russia or China helped revolutionise Marxist thinking about war. Lenin, and later Mao, took his ideas of war as a political instrument and found them compatible with their project of revolutionary transformation.

Clausewitz's great contribution was to recognize irregulars and insurgents as a legitimate warring party. Like other reformers in Germany then, for Clausewitz guerrilla war was part of the theory of war. While war as a continuation of politics applied to all wars, the political character of war determined whether it was to be an Absolute War or a Real War.[2] The idea of an Absolute War aimed at disarming or destroying the enemy was read by Marx, Engels, Lenin and Mao as class war conducted with what Clausewitz defined as 'absolute enmity' (Galle 1978). In both war and politics, identifying and choosing friends and enemies, deciding on absolute versus relative enmity and therefore real war, in which war can be contained or regulated, became of critical importance. When Mao Zedong (1938) stated in his lecture 'On Protracted War' that 'politics is war without bloodshed while war is politics by bloodshed,' he was suggesting that politics is a continuum of which war is one part. Carl Schmitt points out that what Lenin learned from Clausewitz 'was not just the famous formula of war as the continuation of politics. It involved the recognition that in the age of revolution the distinction between friend and enemy is the primary distinction, decisive for war as for politics. Only revolutionary war is a true war for Lenin, because it derives from absolute enmity. Everything else is a conventional game' (2004: 35). According to Schmitt '(t)he question, however, is whether the enmity can be contained and regulated, that is, whether it represents relative or absolute enmity' (2004: 42).

Therefore, for Schmitt, the issue is 'about the quantitative proportion of military action to be conducted by a regular army relative to other methods of class warfare that are not openly military. Mao finds an exact number: revolutionary war is nine tenths non-open, non-regular war and just one-tenth open military war' (2004: 42). However, according to Galle, 'wars are not just politics by other means, war is politics where its aim, methods and intensity change as it proceeds' (1978: 75). Therefore, how one conducts warfare is of critical importance because it influences the desired political objective.

The Indian Maoists are at present in what they describe as a defensive phase of Protracted People's War, a stage which aims to build and organize popular consciousness in order to mobilise people to spearhead a mass struggle as the war progresses. Thus, trying to understand revolutionary warfare requires us to take the politics of war seriously in order to analyse whether and how the Protracted People's War is fulfilling its objectives.

A caveat is necessary here. The nature of the Protracted People's War, indeed even its causation, does not rest with the Maoists alone. The war that the Indian State carries out is also decisive. In the document 'Doctrine for Sub Conventional Operations,' the Indian Army (2006) speaks of sub-conventional operations as the *predominant* form of warfare.' The distinction between fighting the 'enemy' and 'fighting one's own people' is vast. There is a blurring of distinctions between the concepts of front and rear; strategic and tactical; combatants and non-combatants. Therefore, for these operations the document points out that there is a need to change a soldier's mind-set from fighting the 'enemy' in a conventional conflict, for which he is trained, to fighting his 'own people.'

The document states that '... the military operations should aim firstly, at *neutralizing all hostile elements* in the conflict zone that oppose or retard the peace initiatives and secondly, at *transforming the will and attitudes of the* people ... The endeavour should be *to bring about a realization* that fighting the government is a 'no win' situation and that their anti-government stance will only delay the return of peace and normalcy. Therefore, *distancing from the terrorists is in their own interest and the only plausible course of action*. However, the manifestation of *such a realization can take from a couple of years to decades as attitudes take time to form and to change*'(Indian Army 2006, my emphasis).[3]

Since the Indian army's brutal policy forms the bedrock of all counter-insurgency operations, the implication is that the military fights a prolonged war of suppression. Because transforming the will and attitudes of the people is key to understanding the objective behind military suppression, 'Absolute War' is the State's preference.

The Context

Armed struggle by communist revolutionaries in India has a long history starting with what is popularly called the Telengana Uprising in 1946 which lasted until 1951. After 1951, the former Communist Party surrendered its arms and participated in elections. However, sections of the Party were discontented with this policy shift and following the Naxalbari uprising of 1967 some Party veterans broke away to form CPI(ML). Fragmentation of the Naxalbari movement began in the 1970s. Towards the 1990s those who still subscribed to armed struggle drew closer, while those opposed to it began to participate in elections. Eventually, through a merger of various parties, the CPI(Maoist) emerged in 2004.

Since 2009, a series of crackdowns and arrests made by security agencies across India have resulted in the Maoists suffering reverses, while showing how rapidly Maoists could spread across the country. In this sense, critics were wrong to claim that the Maoist strategy of Protracted People's War was leading nowhere. In the Jangalmahal region of West Bengal, the Maoists emerged as a strong popular fighting force just as they did in the Dumka area of Jharkhand, both new to mobilisation. In politico-military terms, meticulously planned looting of armories as well as jail raids to free prisoners showed that they were capable of moving an armed force of between 200 and 500 guerrilla soldiers across a large territory. This required training a team drawn from different units for several months, an operation impossible without a social base in those territories. No longer were the Maoists a rag-tag guerrilla band, but an army in the making. In all these areas, the Maoists have also been actively engaged in building public assets such as ponds and roads as well as organising work teams to develop agriculture and to provide elementary health and education services (Navlakha 2010).

Drawing on the CPI(Maoist) (2007b) document 'Strategy and Tactics of the Indian Revolution,' Chakrabarty and Kujur list the four principal characteristics of India's revolutionary war as: '(a) uneven economic and political development and the semi-colonial and semi-feudal character of Indian Society; (b) The enemy is big and powerful having centralized state machinery and a well-equipped army; (c) The Communist Party, the guerrilla army and the agrarian revolutionary movement in India are still weak and (d) Our country is a prison house of nationalities where some nationalities are engaged in bitter struggles against the Indian state to achieve their right to self-determination' (2010: 73).

The same document points out that, given 'the vastness of the countryside, the inadequacy of the transport and communication system and the isolation of the remote countryside from the military centres, and above all, the inadequacy of the reactionary forces in comparison to the vastness of the country and the population ... can transform the vast tracts of the countryside into red resistance areas, guerrilla zones, guerrilla bases and liberated areas by making use of the favourable terrain which is abundant in some regions of the Indian countryside'(CPI(Maoist) 2007b).

The document goes on to say that 'guerrilla bases will constitute the focal points within the guerrilla zones for the development of a strong party, a strong people's liberation army and a united front while, at the same time, creating favourable conditions for the establishment of liberated areas, expanding the political power in waves and quickening the tempo of the revolution. As the new political power in the guerrilla bases goes on stabilizing, changes should be brought about in the production relations while intensifying the agrarian revolution' (CPI(Maoist) 2007b).[4]

While the Party does not possess 'liberated areas' it does have 'guerrilla bases' and how they consolidate their position there is thus critical to understanding the concept of area-wise seizure of power.

Area-wise Seizure of Power

Here the principal driving force is to gradually exercise control in a specific geographical area so that the nucleus of a parallel administration and the foundations of a new state are laid. However, it is necessary to select suitable geographical locations which are hilly, forested and where the presence of the State is weak. These areas need not be contiguous. There could even be a vast plain area splitting one 'guerrilla zone' from another. Besides, penetration by the Indian State covers a much larger territory and it is confined to a shrinking area as imperialist globalisation seeks newer and cheaper sources of minerals and comes into conflict with people fighting to retain control over their common resources.

If this strategy requires expansion into new areas, what should be its nature? Should party units be equated with guerrilla squads or political mobilisation balanced with guerrilla activities? The concept of 'area wise seizure of power' has some shortcomings when it is applied in India.

The political report of the 9th Congress of the CPI(Maoist) (2007c) was concerned that there were areas where 'grassroots Party organization is weak with insignificant party units at the village level. Some states have formed the party units at the village level but they are non-functional. In many areas *our party activity is still squad centred*. This makes the masses passive supporters and dependent on the squads for taking up struggles and in solving the issues at the village level.'

Another CPI(Maoist) document called *New Circular on Rectification* (undated but issued after the Ninth Congress of the Party in 2007) is important. Rectification campaigns are an integral part of Maoist practice where mistakes are addressed and corrected through a system of criticism. The fact that this document was released after the 2007 Party Congress emphasises its importance.

The document states:

a) In some areas, the lands occupied from landlords in the past are lying fallow due to government repression; when the landlords try to sell these lands, the rich peasants and middle peasants are purchasing them. On such occasions, instead of bringing pressure through the agricultural labourers and poor peasants, who occupied those lands, on those who purchased the lands and stopping the sales, the squads themselves have been thrashing the rich and middle peasants who purchased the lands.

b) In the struggle for the eradication of bad habits like liquor consumption, educating the people with a long term view is lacking; in the struggle to obstruct the manufacture of arrack, instead of rallying the people, especially the women, prominence is being given to squad actions only. Physical punishments are being imposed disregarding class basis.

c) When problems arise in man-woman relations, especially in matters relating to marriage, judgments are being given without taking into view the social problems women face.

d) In various kinds of people's 'Panchayats' instead of listening to the versions of both sides apart from gathering the needed information from others in the villages also, one sided judgments are being delivered, under the effect of sectarianism.

e) When some among the people commit mistakes, when they oppose our mass organisation, or when they are suspected to be working as informers, punishments much beyond their wrongs are being imposed. (CPI(Maoist) undated)

Note the criticism of relying on squad actions instead of mass mobilisation to deal with class issues in areas dominated by the Party. Loss or gain of territory need not be a major deterrent against PPW if subjective forces remain intact. But it does cause problems if, in their areas of control, either the subjective forces are weak or themselves become a cause for concern.

Another report from the Bihar-Jharkhand Special Area Committee on Rectification (CPI(Maoist) 2004-2005) is a candid indictment of certain practices that emerged in *some* areas:

In recent years, large scale relief and reform programmes launched by the government have created a huge battery of contractors and middle-men in the rural areas. They are the social basis of various groups of ruling class parties. Locally, they maintain links with organizers (comrades at zone and even higher levels), appease them, assure block officials and engineers that they can 'manage' the 'new government' and get hold of contracts. During polls, these are the elements who wean away people to polling stations. *That relations with such type of contractors have been maintained by party organizers is a matter of concern.* Some of our comrades use such contractors not only for various works, but also the most secret work of the Party, and they also share their joys and sorrows. Tiffs between contractors over this or that contract have become a cause for contradiction among our cadres. Among cadres ill-feeling arises as they take sides between the contractors; different contractors even take recommendation letters of their 'protector' Party comrades to Block development officials and engineers in order to win in the competition for contracts. For example in Chatra, the so called contradiction between Yadavs and Ganjhus is not a contradiction between toiling masses of these two castes, but between contractors and middle-men of these castes.

Among the recommendations the report calls for is one that Party members do not enter into any 'obligation from contractors' unless it is 'first discussed in the concerned committee' (CPI(Maoist) 2004-2005). It calls for warning and then expelling cadres found to be violating the Party's rule against hobnobbing with contractors and middle-men unless authorised, within limits set by the higher committees.

Concurrently, another issue becomes important. In order to maintain the CPI(Maoist)'s political control over an area it has to decide how it will tackle those who hold opinions different from theirs. Let us consider executions. Maoists claim to have a Constitution for their Janatana Sarkar (People's Government) (CPI(Maoist) 2007a).[5] Under Article 5(a) certain guidelines are laid down for carrying out death sentences. It says that before the People's Court implements a death sentence the local people's government has to obtain permission from the higher courts. Thus summary executions and arbitrary acts were to be contained. However, both Jharkhand-Bihar and West Bengal have reported an increase in summary executions.

It is worth noting, however, that unlike the recklessness that prevailed in Jangalmahal of West Bengal, in Jharkhand there have been comparatively fewer such killings.

By their own account, in the Jangalmahal area, 52 Communist Party (Marxist) or CPM members were killed in just the first seven months of 2009 (Koteswar Rao 2009). Furthermore, these figures do not cover the period from November 2008 to November 2011. It is claimed by the former ruling party, the CPM, that from 2009 to 2011, two hundred and ten of their members were executed by the Maoists (CPI(Marxist) 2012). Numbers apart, what were the charges against those executed? We have only vague explanations that these victims were all cruel and corrupt, so-called 'people's enemies.' So how do we know if the killings of CPM members were actually the execution *of political opponents* or the elimination *of informers* who had committed heinous crimes? Maoists in Jangalmahal appeared to be oblivious to the need for circumspection lest blood-letting rebound on them by creating a constituency of aggrieved people. Kinship and other affiliations can become fertile grounds for mobilising those who are hostile towards Maoists to become pawns in the hands of Government forces.

Take Niyamat Ansari's[6] killing on 2 March 2011. He was engaged in enforcing entitlement under the National Rural Employment Guarantee Scheme in the state of Jharkhand. His suspicious activities were brought to the Party's attention and he was issued a notice to appear before the 'people's court.' While charges against him were serious, including one of settling people on forest land for a price, these in no way deserved a death penalty. But after a summary *trial,* he was beaten with a rifle butt and later died.

So does this example mean that the Janatana Sarkar Constitution is followed only selectively? Is a summary trial not the antithesis of a just procedure, which the Maoists claim for their People's Court? Did it not require an inquiry by the Party into its own practice given that it was a summary trial and he was beaten to death? Instead the Party waited for pressure to mount before ordering an inquiry after six months. Ansari's killing generated a campaign against the Party and became a bone of contention when united programmes were being contemplated in Jharkhand. Participants demanded an explanation for this killing before agreeing to come together to highlight some common concerns.

Another example is how the Maoists responded to the killing of their cadres by the Bihar police who were informed of their whereabouts by members of the Koda tribe in the Jamui district. Here, partial mobilisation appears to have generated caste-based antagonisms in which arms were used against disadvantaged groups. In February 2010, 11 tribals, including women and children, were killed by Maoist squads, 50 others were injured and 36 houses burnt down in the Phulwaria-Kudasi (Korasi) village, creating great upheaval. This event was steeped in local political conflicts, which reflected caste tensions. Kudasi village was not Maoist controlled, although the Maoists were in the forests nearby and had the support of neighbouring villages. This was mainly because the Koda tribals there benefitted from the government's watershed programmes, and a member of their community had won the local election for chief of the Panchayat. Moreover, the Maoist cadres in this area were predominately from a different caste, the Yadavs and the Ravidasis, contributing to the hostility between them and the Kodas.

A caste-based schism between local communities and the Maoists in the Jamui district was behind the killing on July 2, 2011 of a tribal assistant sub-inspector, Lukas Tete. He was one of four police personnel taken hostage by the Maoists and was killed while Yadav sub-inspectors, who were also taken hostage, were freed. While mobilising people to fight for justice remains an important objective for the Maoists, in the exigencies of war, local caste conflicts (here between Yadav Maoist cadres and tribal villagers or the police) appear to take precedence over a struggle which ought to rise above caste divisions.

If the Party's presence in an area is weak, support for its politics, which are meant to protect and encourage the poor to organise themselves for their own emancipation, gets stunted and divisions among the poor lead them to occupy opposing sides. This creates a fissure which can end up harming the movement, as was the case in Jamui. So why and how did they fail to win over Koda tribals in Jamui? How and why did differences with a 'social activist' get out of hand? And why were so many killings passed off as of 'informers' in Jangalmahal when the Party could not even document their crimes? If the Party can admit to some faults, it can be self-critical and correct itself.

It is true that the pent up fury of the oppressed is at times difficult to contain (Rajkumar 2010) or partially true, but this is a limited explanation when, as we saw with the Jamui massacre, the victims also belonged to the oppressed classes. What sense does it make to kill one section of the oppressed in order to satisfy another section baying for blood? Party cadres have to stand up against the very people they mobilise, lest reckless or vendetta killings ensue in the name of fighting 'the class enemy.' In this sense it is a political lapse. The presence or absence of a CPI(Maoist) unit is not a mechanical thing. The task of mobilising people for a revolutionary cause, carrying out work designed to help the 'people's economy,' ensuring participation of people in the task of improving their economy and inspiring them to join the CPI(Maoist) and becoming a guerrilla fighter etc. becomes possible as a result. What is actually happening only widens differences between an oppressed people. This also undercuts the policy of area wise seizure of power where winning the support of the oppressed people matters most if the CPI(Maoist)'s control over an area is to be consolidated.

The Limits of Armed Struggle

If we look at areas where the Party was confident of expanding, its prospects now appear shaky because areas of influence have been lost and the ranks of their political cadres depleted due to killings and arrests. Arrests of Party leaders and cadres are not only due to informers and the intelligence agencies determinedly pursuing them, but also to the erosion of their bases and declining mass struggles in some areas because of over-emphasis on war.

In an interview, the General Secretary of the CPI(Maoist) stated 'we are confident that there is an advantage in the long run which cannot be achieved in a short period ... we want to stretch this war and transform the situation to our advantage favourable to the revolution' (Ganapathy 2010). Another Maoist leader asserted that '(t)he Party and leadership will grow rapidly in times of war ... War is giving birth to new generals and commanders, which we never anticipated in normal times. While it took several years to produce a leader of calibre in relatively peaceful times, it is taking a fraction of that time in the midst of the war situation' (Rajkumar 2010).

This proposition needs investigation, since the risk is that the slow and painful work of political education gets replaced by military concerns. So, how realistic is the proposition of war? Wars do sharpen people's powers of comprehension, and they also help to spread the political appeal of the Maoists. However, it does not mean that political education of the cadres gets replaced by education through war. It may indeed be easier for people to comprehend developments and understand linkages between what appear to be disparate issues under circumstances of war. For instance a CPI(Maoist) leader told Jan Myrdal and myself that when they used the word 'fascism' in the Dandakaranya area prior to 2005, people could not grasp what it meant (Sonu 2011). However, as the State-supported private militia, Salwa Judum, began its brutal campaign, it brought home to the local people what the Maoists had been warning them about. Nevertheless, precisely because war heightens the senses, civil wars, which tend to be dirty wars, can also alienate sections of the people with their needless bloodshed, conflicting loyalties, manipulative propaganda and the machinations of State agencies.

So what are the limits to achieving political objectives through armed struggle in contemporary India? The Party states that 'the mass organizations and mass struggle should serve the war between the people's armed forces and the enemy forces once it has broken out, or should be oriented towards preparation for war'(CPI(Maoist) 2007b). But the Party also says that 'armed struggle cannot achieve success unless it is coordinated with other forms of struggle ... This will amount to leaving behind the masses and going ahead with only the advanced sections'(CPI(Maoist) 2007b). Trying to manage both ends of this requirement is a recipe for conflict.

Take the Jangalmahal area of West Bengal. At its peak, from November 2008 to June 2009, the Jangalmahal struggle encompassed 1100 villages across 1000 sq km and was organised around 150 Gram (village) Committees (GCs) in the Lalgarh and Belpahari blocks. Each GC represented several villages and comprised men and women in equal proportions. While Maoists were the dominant force, there were other political tendencies and groups present in the Peoples Committee Against Police Atrocities (PCAPA).

Simultaneously, the Lalgarh Solidarity Forum grew in urban areas of West Bengal among students, intellectuals and other sections; and the appeal of the Maoist Party grew accordingly. But so did new challenges. Very early in 2008 Maoists were confronted with a Party which also traced its roots to the Naxalbari uprising of 1960s. CPI(Maoist) (2009) accused Santosh Rana, who led CPI(ML), of pushing ahead with demands for an autonomous council for Jangalmahal within the state of West Bengal, and accused him of promoting tribal identity politics, thereby playing into the hands of the Left Front Government. They also accused Rana and his group of covertly extending support to vigilante groups promoted by the ruling CPM. When Santosh Rana said he was willing to accept an independent inquiry into the charge of covert support for vigilantes, the Maoist Party showed little interest.

The Maoists do not oppose identity politics. According to the 'Strategy and Tactics of the India Revolution' document, CPI(Maoist) (2007b) claims to organise Adivasis under the slogans 'rights over the forest belong to people and Adivasis,' 'political autonomy to the Adivasi territories,' 'transform the territory as exploitation-free territory i.e. 'red land,' 'don't be divided, be united,' 'unite the real friends against the real enemies,' 'rights over all the resources including water, forest etc.,' 'the right to protect their own culture and development,' and to mobilise them against economic, political, social and cultural oppression. However, the Maoists are right to stress that divisions among the tribals should neither be lost sight of nor should tribal identity be essentialised and class divisions and struggle underplayed. These revolutionary movements are not just wedded to forests rights, to opposing land grabs by corporations and consequent displacement of people and loss of livelihood. They go further by focusing on class struggle and political power. The Party was clear that the struggle in Jangalmahal was one of the people in general, initiated by the tribals and not a tribal identity struggle per se. Tribal and dalit populations together in the Lalgarh and Belpahari blocks is 55% and 58% . This means that more than 40% of the people did not think of themselves as tribals or dalits and these people had to be mobilised as well. Nevertheless, the accusatory tone of the exchange above mirrored real acrimony at the grassroots level. The situation turned bitter with increased killing of police informers and people's enemies.

A senior Party leader justified these killings by claiming that these are not normal conditions but conditions of war where rules are different. He also said that '(i)n order to tire out informers, the people are adopting a number of methods. On the other side, the state is also trying everything in its power to whet their greed. Thus the number of informers being killed is also mounting. *Had there been some proper system in Jangal Mahal today, the number of informers getting killed would have been far less. In different parts of Dandakaranya, informers are being detained in people's prisons*' (Rajkumar 2009, my emphasis). It is true that in conditions of war, over-ground activities become difficult to carry out. In addition, the difference between combatants and non-combatants becomes decisive and informers or couriers are counted as combatants. However, the Maoists failed to grasp that such killings would carry repercussions, questions would be raised and their recklessness would cause rifts with friends.

The absence of jails was not as important as the fact that Maoist domination of Jangalmahal was weak. As a result, killing more informers was related to a diktat issued to CPM members in Jangalmahal to quit the Party or face social boycott. Perhaps the CPM local units and their members worked as informers and many were cruel and corrupt, but the diktat enabled the CPM, then the ruling party in the province, and government forces to find a way of infiltrating PCAPA. A combination of these factors may have contributed to the surge in informer killings. Furthermore, without politically isolating the CPM or the Trinamool Congress with a popular political campaign, increased killings actually eroded the Maoists' appeal and fractured the urban solidarity movement. Ethical rules of war on the revolutionaries' part are essential to promote their politics and rally real and potential friends or allies.[7]

Another mistake was declaring that they had built and controlled the movement in Jangalmahal. This ran counter to working secretly or in clandestine ways because the Maoist Party is criminalised on the ground. This claim to ownership proved to be a political miscalculation and subverted PCAPA's emergence as a mass movement representing diverse political forces, even while the Maoists remained the dominant force (Bose 2009). This also undermined the open leadership of PCAPA and pushed the CPI(Maoist) to the forefront, thereby exposing them. The emergence of PCAPA was an achievement. Their work in the fields of health, education, small irrigation projects, the help provided to small and marginal farmers, the participation of women etc. was remarkable, despite the efforts made by the state administration and military forces to thwart these activities by physically closing health centres and schools or simply stopping doctors and teachers from entering these areas. All this held out the promise of providing the Maoists with a mass organisation for popular action and for getting around the proscription against open political work.

The urge to take credit and claim leadership of the movement widened the rift and made Maoist control of the PCAPA a divisive issue. This also contributed to the propaganda of the CPM-led Left Front government in West Bengal and the UPA government at the Centre, about PCAPA being a Maoist Front. While the authorities would have demonised PCAPA for being a Maoist front anyway, the Party made it easier to do so. This helped pave the way for a joint forces operation by the government when, knowing full well that such an offensive was imminent, after elections for the 15th Parliament in India (May 2009) were over, the Party ought to have ensured that the united mass front remained intact. This failure contributed to the erosion of their appeal within and outside Jangalmahal. By the time the 2011 state assembly elections drew close, conditions on the ground had altered.

PCAPA members faced a choice to participate in elections, support the Trinamool Congress or boycott the polls. Whereas in the May 2009 parliamentary elections, the voting share was less than 10%, in the 2011 May assembly elections, it reached 60%. What does this imply? That there was no poll boycott campaign in the 2011 polls from the Maoists, unlike in the 2009 Parliamentary elections? Or, that in the 2011 polls the

Maoists encouraged people to vote for the Trinamool Congress? Or, that the difference in voting turnout in 2011 reflectsed a loss of ground since 2009?

The charge against the Maoists for having supported TC, while campaigning fitfully against the jailed leader of PCAPA, Chatrathar Mahato, brings out an old problem. What should be the approach to elections during PPW? If they tweak their own election boycott policy for tactical gains, what would be better: to support one ruling class alliance against another or encourage members of the mass movement to stand? In the Andhra Pradesh elections of 2004, the Maoist Party was accused of campaigning to 'Smash Telugu Desam Party and the Bhartiya Janta Party,' which ended up assisting the Congress Party to sweep the state assembly elections. In West Bengal the main slogan was to 'Defeat the CPM.' Remarkably, neither in Andhra Pradesh in 2004 nor in West Bengal in 2011 were talks held about the Maoists backing Congress or the Trinamool Congress. Their own calculations pushed them to support one ruling class party over another. Considering the decimation of the rank and file of Maoists in Andhra Pradesh from 2004 to 2005 at the hands of the same Congress Party that they supported during the elections, they ought not to have ignored the likelihood of a repeat of the same situation in West Bengal. Indeed in Jangalmahal the arrest and killing of Maoist cadres could be traced to their easy identification by Trinamool Congress members. Both situations forced the Maoists to take a fresh look at their election policy. In West Bengal they could have encouraged PCAPA to put up candidates or backed some local party candidates as a way of enhancing their own political appeal as well as ensuring that the Trinamool Congress did not get to replace the CPM or to consolidate themselves in Jangalmahal.

Armed struggle on its own cannot suffice. Blood-letting may have actually undermined war efforts in that sections of the people were alienated. Guerrillas minus the people's support is an oxymoron.

Other Forms of Struggle

So does this mean that Maoists are averse to other forms of struggle? A senior Party leader (Rajkumar 2010) reminded us that when the Maoist Party mobilised people against feudal landlords in the North Telengana area of Andhra Pradesh in the 1970s and conducted social boycott campaigns against the landlords, military forces were deployed against the Party. According to him, when the Party carried out a peaceful anti-liquor campaign, the police sold arrack and encouraged people to consume alcohol in order to 'foil the anti-liquor agitation of the revolutionaries' (Rajkumar 2010). He recalled that, 'when in the urban areas the colliery workers of Singareni organised themselves under the Singareni Workers Federation in 1981, the union was unofficially banned within three years. An undeclared ban was imposed on the students and youth organizations, women's organizations, workers organizations, cultural organizations and every form of peaceful, democratic space available protest was brutally suppressed'(Rajkumar 2010). He added that 'it is not the forms of struggle and forms of organization adopted by the Party that led to the imposition of bans but the very ban (whether declared or undeclared) on every type of open, legal activity including peaceful public meetings that compelled the revolutionaries to adopt non-peaceful and armed forms of struggle and underground forms of organization' (Rajkumar 2010).

Thus, they may not be averse to other forms of struggle but the ban on their overt political activities restricts their capacity to do so. However, when they succeeded in launching a mass front, and thus overcame the difficulties resulting from banning their Party, their inability to capitalise on this, to 'leap forward,' shifted focus onto the fault-lines in their movement. In order to progress from their forest strongholds to the plains, military victories may be necessary but they remain insufficient because the question remains how do they sustain the movement politically? How can they ensure mass mobilisation and mass struggle if they cannot do it under their own steam? One realises then that the movement either requires the helping hand of radical political formations operating openly and legally, or must expand through political mobilisation under the cover of a broad-based front.

In an interview that the General Secretary of the CPI(Maoist) (Ganapathy 2010) gave in January 2010, he observed the importance of 'partial' victories or reforms. This is evident in areas where the Maoists are present and they encourage people to fight for various entitlements and welfare projects. For people to fight for their rights, mobilisation and organisation is needed. This entails looking again at the popular forces working over-ground, and working with, not against each other. Trying to establish the Party's hegemony with the help of guns undermines revolutionary politics.

What Maoists faced in Jangalmahal was a situation where their political strategy was contested by members of the popular forces. To carry out an acrimonious armed struggle with these forces was problematic. As they drew closer to relatively developed areas, the Maoists found that the freedoms people fought for and won came into conflict with the needs of war. In other words they failed; not only to win over but to neutralise the innate hostility some of these groups entertain for Maoists.

The limitations Maoists face in some areas means that the movement could end up playing a *catalytic role*; one of enabling reform of the existing Indian state. If their practice causes division or subverts the process of unifying 'popular forces', then they may survive for years inside the jungle strongholds but will only play a marginal role outside them. A banned party cannot openly mobilise and organise people, for sure. War also requires the movement to defend itself against relentless attacks. The witch-hunt to which it is exposed, the executions carried out by government forces and the large number of arrests affect their ability to carry out the political education of new recruits. But Maoists exacerbate these issues by antagonising those who work with people over-ground. There was an opportunity in Jangalmahal, where they stood a chance of expanding territorially through an armed takeover of certain areas, but a greater one was to do so politically under the cover of a mass organisation and urban solidarity front. They obviously failed.

Conclusion

Violence can play an emancipatory role when the oppressed are able to defend themselves, when they can save people from being trampled on by a ruthless military force which persistently sides with the rich, powerful and privileged. A call to arms for a political cause does not have to be considered 'evil' because violence is value neutral. It is how violence is harnessed, its purposes, that is relevant. Just because fascists use violence, we need not assume that there is no difference between what they and anyone else does. To claim that all violence is one and the same, grossly misrepresents social reality.

To argue that a death caused by fascists or Maoists is the same just because a person dies is fraught with contradiction. It provides no space for motive, intent, or ideological perspective, and reduces the issue to one of metaphysics. It also blurs the distinction between just and unjust wars, between a war of aggression and a war against oppression. Those who argue that all wars are the same should also accept that all deaths are the same because someone is killed. By this logic rioters killed by security forces are no different from custodial killings carried out by security forces. The fatal lynching of a rapist gangster by slum dwellers would then be the same as a caste panchayat (council) murdering lovers across caste or clan boundaries. This defeats logic and common sense.

The living care about why deaths take place, the motivation and intent behind them. Otherwise the difference between terrorisation of civilians by extreme right wing groups (for whom a community/ethnic group becomes the enemy) and the violence of left wing radicals seeking to end through armed hostilities the material conditions perpetuating the oppression of a people would be inconsequential. So we must ask how the Maoists deploy violence for revolutionary transformation and where they go wrong.

In war, as in politics, choosing strategic friends and allies, as well as fighting the main enemy is decisive. Carl Schmitt points out that '(w)ar finds its meaning in enmity. Because it is a continuation of politics, politics too always involves an element of enmity, at least potentially; and if peace contains within itself the possibility of war – something that by the standards of experience has unfortunately proved to be true – peace too contains a moment of potential enmity'(2004: 41-42). But can the enmity be contained and regulated, that is, does it represent 'relative' or 'absolute' enmity. While war is a continuation of politics by other means, Mao (1938) pointed out that 'war is politics with bloodshed,' meaning that the practice of warfare is part of the political. To treat as an enemy an ideological or political opponent, while enhancing the importance of a tactical ally in the shape of a ruling class, is a dilution of revolutionary politics, which is based on absolute enmity.

But this warfare must combine mass struggle with armed struggle. One without the other makes PPW hollow. In Jangalmahal the needs of war were used to justify indiscriminate killing of 'informers'. Controlling the mass front PCAPA and then publicly declaring it, weakened them just when united mass struggle was most needed.

When a military offensive is imminent, dividing the enemy is tactically useful. But keeping your allies, real as well as potential, with you is even more important. PCAPA was a coalition of class friends and allies. There were others who had joined the struggle earlier but had parted ways. Many were political opponents but remained part of a broad coalition of pro-revolutionary bent. Pushing them out and solving political battles through annihilation was senseless.

Bernard D'Mello (2011)[8] reminds us that '(w)hat makes the implementation of a mass line even more difficult is Article 59 of the Constitution of the Party that directs the Party fraction in the mass organization to dictate terms thereby encouraging 'commandism' which can lead to 'isolationism,' i.e. the Party ultimately failing to gain the support of the non-Party leaders of its mass organizations.'

Against the background of division within the oppressed classes, who are often at odds over common resources, the Party, working to impose its own domination over the mass movement, undermines mass struggles. This throws up contradictions which if not addressed could gravely harm the revolutionary movement. While accepting the legitimacy of armed struggle, we ought to be clear that this does not mean *carte blanche* for killings. We do distinguish between the different manners of death. We mourn the death of our heroes, but will not mourn for tyrants. We mourn when civilians get killed but not when murderous gangs are wiped out. We are outraged by gruesome killings but not appalled by killing combatants in an exchange of fire. These differences are grounded in political ethics. Thus, to be firm in conviction is not to condone cruel and callous behaviour, which undermines revolutionary politics.

Moreover, comparing the Russian and Chinese revolutions, Isaac Deutscher perceptively pointed out that '(i)n Russia the civil war was waged after the revolution, whereas in China it had been fought before the revolution. The question of whether communists enter the civil war as a ruling party or as a party of opposition is of the greatest consequence for their subsequent relationship with all classes of society' (1964: 31). He goes on to say:

> The establishment of the single party system in China was not the painful and dramatic crisis it had

been in Russia, for the Chinese had never had the taste of any genuine multiparty system. No Social Democratic reformism had struck roots in Chinese soil. Maoism has never had to contend with opponents as influential as those that had defied Bolshevism: there were no Chinese Mensheviks or Social Revolutionaries ... Maoism was never in the throes of a deep conflict with its own past, such as troubled the Bolsheviks' mind when it was being forced into the monolithic mould. (1964: 30-32)

In India, the PPW takes place in a context where both 'politics without bloodshed' as well as 'politics with bloodshed' are present, side by side and overlapping. Political plurality in India also has a different history and contestation within the Indian Left with its multiple communist formations, parliamentary and extra-parliamentary parties, a six decades-long multiparty system, a large middle class, funded or non-funded activists and, above all, a multi-national and multi-ethnic lived culture. The fact that Maoists have been able to negotiate this complex terrain and have retained the support of the most oppressed classes, lends legitimacy to their movement. But, social and political divisions can easily be stoked and exploited by the ruling class(es). When this is combined with moments of elation such as when a corrupt party is removed from power in elections, or when the government bows to pressure to pass a law or modify draconian law or a judgment questions the notion of 'guilt by association,' rejects a charge of sedition, or upholds people's right to land, a concerted popular campaign can succeed. Saner voices in the judiciary and among political leaders do triumph at times and create the impression that it is possible to get things done within the confines of the prevailing system. This impression enables the Indian state to ride roughshod over dissent and popular discontent, and, to emerge intact. All the more reason then to pay careful attention to distinguishing between friends and enemies when wageing mass struggle.

Fault lines in the Maoist movement prevent it from winning over other sections of the working class, oppressed people and sections of urban wage earners, without which their movement cannot grow stronger. The presence of Maoists and their proficiency in armed warfare does act as a check and counter to the 'savage war for development' that is going on in India. The fear of people joining the Maoist ranks when state repression increases persuades the State to take *reformers* seriously. Maoist armed struggle is also a check on the proclivity of Left parties to indulge in reformism, legalism and electoralism.

Class war demands that the revolutionaries, through their own practice, mark out their differences from the reactionary classes. The niceties of ethical warfare or the Geneva Convention and Protocol are not just an attempt to undermine class war, if not to tie it down with too many principles, while the ruling classes carry out 'dirty wars'. The politics of revolutionary warfare are designed to win over large numbers of people, supported by armed cadres for the seizure of power. Winning popular recognition for their armed struggle as legitimate belligerents pushes the political to the forefront and focuses resistance on the 'savage war for development' being waged by the State. If some practices of PPW impede or undermine the movement's legitimacy, a fresh look at the strategy and tactics of revolutionary warfare in India is called for. The people's will to change must prevail over any attempt to change the will of the people. This is the challenge posed to Maoists in India.

Notes

Acknowledgements. My interest in the subject of revolutionary warfare was triggered by conversations with Jan Myrdal. These began when, together with him, I met senior leaders of the CPI(Maoist) in January 2010. During our meeting, I raised the issue of the CPI(Maoist) accepting the public appeal of the Indian civil liberties movement to adhere to the Geneva Convention and its Protocol II. Reference to this meeting can be found in Jan Myrdal's (2012) book *Red Star over India: As the Wretched of the Earth are Rising*. Our conversation carried on thereafter and Jan Myrdal drew my attention to the history of the Geneva Convention. Thanks to him I was able to access some of the material available in English on the question of partisans/irregulars and how they became de-criminalised as belligerents, on the difference between 'absolute' and 'real' war and on the evolution of the Geneva Convention. I also became familiar with how Prussia violated every tenet of the Geneva Convention during the war against the Paris Commune, how the Versailles' regime massacred more than 70,000 Parisians while the Paris Commune killed 70. And yet the latter are vilified not the former, just as in our own times bigger war mongers and war criminals, such as the US-led NATO, escape prosecution for crimes against humanity while leaders of smaller African and Balkan states are brought to justice. What follows, however, is mine alone. I am also obligated to Bernard D'Mello for drawing my attention to several issues of Socialist Register that critiqued Maoism.

1. I have also benefitted immensely from the clarity and lucidity with which the phenomenon of war is discussed by Carl Schmitt (2004). Schmitt is a controversial scholar with ties to the Nazi party. This fact, combined with his belief in majoritarianism and dictatorship, makes him a problematic figure. However, the value of his scholarship cannot be denied when one reads his work on politics and the significance of partisans. That said he has to be read critically. People are not an undifferentiated mass. Thus all so-called 'People's Wars' need to be examined. For instance the Taliban, as partisans, may appear to be freedom fighters. But that is not all that can be said about them. They represent a world view which is problematic to say the least. If war is politics, the specificities of each war – in particular revolutionary warfare – cannot be innocent of political ethics. This is closer to a Clausewitizian understanding which advocates understanding the specificities of each war. That is to say that each war has to

be understood against the social context within which it takes place, rather than collapsing all sub-conventional wars into a single category.

2. Real War 'is a wonderful trinity, composed of the original violence of its elements, the play of probabilities and chance that make it a free activity of the soul, and its subordinate nature as a political instrument, in which respect it belongs to the province of Reason' (Clausewitz cited in Galle 1978: 49- 50). Lenin (1916) in 'The Military Programme of the Proletarian Revolution' also reminds us that 'national wars under imperialism' as well as 'civil wars, which in every class society are natural, and under certain conditions inevitable' cannot be denied. Lenin also offered a thesis advancing the socialist cause by using the opportunity offered by the 'capitalist war.' Much of contemporary social life continues to be and will be dictated, influenced or caused by war(s), whether it takes the shape of Afghan Resistance against US-NATO invasion, a civil war to overthrow a military dictatorship or to overthrow oppressive class rule, a popular resistance against national tyranny such as the Palestinian struggle against Israel etc. or class wars such as the PPW of CPI(Maoist).

3. See also Navlakha (2007).

4. The same document also says 'Guerrilla bases are transitory in nature and it is not a separate phase in itself. If we want to wage guerilla war powerfully, if we want to change the Guerrilla zones into Liberated Areas, then the question of establishment of guerrilla bases will have a special importance. These guerrilla bases will constitute the focal points within the guerrilla zones for the development of a strong party, a strong people's liberation army and a united front while, at the same time, creating favourable conditions for the establishment of liberated areas, expanding the political power in waves and quickening the tempo of the revolution. As the new political power in the guerrilla bases goes on stabilizing, changes should be brought about in the production relations while intensifying

the agrarian revolution. Land should be distributed on the basis of land to the tiller and cooperative movement among the people should be promoted for the development of agriculture. The embryonic form of the new democratic state should be consolidated. Therefore it should be understood that formation of the guerrilla base means a significant advance in the process of building base area. This will create a strong impact on the people in the areas around the guerrilla base and will inspire them to participate in the people's war more extensively' (CPI(Maoist) 2007a).

5. See especially the second part of the document 'Structure of Government' with particular reference to the People's Judicial Department.

6. In response to criticism by civil liberties groups in India, the Bihar - Jharkhand – North Chhattisgarh -- UP Territorial Regional Committee issued an apology on September 1st 2011. But they insisted that there were charges against Niyamat Ansari for grabbing land benefitting a section of the villagers. A press release issued on September 3, by Koyal Shankh Zonal Committee of the CPI(Maoist), says that 'he (Niyamat Ansari) was killed, not because of his role as an Mahatma Gandhi National Rural Employment Guarantee Act (MGNREGA) activist, but because he along with his associate, one Bhukhan Singh, was found guilty of capturing forest land in Jerua village for agricultural purpose for which he was subjected to beating.' The situation is murky as there are competing arguments and a certain section of the villagers wanted the forests to remain intact since minor forest produce forms an integral part of forest dwellers lives. It is nevertheless clear that the punishment exceeded the crime.

7. Carl Schmitt, while recognizing the significance of the Geneva Convention as an attempt to regulate war(s), does not specifically take up the issue of the ethics of war, let alone revolutionary ethics. His focus was on the emergence and significance of the 'Partisan' and 'People's Wars.' Although the Geneva Convention itself represents, for all its

shortcomings of non-compliance, an attempt at regulating conduct of war. And in so doing it accords legitimacy to the Partisan/People's War. However, Schmitt does not go beyond this to examine the political ethics embedded in revolutionary war. For instance notions of collateral damage or civilian casualties during war are central to regulating wars as much as providing some protection for combatants when they are injured or taken prisoner. This is certainly a post-second world war phenomena, especially during the Indochina wars. Indeed, these concerns occupy a significant part of reportage from battlefields and analysis of military matters.

8. This is the longer version of a chapter included in this volume originally presented at the workshop where the papers produced here were discussed. Article 59 of the CPI(Maoist) (2007a) Party Constitution says 'The Party fractions shall be formed in the executive committees of mass organizations. Party fractions will guide the executive committees of the mass organizations adopting suitable method in accordance with the correct concrete situation. Fractions will function secretly. The opinions of a Party committee/member guiding the fraction shall be considered as a final opinion. If fraction committee members have any difference of opinion, they will send their opinions in writing to the concerned party committee/higher committee. The concerned Party committees shall guide fraction committees of different mass organizations at their own level.' The article's ambiguity has led many cadres to interpret it as a justification for commandism.

References

Bose, R. 2009. Fight is not over, says Maoist leader. *The Hindu*, 26 July (available on-line at: http://www.thehindu.com/todays-paper/tp-national/fight-is-not-over-says-maoist-leader/article239404.ece, accessed 13 August 2015).

Chakrabarty, B. & R. Kumar Kujur 2010. *Maoism in*

India: Reincarnation of ultra-left wing extremism in the twentieth-first century. Abingdon: Routledge.

D'Mello, B. 2011. *Insurgent Comrades: Maoist Learnings-by-doing in India, 1967-2010.* Unpublished.

Deutscher, I. 1964. Maoism – Its Origins, Background and Outlook. *Socialist Register* 1, 11-37.

Galle, W. B. 1978. *Philosophers of Peace and War: Kant, Clausewitz, Marx, Engels and Tolstoy.* Cambridge: Cambridge University Press.

Ganapathy, General Secretary of CPI(Maoist). 2010. Interviewed by Gautam Navlakha and Jan Myrdal (available on-line at: http://www.sanhati.com/articles/2138, accessed 10 July 2015).

Indian Army. 2006. *Doctrine for Sub Conventional Operations.* Simla: Headquarters, Army Training Command.

Kipnis, A. 2003. The Anthropology of Power and Maoism. *American Anthropologist* 105: 2, 278-288.

Koteswar Rao, M. 2009. Interviewed by Suhrid Sankar Chattopadhyay. *Frontline* 26: 22 (available on-line at: http://www.frontline.in/navigation/? type=static&page=archive, accessed 12 August 2015).

Lenin, V. I. 1916. The Military Programme of the Proletarian Revolution. In *Collected Works 4th English Edition* (trans. J. Fineberg & G. Hanna). Moscow: Progress Publishers.

Lew, R. 1975. Maoism and the Chinese Revolution. *Socialist Register* 12, 115-159.

Myrdal, J. 2012. *Red Star Over India: As the Wretched of the earth are Rising*. Kolkata: Setu Prakashani.

Navlakha, G. 2007. Doctrine for Sub-Conventional Operations: A Critique. *Economic and Political Weekly* 42: 14, 1242-1246.

_____ 2010. *Days and Nights in the Heartland of Rebellion* (available on-line at: http://sanhati.com/articles/2250, accessed 10 July 2015).

Rajkumar, C. 2010. Interviewed by Siddartha Vardarajan. *The Hindu*, 14 April (available on-line at: http://www.thehindu.com/news/resources/edited-text-of-12262word-response-by-azad-spokesperson-central-committee-cpi-maoist/article396694.ece, accessed 10 July 2015).

Rana, S. 2009. *Reply to the Eastern Bureau of the Central Committee of the Communist Party of India (Maoist)* (available on-line at: http://www.atik-online.net/english/2009/10/letter-of-the-cpimaoists-to-santosh-rana-and-reply-from-the-cpiml, accessed 10 July 2015).

Schmitt, C. 2004. *The Theory of the Partisan: A Commentary/Remark on the Concept of the Political*. Ann Arbor, MI: University of Michigan Press.

Sonu, Committee Member of CPI(Maoist). 2011. Interviewed by Gautam Navlakha and Jan Myrdal. Unpublished.

Zedong, M. 1938. *On Protracted War* (available on-line at: http://www.marxists.org/reference/archive/mao/selected/works/volume, accessed 10 July 2015).

Unpublished Sources

CPI(Maoist). 2005. *Bihar-Jharkhand Special Area Committee on "Rectification": People's War.* Central Committee.

_____ 2007a. *Policy Program of Revolutionary People's Committee.* Central Committee.

_____ 2007b. *Strategy and Tactics of the Indian Revolution* (available on-line at: http://www.satp.org/satporgtp/countries/india/maoist/documents/papers/strategy.htm, accessed 10 July 2015).

_____ 2007c. *Political Organisational Report: People's War.* Central Committee.

_____ 2009. *Letter to Santosh Rana* (available on-line at: http://www.atik-online.net/english/2009/10/letter-of-the-cpimaoists-to-santosh-rana-and-reply-from-the-cpiml, accessed 10 July 2015)

_____ 2011. Bihar-Jharkhand-North Chhattisgarh-IP Territorial Regional Committee. *Letter to Civil Liberties Organisations* (available on-line at: http://www.radicalnotes.com/2011/09/19/cpi-maoists-letter-to-civil-liberties-organisations/, accessed 10 July 2015).

_____ Undated. *New Circular on Rectification.* Unpublished.

CPI(Marxist). 2012. *Draft Political Resolution for the 20th Party Congress.* Kolkata: Central Committee.

Chapter 3

UNCONVENTIONAL POLITICS: PRELUDE TO A CRITIQUE OF MAOIST REVOLUTIONARY STRATEGY IN INDIA

Bernard D'Mello

Abstract *This chapter argues that the Chinese strategy of Protracted People's War (PPW) may not be the most appropriate road to revolution in India today, for India is not a semi-feudal, semi-colonial country and the international context is totally different from what it was in the 1930s and 1940s. The Communist Party of India (Maoist)'s erroneous characterisation of Indian society and the failure of its PPW strategy are reflected in the fact that even after 48 years the fight is still in an initial stage of 'strategic defence' and the revolutionary forces have not been able to establish 'base areas'. This error stems from the Party's narrow conception of practice and the restricted range of vision attributed to Mao's practice theory of knowledge. Uneven development in an underdeveloped capitalist system with a strong oligopolistic segment and a sub-imperialist proclivity makes it doubly difficult to succeed in seizing power.*

Vadkapur Chandramouli (comrade BK), a Central Committee (CC) member of the Communist Party of India (Maoist) [CPI(Maoist)] and a member of its Central Military Commission, and his comrade-in-arms and partner Karuna, a barefoot doctor and guerrilla fighter, were on their way to the Party's Unity Congress when they were arrested in the Eastern Ghats on the Andhra Pradesh (AP)-Orissa border, brutally tortured and assassinated on December 29, 2006. The Special Intelligence Bureau of the AP police (APSIB), which allegedly apprehended Chandramouli and Karuna, was however not able to extract even a clue from them as to the venue of the Party Congress, information that would have caused grave harm to the CPI(Maoist) (referred to as the Party from hereafter) and the revolutionary movement. This was the Party's first Congress after the coming together of two major streams – the CPI(Marxist-Leninist) (People's War) [CPI(ML) (PW)] and the Maoist Communist Centre of India (MCCI) – of the Maoist movement in September 2004. It decided, among other things, to advance the Protracted People's War (PPW), turn some of the nine guerrilla zones[1] into base areas,[2] the guerrilla war into a mobile war, and further develop the People's Liberation Guerrilla Army (PLGA) – that insurgent comrades like Chandramouli and Karuna had helped build – into a People's Liberation Army (PLA).

A decade after this union of the main Maoist streams, the Party is nowhere nearer to achieving its objectives; indeed, after the launch of Operation Green Hunt (OGH) by the Indian state in September 2009, some of its guerrilla zones have almost reverted back to 'white areas.'[3] Soon after the formation of the new Party in September 2004, from January 2005 onwards, the APSIB, having (probably) infiltrated the Party's political structure, together with the province's elite counterinsurgency force, the Greyhounds, began apprehending and either incarcerating or (allegedly) assassinating the leadership of the revolutionary movement in AP. Concurrently, civil vigilante groups, secretly sponsored and supported by the police, spread terror and killed many leaders of the Party's mass organisations. The repercussion was a severe setback to the Party and its mass organisations, so much so that north Telangana no longer has any guerrilla zones. The same counterinsurgency tactics have been adopted with some success elsewhere in India too.[4] The net result is that the number of CC and Politburo members of the Party elected at the Unity Congress in January 2007 has been dwindling as comrades are arrested or killed. The few who remain outside have been forced to scatter in isolated Party cells. But sheer determination, sacrifice and commitment has, in the past, brought the movement back from the brink of disaster. There is no reason not to expect that the Maoists will retreat, regroup, learn from their mistakes, and fight on to ensure that their comrades didn't die in vain. It is remarkable that right in the midst of the civil war the Maoists have put in place *Janathana Sarkars* – people's governments in an embryonic form at the primary level – in their guerrilla bases, pockets in the Dandakaranya guerrilla zones where their writ runs and which serve as a kind of 'rear' for the guerrillas (Navlakha 2012).

The quest of the original Party – the CPI(ML) whose formal existence dates to April-May 1969 – for an area-wise seizure of political power began even before it was formed. The armed struggle originated in Naxalbari[5] in March-May 1967 and in Srikakulam[6] later that year. A few years later, learning from early setbacks, a section of revolutionaries led by Kondapalli Seetharamaiah and his close associates in north Telangana created mass organisations of writers, performing artists, students, youth, women, peasants and mineworkers.[7] They then tried to integrate 'mass-line' politics and mass organisations as necessary complements to armed struggle, for, as Mao (1934) had put it, 'the revolutionary war is a war of the masses; it can be waged only by mobilizing the masses and relying on them.'

With some success on this score, the Maoist movement spread into parts of the districts of Nizamabad, Adilabad, Karimnagar, Warangal, and Khammam in north Telangana. It further extended into segments of Dandakaranya, the forest area situated on the border and adjoining tribal districts of the states of AP, Chhattisgarh (then part of Madhya Pradesh), Maharashtra and Orissa.[8] Merger with another Maoist stream, the CPI(ML) (Party

Unity), in 1998 strengthened the Maoist camp in Jharkhand and Bihar, and the movement then unrolled in Jangalmahal in West Bengal. Besides, it had already fanned out into the forest areas of the East Godavari and Vishakhapatnam districts of AP, and the Malkangiri and Koraput districts in the province of Orissa. In AP, apart from some strongholds in north Telangana, the movement had also made inroads into sections of the Nalgonda, Mahbubnagar, Medak and Rangareddy districts in south Telangana, and in the Nallamala hilly-forest range (a section of the Eastern Ghats) of the Mahbubnagar, Guntur, Prakasam, Kurnool and Cuddapah districts.

Parts of north Telangana were turned into guerrilla zones in 1995,[9] as well as parts of the old Bastar district, then in the province of Madhya Pradesh (now in Chhattisgarh), and a People's Guerrilla Army was formed in 2000. One of the main achievements of the Maoists in their guerrilla zones was that they helped transform class-power relations. A section of the workers, the poor peasants and landless labourers, dalits and the tribal people stood up – they now had a voice of their own, with the courage to speak out against oppression and exploitation, and fight against their domination. The merger of the CPI(ML) (PW) and the MCCI, and the formation of the CPI(Maoist) in September 2004, catapulted the Maoist armed struggle into an orbit where expectations ran high. It helped consolidate the armed struggle in north Bihar and the Magadh (central Bihar), and in Jharkhand. Moreover, the movement had also, by now, taken root in pockets (a few villages in some districts) of the Western Ghats in Karnataka and in Uttar Pradesh and Uttarakhand.

The launch of the PPW strategy in India goes back 48 years. Now, if one were to date the beginning of the PPW undertaking to where it originated in the Hunan province of China in 1927, then the 'new democratic revolution' (NDR) took 22 years, from 1927 to 1949, to bring the Communist Party of China (CCP) to power in mainland China.[10] If 22 years of people's war deserves the appellation 'protracted,' then the passage of 48 years in India in the first stage of the PPW, that of the 'strategic defensive,' calls for a critique of the choice of such a strategy – the whole set of politics, the forms of political organisation, the entire question of how to take power in a country like India. While revolutionary violence is a necessary evil, I do not think that the PPW of the Chinese Revolution can be successfully copied to bring about revolution in India. In the PPW model, the PLA and the Communist Party rely on peasants and rural proletarians to build rural base areas, carry out 'land to the tiller,' 'full rights to the forests,' and other social policies in these areas (run democratically as miniature, self-reliant states) thereby building up a political mass base in the countryside to finally encircle and 'capture' (politically win over) the cities. There is thus territorial dual power in the course of the revolution, with the communists in power in these self-administered, liberated areas.

I argue that the Indian revolution cannot be a repeat of such a model, for India is not a semi-feudal, semi-colonial country, and the international context is totally different today[11] from what it was in the 1930s and 1940s. But first it is necessary to state a clear view of history and the present, since the here and now is the outcome of more than four centuries of the history of capitalism, right since its beginnings in the process of primitive accumulation. Capitalism, based as it is on the exploitation of the labour of human beings and of nature, generates inequality and, when it works with 'the gloves off', as it does today, exploitation is greatly exacerbated. It has created islands of wealth, luxury and civilization in a vast sea of poverty, misery and degradation. On the one hand, there are what Samir Amin (2003) has called the 'precarious classes' (they constitute more than 90% of the workforce in India) that are denied the right to live and work with dignity, and on the other, a minority that has appropriated for itself – and for those who manage the system on its behalf – most of the wealth, luxury and fruits of civilisation that human labour and ingenuity has produced, and now, humanity and other forms of life are heading towards catastrophe as a result of the cumulative ecological degradation that capitalism has caused.

People's Wars and revolutions – costly in terms of human lives and suffering – are not as much a matter of preference as of necessity; they spring from the internal contradictions of the capitalist-imperialist system. Tragically, so far, they have not succeeded in doing away with the very system (capitalism-imperialism) that breeds them. The dominant classes have managed, by doing all they could (including armed counter-revolution), to preserve their monopoly over wealth, privilege and power. The question therefore is not whether revolution will take place but how, this time around, it can possibly succeed in doing away with the system that continues to breed it.

In India, the costs of maintaining the status quo are atrociously extortionate for the exploited, the dominated and the oppressed – who constitute the majority – and yet there is an overwhelming bias in elite circles against revolutionary violence, which has become a tragic necessity. Need we remind the elite that the costs to the exploited, the dominated and the oppressed of going without a revolution are accumulating at an atrocious rate, including the tragedies of the victims of Hindutvadi proto-fascism and the long army occupations of the Kashmir Valley and parts of the North-East.

Let us then come to the layout of this chapter. Section 2 critically comments on the Party's understanding of Maoism and pleads for a fresh approach in which Maoism is conceived of as open-ended and adaptable to new and changing historical situations. Such a perspective calls for a widening of the range of vision attributed to Mao's practice theory of knowledge. Sections 3 and 4 critically examine the Maoist thesis that India is semi-feudal and semi-colonial. India is an underdeveloped capitalist country[12] with one of the most dynamic bourgeoisies in the periphery of the world capitalist system. Section 5 argues that India is exhibiting tendencies that seem to suggest that it is on the road to emerging as a sub-imperialist power.

From all this it is clear that the principal contradiction is certainly not what the CPI(Maoist) claims it is, namely, the contradiction between caste-based semi-feudalism and the broad masses of the people. Section 6 contends that the Party's wrong identification of the *principal* contradiction among the set of four major contradictions – internal conflicts tending to split the functionally united Indian socio-economic system – compounds its errors in the strategic realm. The Party's errors in understanding the nature of Indian society, the character of the state, the main contradictions and in pinpointing the principal contradiction leads it seriously to underestimate the stability, power and strength of the Indian state, the economy, and the ruling classes. Uneven development in an underdeveloped capitalist system is fundamentally different from uneven development in a semi-feudal, semi-colonial one, which makes it doubly difficult to succeed even in the first stage of the PPW, 'the strategic defensive,' and establish base areas. Given that the Indian system is not semi-feudal and semi-colonial, its internal logic and contradictions have not produced the main characteristics that semi-feudal, semi-colonial China had in its pre-revolutionary period. Section 7 puts together the various elements of this prelude to a critique of Maoist revolutionary strategy in India and suggests that the Maoists need to attribute a wider range of vision to Mao's practice theory of knowledge and take a hard look again at the abyss that is India – its history, economy, society and polity, and potentialities – and then, after a radical self-critical review, reformulate their political programme, strategy and tactics anew.[13]

An Approach to Maoism

'Marxist-Leninist-Maoist theory' has been the main guiding light in the CPI(Maoist)'s understanding of Indian society, its class structure and contradictions, and the nature of the Indian state. This theory has provided the basis for the Party Programme that has guided the formulation of strategy, which in turn has shown the way to tactics. Given this logical framework of the Party's approach to revolutionary strategy and tactics, we first need to examine the CPI(Maoist)'s understanding of Marxism-Leninism-Maoism.

According to the Party, Marxism, founded by Marx and Engels, was developed by Lenin and Stalin into Marxism-Leninism (M-L), and Mao later took the doctrine to its present (third) stage (CPI(Maoist) 2004). Mao is considered the true interpreter of Marx, Lenin and Stalin. His 'strategy and tactics,' 'military science,' 'theory of New Democracy' and the New Democratic Revolution (NDR), his 'theory regarding the nature and the path of the revolution for the colonial, semi-colonial and semi-feudal countries' of 'following the path and the principles underlying the strategy and tactics of the Chinese revolution,' his 'basic method of leadership' in the 'mass line,' his 'three magic weapons' – the Party, the PLA and the four-class Revolutionary United Front (RUF) – his further development of Lenin's ideas on imperialism and the national question, etc. are all considered the latest 'proletarian science.' The Party tract concludes thus: *'Maoism is the Marxism-Leninism of the present-day'*. Indeed, '[t]o *negate Maoism is to negate Marxism-Leninism itself'* (2004: 39; my emphasis).

What does one make of this 'ideology'? At one time Joseph Stalin was considered the infallible 'applier' of M-L, the great social engineer; now, it is Mao, more than 75 years after he formulated some of his main ideas. Indeed, if what is important to Marxism is its method, then even this is reduced to orthodoxy, for it is Mao's 'On Contradiction' (1937) and 'On Practice' (1937) that are considered the last word on such method.

Contrary to the Party, in my view, Maoism, based, as it was, on a particular version of the M-L of Lenin's and Stalin's times, evolved in the context of China's backwardness and its peasant-based, militarised communist party-led revolutionary movement. A Marxist understanding of it (D'Mello 2010: 21-54) is perhaps the best way to begin. From such a study, in my view, the distinctive features of Maoism are the following:

- An '-ism' that is (or rather, *should be*) open-ended and adaptable to new and changing historical situations, wide open to empirical evidence and thus able to grapple with social reality as it unfolds;
- The postulation of open-ended interrelations among and between the forces of production, the relations of production, and the superstructure;
- Stress on egalitarianism even where the forces of production have not yet been developed enough to produce and satisfy all reasonable human needs (notion of the 'iron rice bowl');
- A 'practice theory of knowledge' – 'practice, knowledge, again practice, and again knowledge,' 'repeating itself in ... cycles,' but, with each cycle, the content of practice and knowledge raised to a higher level (Mao 1937);
- In a semi-feudal, semi-colonial country, the poor peasantry and rural landless wage-workers of the interior rather than the urban proletariat constitute the mass support base of the revolutionary movement;[14]
- The central idea that contradictions – the struggle between functionally united opposites– at each stage drive the process of development on the way to socialism, which is sought to be brought about in a series of stages, where the existing stage, at the right time, is impregnated with the hybrid seeds of the subsequent one, thereby dissolving the salient contradictions of the former and ushering in the latter;
- A theory of revolution by stages as well as 'uninterrupted revolution,' implying a close link between successive stages and an imperative that the political party and other organisations of the revolutionary classes leading and continuing the revolution must be free of all the debilitating influences coming from the exploiting classes and need to maintain their independence and

uncompromising opposition to those classes if the revolution is to be taken to its logical end;

- An incisive critique of Stalin's philosophy, politics and economics, and especially, a rejection of the Stalinist practice of 'primitive socialist accumulation' which was against the interests of the peasantry and, in fact, dealt a severe blow to the worker-peasant alliance in the Soviet Union, and led to the build-up of a many-times-more repressive state there;
- Progression from land to the tiller to mutual aid teams, and then to *elementary* cooperatives (where incomes are based on productive capital ownership *and* on labour time committed to cooperative production with the ratio of the labour to capital share of net output increasing over time), followed by *advanced* cooperatives (wherein the capital share of net output is done away with), and, over a period of time, turning the latter into larger units of collective economy and government – the communes;
- Democratic centralism ('freedom of discussion, unity of action') *plus* the 'mass line' (the leadership principle 'from the masses, to the masses') thereby ensuring that 'democracy' doesn't take a backseat to 'centralism' and the Party vanguard genuinely legitimises its guidance of the people by following certain participatory democratic methods of programme formulation and implementation (Mao 1943; Young 1980). Practice of the mass line must also be seen as a process of collective learning and an application of Mao's practice theory of knowledge;
- In the period of transition to socialism, the need for a series of Cultural Revolutions (CRs) – mass mobilisation and initiative on the part of students, workers and peasants in major 'class struggles' against a powerful and privileged stratum that has a tendency to emerge in the party, the government, the enterprises, the communes, the educational system, and so on, and which develops a stake in

maintaining its favoured position and passing it on to its progeny (a ruling class in the making);[15]

- For semi-feudal, semi-colonial countries, the stage of NDR, which does away with semi-feudalism, frees the country from imperialist domination, and renders the big bourgeoisie politically impotent by expropriating its wealth, thereby making capitalism much more compatible with democracy, and aiding the transition to socialism;

- For the NDR, the revolutionary path and strategy is one of PPW with the PLA and the Communist Party at its core, which (as already mentioned) relies on the peasants, builds rural base areas, carries out 'land to the tiller' and other social policies in these areas (run democratically as miniature, self-reliant states) thereby building up a political mass base in the countryside to finally encircle and 'capture' (politically win over) the cities;

- A conception of 'base areas' – self-administered, liberated areas, miniature 'new democratic' republics of the revolutionary forces, albeit under siege, but serving as places of refuge and remobilization for the PLA – and the way to establishing them;

- The importance of women's emancipation ('women hold up half the sky') even during the NDR; and,

- 'Capturing' (winning mass support in) the cities by demonstrating a brand of nationalism that is genuinely anti-imperialist, thereby re-orienting an existing mass nationalist upsurge in favour of the completion of the NDR.

What emerges is not simply the application of Marxist-Leninist principles in the Chinese context, but an '-ism' that is collective, international and universal in its connotation. And, in keeping with its openness, it then becomes a guide to revolutionary change not merely in semi-feudal, semi-colonial countries, but all over the periphery of the world capitalist system.

But in the context of its application to understanding and changing Indian society, it might be relevant to highlight the –ism's practice theory of knowledge (Mao 1937). What is meant by the Maoist maxim 'learn truth from practice?' As I understand it, the saying exhorts us to learn truth 'from history, from economics and politics ... from the real world of social relations and class struggle' (Sweezy 1985: 1) in combination with and from one's own political practice. In keeping with this, Maoists need to take a hard relook into the abyss that is India – its history, economy, polity and society, and potentialities while formulating their strategy and tactics. The failure of the PPW to advance even within the initial stage, that of the 'strategic defensive,' after 48 years of the practice of armed struggle calls for a radical, self-critical review of the same. Mao offered no one revolutionary path for all times and places, but he left us with his *Weltanshauung*, his method of analysis – materialist dialectics – his values and his vision.

Knowledge which is subordinated to practice, narrowly conceived, will be incapable of guiding it to achieve its goals. This is precisely because if knowledge has to serve the goals of a particular practice, it needs a wider range of vision than the one defined by the immediate goals of that specific practice. I mention this because I think that Maoist knowledge *and* practice in India have suffered due to a reluctance to even admit to, let alone transcend the restricted range of vision attributed to Mao's *practice* theory of knowledge. Take, for instance, the Maoist thesis that Indian society is semi-feudal – which I will look at next – formulated mainly from knowledge derived from their political practice in the most underdeveloped areas of rural India. Instead of concluding from their deep knowledge of such districts that Indian society as a whole is semi-feudal, a wider vision would suggest that the process of capitalist development is marked by persistent disparities across regions – and even spatially within regions – in the levels and rates of socio-economic development, and that such uneven development is an intrinsic characteristic of the capitalist economic process itself. Marx's method tells us that the truth is in the whole, arrived at from an explanation of 'facts' generated through historical and empirical research. It cannot be arrived at solely on the basis of the fragments of knowledge derived from one's own practice alone.

Let us then move on to the main Maoist formulations on India.

Is Indian Society Semi-Feudal?

The CPI(Maoist) believes that Indian society is 'semi-colonial and semi-feudal under a neo-colonial form of indirect rule, exploitation and control,'[16] and in this it adheres to what the original CPI(ML) held in its first Party Congress in 1970. In the interplay of continuity with change, the Party seems to emphasise continuity rather than change. Indeed, if one looks at the Party Programme adopted by the original CPI(Marxist-Leninist) at its first Party Congress in May 1970 and compares this with the Party Programme established at the time of the merger and formation of the new Party in September 2004 (CPI(Maoist) 2004b) or the one passed at the first Congress of the CPI(Maoist) in 2007 (CPI(Maoist) 2007a), in the characterisation of Indian society as semi-colonial and semi-feudal, the character of the Indian state, the four major contradictions, the two fundamental contradictions, the principal contradiction, the character of the Indian big bourgeoisie, the stage of the Indian revolution, the four-class RUF, and so on, they are all essentially the same.

I do not agree with the CPI(Maoist)'s characterisation of Indian society as semi-feudal[17] and the proposition that the contradiction between feudalism and the 'broad masses of the people' is the *principal* contradiction.[18] The semi-feudal thesis has already been the subject of a scholarly debate in the 1970s,[19] but we need to pose the main questions from a more radical perspective. Doesn't the CPI(Maoist)'s understanding that unless 'free labour' (in the double sense)[20] in Indian agriculture becomes generalised, the system is still semi-feudal, smacking of an 'ideal-type,' un-Marxist approach? As things stand, the big landlords own a relatively small proportion of the total arable land and semi-feudal tenancy is a minor part of the system of land tenure, though poor peasants eking out a living through intensive labour on the small plots of land that they own or lease, low crop yields, inadequate reinvestment of the surplus, caste oppression and subjugation, usury and high merchant margins, are all widespread (Basole and Basu 2011).

What then of the predicament of poor peasants? Are they subject to semi-feudal exploitation? Should we view the extraction of high merchant margins, usurious rates of interest, and for a small proportion of the poor peasants, extortionate rates of rent, all as forms of semi-feudal exploitation? In answering 'no,' I recall Marx's sharp comment on the plight of the small peasant in *The Eighteenth Brumaire of Louis Bonaparte, 1848-1850*:

> ... [I]n the course of the nineteenth century the urban usurer replaced the feudal one, the mortgage replaced the feudal obligation, bourgeois capital replaced aristocratic landed property. The peasant's small holding is now only the pretext that allows the capitalist to draw profits, interest, and rent from the soil, while leaving it to the agriculturist himself to see to it how he can extract his wages. (Marx 1937 [1852]: 64)

If this is, to an extent, the predicament of Indian poor peasants too, then, for all practical purposes, are not a significant proportion of them already virtually a part of the rural proletariat? We are reminded of the following comment from Lenin in the conclusion of chapter 2 on the 'Differentiation of the Peasantry' in his classic *The Development of Capitalism in Russia* (1899), made after arguing why a significant proportion of the poor peasants already virtually belong to the rural proletariat:

> ...our literature frequently contains too stereotyped an understanding of the theoretical proposition that

capitalism requires the free, landless worker. This proposition is quite correct as indicating the main trend, but *capitalism penetrates into agriculture particularly slowly and in extremely varied forms. ...* In assigning the indigent peasants to the rural proletariat we are saying nothing new. *...the mass of the "peasantry" have already taken a quite definite place in the general system of capitalist production.* (Lenin 1964 [1899]: 178-179, my emphasis)

If we compare Lenin's comment on the situation of poor peasants in backward Russian agriculture at the end of the 19th century to Marx's astute reflection on the plight of peasants in the undeveloped French agricultural sector of the 1840s, the two remarks suggest that both Marx and Lenin chose to understand the predicament of French and Russian peasants in their historical transformation – for both authors those peasants were no longer subject to the feudal relations of production that they had historically emerged from. Nevertheless, the classic *peasant question* in a country like India, namely, how to draw the majority of the peasantry into a revolutionary movement, is more complex than elsewhere. For we have in the Indian middle and rich peasants, not only a combination of the proprietor *and* the worker, but also one imbued with *caste* consciousness, which drives him or her to strive to give up the use of family labour in tilling the soil and other manual tasks, and this is the biggest impediment to his or her solidarity with the poor peasant and the landless labourer. The institution of caste impedes class solidarity and class consciousness, and buttresses landlordism.

In this context, if one goes by the National Sample Survey (NSS) data on 'Household Assets and Liabilities in India' for the year 2002, then over the years 1981-2002 a new set of landlords in the form of 'non-cultivating peasant households' (NCPHs) have appeared on the Indian rural scene, except in Haryana and Punjab (Vijay 2012), and they appear to have emerged mainly from the ranks of rich peasants, even in areas like the Krishna-Godavari belt which used to be a bastion of the latter.[21] Interestingly, the data also show a more or less stable proportion of agricultural labour households in total rural households – 14.6% in 1971, 11.3% in 1981, 14.2% in 1991, and 14.4% in 2002. Further, over time, land does not seem to be getting concentrated in the hands of the rich peasants. Village survey data (nine villages in Andhra Pradesh)[22] show that although these NCPHs constitute 5.5% of the rural households, they own 19.6% of the land. They are the major player on the lessor side of the land lease market, where poor peasants are by far the largest lessees. And the NCPHs are the only net purchaser of land among the different categories of households residing in the village.

What conclusion might one then draw from the facts in Basole and Basu (2011) and Vijay (2012) and the functional logic in Marx's and Lenin's writings with regard to the question of whether semi-feudalism or underdeveloped capitalism prevails in Indian agriculture? All we can possibly say is that capitalism has to be understood in its historical coming-to-be. Underdeveloped capitalism in the contemporary setting has retained 'un-free labour,' usurious credit, high absolute rent (in some pockets), and high trade margins. These modes of exploitation along with 'backwardness,' namely, the lack of development of the productive forces in agriculture and unorganised industry and services, make for low wages in the advanced part (the plantations and capitalist agriculture, more generally, and organised industry and services) of the economy, even though labour productivity is high there. Indeed, all these attributes are the markers of exploitation in an underdeveloped capitalist system, characterised as it is by various forms, including that of 'free labour.' The relations of production between landlords, old and new, and their poor peasant-tenants may appear to be semi-feudal, but the former are wholly oriented towards the national (and even, in some crops, the international) market and seek to maximise their profits – from credit, trade, and/or rent. Certainly, the significant prevalence of mercantile capitalist exploitation and 'semi-feudal' relations of production affects the accumulation (the saving of part of the surplus and its investment in agriculture and elsewhere) process, but at its core, this part of the business operation is an underdeveloped capitalist, and *not* a semi-feudal, one.

In the Maoist view, though, the existence of semi-feudalism is the reason for India's backwardness, and it is imperialism that explains the *persistence* of that backwardness, and underdevelopment. Hence the Maoists stress the need for the NDR, which will do away with semi-feudalism and free the country from the influence of imperialism thereby overcoming backwardness and underdevelopment.

Is India Semi-Colonial and Semi-Feudal?

Maoism does understand global capitalism as a system of dominating/exploiting and dominated/exploited national capitals together with their respective nation-states, yet it seems to be ambivalent with regard to the idea that the *Communist Manifesto*'s sequence of feudalism, bourgeois revolution, industrialisation, and class polarisation, followed by socialist revolution has to apply in each underdeveloped country too. In its view, imperialism exercises its political domination of the backward countries by striking alliances with the most reactionary classes – the native, big capitalists turned into compradors, and the landlords.[23] The former hinders the development of a *national* bourgeoisie thereby preventing *independent* capitalist development, and the latter preserves agricultural backwardness. Besides, imperialism also, directly and/or indirectly (the latter, via other junior partners and through local collaborators) provides armaments and trains the repressive apparatus of the 'semi-colonial' state; it culturally penetrates the educational system, media, etc., drawing the local intelligentsia into its hegemonic orbit. Thus, according to the CPI(Maoist), the other *fundamental* contradiction is between imperialism and the Indian people, in addition to the two other *major* contradictions – between capital and labour, and the internal contradictions among the ruling classes. The Indian state is the joint dictatorship of the big comprador bureaucrat bourgeoisie[24] (CBB) and the big landlords, the former collaborating with imperialism and allying with feudalism.[25]

Following this, a few critical comments would now seem to be in order. First, can we agree with the Party's characterisation of the Indian big bourgeoisie as comprador? Certainly, an industrial bourgeoisie can possibly be comprador. According to Mao's (1926) criteria, if the majority of the Indian big bourgeoisie is an appendage of the international bourgeoisie, depending upon imperialism for its survival and growth, then that bourgeoisie would be comprador. This is not the place to look at the reality in detail, but I would find it difficult to characterise the Tata group, for instance, as comprador – in April 2007, Tata Steel Ltd acquired 100% of the equity capital of Corus Group Plc (UK) for $12.695 billion, taking management control of the latter. Another Tata group company, Tata Motors acquired the South Korean truck manufacturer Daewoo Commercial Vehicles Company in 2004, and the British premium car manufacturer Jaguar Land Rover in 2008. Or take another Indian big business bloc, the Aditya Birla group – in May 2007, its Hindalco Industries Ltd acquired 100% of the equity capital of Novelis Inc (US) for $5.766 billion, placing itself in the saddle of the latter.

Frankly, we do not know of any historical instance of a comprador bourgeoisie acquiring companies of a significant size and market power headquartered in the imperialist countries. Indeed, in our view, the Indian big bourgeoisie is one of the most dynamic capitalist classes in the periphery of the world capitalist system. Yet, there is a long-standing relationship of subordination of the Indian state and the big bourgeoisie to imperialism, which deepened following the collapse of the Berlin Wall and the demise of the Soviet Union. The Indian government quickly made a somersault in its foreign policy and subsequently entered into a strategic alliance as a junior partner with US imperialism.[26]

Unfortunately, the concepts 'semi-feudalism' and 'semi-colonialism' deployed by the CPI (Maoist) are *not* open-ended; neither have they been adapted to the new and changing historical situation since the 1970s. Hence, they do not seem to be of much use in an understanding of 'the present as history,' i.e. in comprehending what is new, along with the equally vital task of seeing the longer process. Today, the two most significant contemporary global capitalist triumphs are the imperialist system's ability to attenuate inter-imperialist rivalry and to appear as the main promoter of political democracy worldwide.[27] The first deprives revolutionary forces like the CPI(Maoist) from taking advantage of inter-imperialist contradictions and consequent divisions within the country's native big bourgeoisie, while the second poses a challenge and an opportunity for these forces, namely to prove in practice that the process of real democratisation (political *and* economic) is only possible with the transition to socialism. At present, this entails the Maoists in India adopting the position that political democracy (provision for a multi-party political system in their 'New Democratic' constitution) will be part and parcel of their 'New Democracy' – and indeed, the latter has to be a form of political *and* economic democracy qualitatively superior to bourgeois democracy.

At least on paper, India has instituted a liberal, political democratic system, but, in practice, the Indian big bourgeoisie has failed to complete the bourgeois-democratic revolution and instead, in alliance with landlordism, is engaged in a conservative modernisation from above. This enterprise not only keeps the masses in poverty and degradation, but importantly, the state and the ruling classes, at best, can only practice a *decomposed* form of liberal-political democracy, never mind the tall claims made by their apologists.

Nevertheless, if India is not semi-feudal and semi-colonial, what are the main characteristics of its political-economic system?

Is India Becoming a Sub-Imperialist Power?

India is an *underdeveloped* capitalist country, permeated with the following characteristics, tendencies and trends, some of which are reinforcing its emergence as a *sub-imperialist* power:[28]

- The emergence of a powerful 'financial aristocracy' (financial big bourgeoisie) – following the opening of the energy, mining, telecommunications, civil aviation, infrastructure (ports, highways, airports, etc.), banking, insurance, and other sectors to private capital – which is increasingly calling the shots in the corridors of power (Bernie 2012);
- Oligopolistic market structures in the modern industrial and services sector, buttressed, no doubt, by foreign capital;
- The increasing influence of foreign capital in modern industry[29] and services, especially in the financial system, and in information technology and business process outsourcing services,[30] especially from 2003 onwards, as also significant *outward* foreign direct investment (Indian transnational corporations)[31] from 2005 onwards;
- Globalisation of the country's financial markets[32] – gross capital inflows and outflows as a percentage of GDP increased from 15.1% in 1990-99 to 53.9% in 2010-11 – and the imperative to follow conservative fiscal and monetary policies (Chandra 2008: 39-51);
- Rapid decline in the share of agriculture, relative stagnation in industry's share, and a rapid rise in the share of services, in gross domestic product from the 1980s onward but with the corresponding changes in the proportions of employment, especially that of agriculture declining much less, in turn, having serious implications for mass living standards (Patnaik 2011: 299-325);[33]
- Huge wage-relative-to-labour-productivity gaps vis-à-vis the developed capitalist countries and, in the

presence of disadvantageous export-import market structures,[34] consequent unequal exchange in international trade;

- An increasing proportion of exports of primary commodities, manufactured goods, and services routed via the trade and investment networks of transnational corporations;
- Outward 'temporary' migration of 'knowledge workers' under Mode 4 of the World Trade Organisation's General Agreement on Trade in Services, constrained by political restrictions in the recipient high-wage countries;
- A systematic dependence on import of technology as far as the islands of high productivity in the economy – in agriculture (including hybrid-seed R&D), industry and services – are concerned;
- A *La Grande Bouffe*, so characteristic of consumer society, confined to the local elite, which imitates the consumption patterns of its counterparts in the developed capitalist countries;
- Islands of undreamt wealth-luxury in a vast sea of poverty-misery (Bernie 2012; Chandra 2010: 279-317; Patnaik 2004: 9-35, 2010: 1-4; Shetty 2011: 86-147);[35]
- Dispossession of the peasantry via class differentiation *and,* increasingly, through displacement and environmental degradation (Patnaik 2011a: 217-239);[36]
- Political subordination to US imperialism and working with it to advance mutual strategic interests (Research Unit for Political Economy 2006);[37]
- Bolstering of the semi-fascist project of the Hindutva forces (whose parliamentary political front, the *Bharatiya Janata* Party is now in power at the national level) following the US' 'war on terror' in the aftermath of 9/11; and,
- Intensification of coercive institutional mechanisms internally[38] *and* extra-territorially, as regards the latter, where the Indian state teams up

with Indian business to advance mutual interests, influence and power beyond its national borders, for instance, in Nepal,[39] Afghanistan[40] and Sri Lanka.[41]

All this cannot be elaborated upon here, and the Maoists too touch on some of the above characteristics, tendencies and trends. The question however is: where would the contradiction between caste-based feudalism and the broad masses of the people, what the Maoists say is the *principal* contradiction among the set of four major contradictions, figure as an explanation for the tendencies and trends mentioned above? The answer is, almost nowhere. Further, and in order to emphasise the point: is this contradiction the most critical and the most decisive one in terms of the main consequences/tendencies/propensities outlined above (for, after all, a system's *tendencies* are a function of its very *character*)? Is this the contradiction according to Mao (1937) 'whose existence and development determine or influence the existence and development of the other contradictions?'[42] Emphatically, the answer is no.

Main Implications of the Wrong Characterisation of Indian Society

Clearly, this point of disagreement with the Maoists is a fundamental one – it has revolutionary implications. The CPI(Maoist)'s programme has followed mainly from the party's class analysis of the society, the character of the Indian state and understanding of the major contradictions, the two fundamental ones from among them, and from these two, identifying the principal contradiction, and strategy has been formulated based on that programme. However, if there is a major error in understanding the class structure and nature of class relations, the character of the state, the nature of the main contradictions, and in pinpointing the principal contradiction, then the party programme and consequent strategy and tactics would be inappropriate and erroneous, as they would be based on a serious underestimation of the stability, power and strength of the Indian state, the economy and the ruling classes. Uneven development in an underdeveloped capitalist system is fundamentally different from the same in a semi-feudal, semi-colonial setup, making it doubly difficult to succeed in even the first stage[43] of the PPW and establish a series of base areas from which the movement can then be steered to move beyond the stage of the 'strategic defensive' and expand further.

Moreover, the CPI(Maoist) and its PLGA do not have the 'socialist' *rear* that they may have had if Maoism had not been abandoned in China, nor do they, as yet, have base areas. Unlike China during the period 1927-49 when the CCP was fighting its PPW, in India today there are no imperialist enclaves (the imperialist powers had seized and 'leased' parts of Chinese territory, and exacted huge indemnities), no *numerous* unequal treaties, no imperialist control of important trading ports, all of which gave rise to inter-imperialist rivalry that bitterly divided the Chinese big bourgeoisie.[44]

In India today, unlike in China then, there are no vast stretches of country where the writ of warlords prevails; the system of land tenure is nothing compared to landlords (who were also military and political officials) owning a significant part of the total arable land and leasing large parts of it under semi-feudal tenancy (poor peasants – who together with farm labourers, comprised 70% of the rural population – were subject to high rates of rent and the millstone of usury) with the bulk of the peasantry (poor and middle peasants) eking out a living by intensive labour on small plots of mainly leased in land. There is no widespread military authoritarianism, no 'failed state', not a semblance of the semi-colonial political-economic influence that inhibited China's industrial development then – factors, in addition to the above, that made the PPW more feasible in semi-colonial, semi-feudal China, but are absent in underdeveloped-capitalist India today.

The contradictions between India and the collective triad of imperialist powers (the United States, Western

Europe, and Japan) led by the US, within the Indian ruling classes, between the Centre and the States, and between the political parties of the Establishment are not of the same kind or intensity as the contradictions between China and the imperialist powers, within the *Guomindang* (GMD), and between the GMD and the warlords between 1927-1937. It was the latter contradictions that made it possible for Red base areas to exist in China even when they were almost completely surrounded by White areas. If the Indian system is semi-colonial, semi-feudal, as the CPI(Maoist) thinks it is, then its internal logic should have produced at least some of the main characteristics that China had in its pre-revolutionary period.[45]

Thus the conditions that the Maoist revolutionaries in India are facing are very unfavourable and this has been the case from the very start of the movement in 1967 right up to the present. In taking on the might of one of the most powerful capitalist states and ruling classes in the periphery of the world capitalist system, the CPI(Maoist) is inevitably getting increasingly militarised in the course of the PPW. Indeed, as Gautam Navlakha's chapter shows, the Party now shapes and orients its mass organisations in accordance with the advance or retreat of the armed struggle. Frankly, if it persists in viewing the role of mass organisations and mass struggles within such circumscribed limits, it will not make much headway in the struggle to gain the support of the 90% that Maoism claims as its constituency in semi-feudal, semi-colonial countries. As it is, working class, peasant and middle-class Maoist intellectual leadership has nowhere come to the fore in the political, cultural and ideological realms across the country. But without this, the Revolutionary United Front, which seeks to win over the working class, the peasantry, the middle class and the 'national bourgeoisie' – the 90% – will not grow. Importantly, it is only through winning widespread legitimacy that the revolution can be accomplished with a minimum of violence. The CPI(Maoist) is not yet a major party, national in scope, even 46 years since the formation of the original party; the Maoist movement is yet to win widespread legitimacy among the people. Except in some pockets in the guerrilla zones, the Party's mass-line politics has nowhere emerged as the real-life alternative to India's rotten liberal-political democracy.

Conclusion

This chapter has argued that since India is an underdeveloped capitalist country emerging as a sub-imperialist power in South Asia, and *not* a semi-feudal, semi-colonial country akin to China in the late 1920s, and considering that the international context is also very different, the Chinese path of PPW may not be the most appropriate road to revolution here in the 21st century. In its erroneous characterisation of Indian society as semi-feudal and semi-colonial, the CPI(Maoist) has seriously underestimated the stability, power and strength of the Indian state, the economy, and the ruling classes, especially the Indian big bourgeoisie. The resilience of the latter, the very formidable repressive apparatus of the Indian state, and the institutions of Indian civil society increasingly coming under the ideological hegemony of the ruling classes, are the main reasons why the Maoist movement in India, despite the practice of PPW over 48 years, has still remained in the initial stage of the 'strategic defensive' and has not been able to establish base areas. Uneven development in an underdeveloped capitalist system with a strong oligopolistic segment and a sub-imperialist proclivity is fundamentally different from the same in a semi-feudal, semi-colonial one, making it doubly difficult to succeed in the area-wise seizure of power. The CPI (Maoist) continues to apply Mao's *practice* theory of knowledge as the only way to foolproof knowledge *and* correct revolutionary practice, but, as we have suggested, the theory itself needs a wider range of vision.

Now, even as I have pleaded for a fresh approach to Maoism as an –ism that ought to be open-ended and adaptable to new and changing historical situations and engaged in a prelude to a critique of the CPI(Maoist)'s political programme, strategy and tactics, I still admire its insurgent comrades – their simplicity, their singleness of purpose, their high spirits in the course of the fight, their sense of misery when one of their comrades gives up the fight or submits to the powers-that-be, their ever-willingness to excuse the gullibility of the masses but nevertheless still detest any signs of servility. The vital spark of the brutally assassinated couple, comrades Chandramouli and Karuna, with whom this chapter began, is still glowing; so is the self-confidence and determination to carry on to the very end – the fighting spirit of the Maoist movement is still alive and well. But, as suggested here, the Maoists need to go beyond their restricted range of vision in applying Mao's practice theory of knowledge and take a fresh relook into the abyss that is India – its history, its economy, society and polity, its potentialities. Then, after acknowledging that India is an underdeveloped capitalist country with a strong monopoly segment and a sub-imperialist proclivity, they must undertake a radical self-critical review and reformulate their political programme, strategy and tactics anew.

Notes

Acknowledgements. The author is grateful to Alpa Shah, Luisa Steur, P. A. Sebastian, Stephan Feuchtwang, Sumanta Banerjee, Swapna Banerjee-Guha and Tilak Dasgupta for critical comments on what was then an altogether different draft, Gautam Navlakha, Venugopal Rao Nellutla and Varavara Rao for clarifications, and the participants of the Oxford workshop on 'Marxist Revolutionary Movements Across the World: Comparing the Changing Strategies and Tactics,' held on 11-12 July 2011, for creating an ambience conducive to lively discussion. He also thanks Demeter Chanter for copy-editing the manuscript. The usual disclaimers apply.

1. These are the tracts where the agrarian revolutionary movement is strong, but where the party and its mass organisations are in power only as long as the guerrillas have the upper hand over the state's forces. Power reverts

to the Indian state when the guerrillas are forced to retreat.

2. Base areas are self-administered, liberated areas, miniature 'new democratic' republics of the revolutionary forces, albeit under siege, but serving as places of refuge and remobilisation for the people's army.

3. Terms such as Red areas and White areas are from Mao (1938a). A White area is one where the enemy is in power, whereas a Red area is one where the revolutionaries are in the saddle. So the terms, Red Army and White Army also refer to the respective armed forces of the revolutionary and reactionary camps.

4. State-sponsored vigilante gangs – the Salwa Judum in Chhattisgarh, the Nagarik Suraksha Samiti and Gram Raksha Dal in Jharkhand, the CPI(Marxist)'s Gana Pratirodh Committee and Harmad Bahini, and the Trinamool Congress' Bhairab Bahini in Jangalmahal, the forest areas of the districts of West Midnapore, Bankura and Purulia in West Bengal, the Shanti Sena in Gadchiroli (Maharashtra) and parts of Orissa – routinely attack the leaders, members and supporters of the revolutionary movement. The big bourgeoisie supports these vigilante gangs – the Federation of Indian Chambers of Commerce and Industry has recommended that the Indian state continue to back such counterinsurgency tactics.

5. Naxalbari is an area in north Bengal bordering Nepal to the west, Sikkim and Bhutan to the north, and the then east Pakistan (now Bangladesh) to the South. For an account of the armed struggle there, see Banerjee (2008: chapter 4).

6. Srikakulam district is in North-Eastern Andhra Pradesh. For an account of the armed struggle there, see Banerjee (2008: chapter 5).

7. The Revolutionary Writers' Association in 1970, the Jana Natya Mandali in 1972, the Radical Students' Union in 1974, the Radical Youth League in 1975, and later, after the formation of the CPI(ML) PW) in 1980, the Rythu Coolie

Sangham, the Singareni Karmika Samakhya and the Mahila Vimukti Sangham.

8. The two main mass organisations are the autochthonous peasants and workers' Dandakaranya Adivasi Mazdoor Kisan Sanghatan and the autochthonous women's Dandakaranya Krantikari Adivasi Mahila Sanghatan.

9. For the CPI(ML) (PW)'s version of the Maoist movement, 1969-99, see People's March (1999).

10. See Mao's (1927) controversial 'Hunan Report,' presented to the CCP in January of that year.

11. With the 'great leap backward' to capitalism in China, the fall of the Berlin Wall in 1989, the reversion to capitalism in the former Soviet Union, 9/11 and the nakedness of US imperialism in its aftermath, the very idea of revolution as the road to human emancipation is being obliterated from the horizon of the present epoch.

12. An underdeveloped capitalist country is one in which (a) domestically, backwardness (a low level of development of the forces of production) prevails in significant parts of the economy, with these spheres dominated by mercantile (and credit) capital, this state of affairs concomitant with retrograde relations of production and sub-standard institutions of state and civil society, and (b) internationally, its state and capitalist class are largely dependent entities in the world system. This definition may seem 'technological determinist,' so I should clarify that I am postulating open-ended interrelations among and between the forces of production, the relations of production, the state and civil society.

13. Indeed, Dominique Caouette in this volume argues that this is what the Communist Party of Philippines has been able to do.

14. In the section on 'Vanguards of the Revolution' in his *Report of an Investigation of the Peasant Movement in Hunan*, Mao (1927) states: 'Leadership by the poor

peasants is absolutely necessary. Without the poor peasants there would be no revolution. To deny their role is to deny the revolution.'

15. CR is meant to prevent 'capitalist restoration'; its focus is on the political, ideological and cultural superstructure – institutions that wield power and instil or alter the ideas and values held by individuals and classes in the transitional society.

16. The Party's view on why it characterises India as semi-colonial and semi-feudal, its statement of the major contradictions in Indian society, the fundamental contradictions and the principal contradiction, the class character of the Indian state, and the targets of the Indian revolution are contained in CPI(Maoist) (2007: chapter 2).

17. For the Party's semi-feudal thesis, see the sub-section 'Why do we call India semi-feudal?' in CPI(Maoist) (2007: chapter 2).

18. For the principal contradiction, see CPI(Maoist) (2007a: section 19).

19. Drawing, among other things, on Marx's analysis of 'primitive accumulation' and his theory of ground rent, Lenin's and Kautsky's analyses of the development of capitalist relations in agriculture, and Mao's investigation of the peasant movement in Hunan and his analysis of classes in rural areas in semi-feudal China, there has been a very rich debate on the mode of production in Indian agriculture. See Patnaik (1990), wherein I would like to particularly draw our readers' attention to Rao's (chapter 2:33-37) and Banaji's (chapter 19:234-250) essays.

20. The notion of 'free labour' in the double sense is explained in chapter 6 of Marx's *Capital, Vol.I*. Basically the labourer is free to sell her/his labour-power to the employer of her/his choice. She/he cannot realise the value of this labour-power in any other way because she/he does not have the means of production, in other words, because

she/he has been 'freed' from ownership of the means of production.

21. Besides these new landlords, there are, of course, those landlords who own land in the villages but reside in urban India, and this category of absentee landlords is not taken into account in the NSS data.

22. Vijay (2012) draws on Rao and Bharathi (2010).

23. For the Party's version, see the sub-sections 'Why do we call India semi-colonial?' (CPI(Maoist) 2007: chapter 2) and 'Comprador Bureaucratic Bourgeoisie' and 'National Bourgeoisie' (ibid: chapter 3).

24. 'Bureaucrat capital,' in pre-liberation China, was capital unduly dependent on the state for its accumulation.

25. See the sub-section 'Class Character of the Indian State' (CPI(Maoist) 2007: chapter 2).

26. Imperialism, in my view, is a process whereby the main corporations and the state of a developed capitalist country get together to expand their activities, their interests, and their power beyond their borders. It has changed very significantly from the time when Lenin wrote about it.

27. See Amin (2010).

28. I first began theorising about this phenomenon 17 years ago. See D'Mello (1998: 38-40). A sub-imperialist power acts in the manner of an imperialist power in its regional setting and at the behest of an imperialist power, but can only do so as a junior partner in a strategic alliance with such a power. An example is Israel in the Middle-East as a junior partner of the United States. I have defined imperialism in footnote 26.

29. The TNCs reacted very favourably to the new economic policies of 1991 – in many cases, they ousted their Indian partners, acquired Indian enterprises, expanded and engaged in green-field entry in India's manufacturing

sector (see Chaudhuri 1995: Section IV; Nagaraj 2003: Section V). Also see Chaudhuri (2012) on the enhancement of transnational management control and market power in the Indian pharmaceutical industry as a result of the reintroduction of strong product patent protection.

30. Recent economic growth has been led by services, and India is now a 'global player' in information technology (IT) and IT-enabled, including business process outsourcing, services exports. The share of the services sector in both inward and outward foreign direct investment has increased dramatically in the 2000s, and is poised to do so even further as India continues to liberalise policy related to banking, insurance, and other financial services, civil aviation, telecommunications, and retail trade.

31. See Nagaraj (2006).

32. I allude to the contradictions between India and international financial capital, the latter, not the 'finance capital' of Lenin's time. This capital is, relatively speaking, disengaged from any particular national capitalist interests.

33. An earlier episode was in colonial India from 1881 to 1931 (Patnaik 2011: 301).

34. The value of exports and imports of goods and services as a percentage of GDP has increased from 22.9 in 1990-99 to 50.4 in 2010-11. Note disadvantageous import and export market structures in the context of the Singer-Prebisch proposition with respect to exports of agricultural and mineral commodities, and its possible extension to exports of low-tech manufactured commodities in relation to imports of high-tech manufactured products, and in the context of the inroads that the trading arms of transnational corporations have made in India's commodities trade, including buyer-driven global commodity chains in low-tech manufactured goods. See Chandra (1997: 173-174).

35. Patnaik's (2010: 1-4) own estimates of the proportion of the rural and urban populations unable to reach the minimum

nutrition norms in 2004-05 are 86.7% and 64.5% respectively.

36. Patnaik (2011a), among other things, links displacement due to special economic zones with rural landlessness.

37. What is of crucial significance is Washington's 'Pivot to Asia' strategy in the wake of China's rapid economic development over the last 30 years, Beijing's securing of international energy and raw material sources and transportation routes for the same, and her accompanying geo-political ascendency, all of which have upset the long-established US imperialist dominated order in Asia. The US' strategic alliances with Japan, Australia and India are aimed at containing China through political, diplomatic and military means, and Washington's three strategic partners have in turn forged strategic ties with each other. As a junior partner of the US Navy, the Indian Navy is fast becoming the chief policeman of the Indian Ocean. And, the Indian military's dependence on the US military-industrial complex is increasing, this also via military hardware and software deals with Israel.

38. On the whole, this alludes to state repression of the nationality movements in Kashmir, Nagaland, Mizoram, Assam and Manipur, and, of course, the Maoists and their support base in parts of central, eastern and southern India, aided by laws such as the Armed Forces (Special Powers) Act 1958, which gives the armed forces immunity from prosecution for rape, abduction, torture and summary execution in the course of the counter-insurgency in Kashmir and the North-East, and the Unlawful Activities (Prevention) Act, which outlaws politics and political parties that threaten the status quo.

39. Since 2005, India has played a leading role in ending the Nepali Revolution. The question being asked in radical left circles today is whether the 12-point agreement of 22 November 2005 with the seven parliamentary parties (SPP), the 8-point agreement of 16 June 2006, the Comprehensive Peace Agreement of November 2006, the 18 June 2008

deal, and all the rest of the pacts, taken together, that the Nepali Maoists entered into were part of the Washington-New Delhi combine's grand design – in alliance with the SPP – to end the Nepali revolution. Earlier, following the murder of King Birendra on 1 June 2001, the US intervened militarily in Nepal, and India closely coordinated with US strategy to ensure the military defeat of the Maoist-led People's War there (Mage 1997). But later, at India's insistence, the US changed tack. Indeed, with the US-India strategic alliance that followed, on South Asian affairs, Washington does, on occasion, defer to New Delhi on matters of regional security.

40. In concurrence with Washington, and as part of the Indian state's ambition to establish itself as the number-one regional power in South Asia, since 2001, India has emerged as Afghanistan's fifth largest bilateral 'aid' donor, after the US, UK, Japan and Germany. Indian business and the Indian government are closely involved in infrastructural projects, the most important of which is said to be the highway that will link the Iranian port of Chabaha to Afghanistan's main highway network. This will then be the main transport route for Indian exports to Afghanistan, circumventing Pakistan. Moreover, in October 2011, New Delhi entered into a bilateral Strategic Partnership Agreement with Kabul that envisages armaments supply, counterinsurgency and high-altitude warfare training to the Afghan army, air force and police.

41. Not long ago, even as New Delhi kept placating public opinion in Tamil Nadu (bitter memories still linger of the despicable role of the so-called Indian Peace Keeping Force in Sri Lanka in the 1980s), it supported Colombo all the way in its vicious military campaign that wiped out the Liberation Tigers of Tamil Eelam. The way has been cleared for a Comprehensive Economic Partnership Agreement with Colombo to be wrapped up; after all, most of India's foreign direct investment in South Asia is centred on Sri Lanka.

42. This is how Mao (1937) explains what he means by *principal* contradiction.

43. In Mao's (1938) theorisation of the PPW, in its first stage – the 'strategic defensive' – the see-saw of the enemy's 'encirclement and suppression' followed by the communists' 'tactical counteroffensive' ultimately takes the PPW into a state of 'equilibrium' and a 'strategic stalemate' is reached, which is stage-2 of the PPW.

44. This characterisation of the contrasting situation in China during its NDR relies on Mao (1939).

45. It may also be mentioned that the capacity to sustain a Long March, abandoning one but linking the other base areas in order to settle in and expand the base area with Yan'an as its capital in north-central China, is beyond the CPI(Maoist)'s military strength. And, revolution as national liberation from a colonial occupier, plus the provisional alliance with the GMD against Japanese occupation has no parallel whatsoever in India.

References

Amin, S. 2003. World Poverty, Pauperisation and Capital Accumulation. *Monthly Review* 55: 5 (available on-line at: http://monthlyreview.org/2003/10/01/world-poverty-pauperization-capital-accumulation/, accessed 24 July 2015).

_____ 2010. The Battlefields Chosen by Contemporary Imperialism: Conditions for an Effective Response from the South. *MRZine*, 2 February (available on-line at: http://mrzine.monthlyreview.org/2010/amin070210p.html , accessed 24 July 2015).

Banaji, J. 1977. Capitalist Domination and the Small Peasantry: Deccan Districts in the Late Nineteenth Century. *Economic and Political Weekly* 12, 1374-1404.

Banerjee, S. 2008 [1980]. *In the Wake of Naxalbari*. Kolkata: Sahitya Samsad.

Basole, A. & D. Basu 2011. Relations of Production and Modes of Surplus Extraction: Part I – Agriculture. *Economic and Political Weekly* 46: 14, 41-58.

Bernie. 2012. All Sorts of Roguery? The 'Financial Aristocracy' and Government à Bon Marché in India. *MRZine*, 19 August (available on-line at: http://mrzine.monthlyreview.org/2012/bernie190812.html , accessed 24 July 2015).

Bharathi, M. & R. S. Rao 2010. Comprehensive Study on Land and Poverty in Andhra Pradesh. In *In Search of Method: Collection of Articles* (ed.) M. Bharathi, 323-367. Hyderabad: Collective and Centre for Documentation, Research and Communication.

Chandra, N. K. 1997. Trade Technology and Development. In *Trade and Industrialisation* (ed.) D. Nayyar, 169-224. New Delhi: Oxford University Press.

_____ 2008. India's Foreign Exchange Reserves: A Shield of Comfort or an Albatross? *Economic and Political Weekly* 43: 14, 39-51.

_____ 2010. China and India: Convergence in Economic Growth and Social Tensions? In *China after 1978 – Craters on the Moon: Essays from Economic and Political Weekly* (ed.) Economic and Political Weekly, 279-317. Hyderabad: Orient Blackswan.

Chaudhuri, S. 1995. Government and Transnationals: New Economic Policies since 1991. *Economic and Political Weekly* 30: 18/19, 999-1011.

_____ 2012. Multinationals and Monopolies: Pharmaceutical Industry in India after TRIPS. *Economic and Political Weekly* 47: 12, 46-54.

D'Mello, B. 1998. Does Indian Sub-Imperialism Drive the

Bomb? *Frontier* 31: 8/11, 38-40.

_____ 2010. What is Maoism? In *What is Maoism and Other Essays* (ed.) B. D'Mello, 21-54. Kharagpur: Cornerstone Publications.

Gough, K. 1974. Indian Peasant Uprisings. *Economic and Political Weekly* 9: 32, 1391-1412.

Lenin, V. I. 1899. The Differentiation of the Peasantry. In *The Development of Capitalism in Russia* (available on-line at: http://www.marxists.org/archive/lenin/works/1899/dcr8ii/index.htm, accessed 24 July 2015).

_____ 1975 [1916]. *Imperialism: The Highest Stage of Capitalism*. Peking: Foreign Languages Press.

Mage, J. 2007. The Nepali Revolution and International Relations. *Economic and Political Weekly*, 42: 20, 1834-1839.

Mao Zedong. 1926. *Analysis of the Classes in Chinese Society* (available on-line at: http://www.marxists.org/reference/archive/mao/selected-works/volume-1/mswv1_1.htm, accessed 24 July 2015).

_____ 1927. *Report of an Investigation of the Peasant Movement in Hunan* (available on-line at: http://www.marxists.org/reference/archive/mao/selected-works/volume-1/mswv1_2.htm, accessed 24 July 2015).

_____ 1934. *Be Concerned with the Well-being of the Masses, Pay Attention to Methods of Work* (available on-line at: http://www.marxists.org/reference/archive/mao/selected-works/volume-1/mswv1_10.htm, accessed 24 July 2015).

_____ 1937a. *On Contradiction* (available on-line at:

http://www.marxists.org/reference/archive/mao/selected-works/volume-1/mswv1_17.htm, accessed 24 July 2015).

_____1937b. *On Practice: On the Relation between Knowledge and Practice, Between Knowing and Doing* (available on-line at: http://www.marxists.org/reference/archive/mao/selected-works/volume-1/mswv1_16.htm, accessed 24 July 2015).

_____1938a. *On Protracted War* (available on-line at: http://www.marxists.org/reference/archive/mao/selected-works/volume-2/mswv2_09.htm, accessed 24 July 2015).

_____ 1938b. *Problems of War and Strategy* (available on-line at: http://www.marxists.org/reference/archive/mao/selected-works/volume-2/mswv2_12.htm, accessed 24 July 2015).

_____1939. *The Chinese Revolution and the Chinese Communist Party* (available on-line at: http://www.marxists.org/reference/archive/mao/selected-works/volume-2/mswv2_23.htm, accessed 24 July 2015).

_____ 1940. *On Policy* (available on-line at: http://www.marxists.org/reference/archive/mao/selected-works/volume-2/mswv2_37.htm, accessed 24 July 2015).

_____ 1943. *Some Questions Concerning Methods of Leadership* (available on-line at: https://www.marxists.org/reference/archive/mao/selected-works/volume-3/mswv3_13.htm, accessed 24 July 2015).

Marx, K. 1852. *The Eighteenth Brumaire of Louis Bonaparte, 1848-1850* (available online at: http://www.marxists.org/archive/marx/works/download/pdf/18th-Brumaire.pdf, accessed 24 July 2015).

_____1853. *The British Rule in India* (available on-line at: http://www.marxists.org/archive/marx/works/1853/06/25.

htm, accessed 24 July 2015).

_____ 1954 [1867]. *Capital, Volume I*. Moscow: Foreign Languages Publishing House.

Nagaraj, R. 2003. Foreign Direct Investment in India in the 1990s: Trends and Issues. *Economic and Political Weekly* 38: 17, 1701-1712.

_____ 2006. Indian Investment Abroad: What Explains the Boom? *Economic and Political Weekly* 41: 46, 4716-4718.

Navlakha, G. 2012. *Days and Nights in the Heartland of Rebellion*. New Delhi: Penguin Books.

Patnaik, P. 2010. Notes on Contemporary Imperialism. *MRZine*, 20 December (available on-line at: http://mrzine.monthlyreview.org/2010/patnaik201210.html, accessed 24 July 2015).

Patnaik, U (ed.) 1990. *Agrarian Relations and Accumulation: The 'Mode of Production' Debate in India*. Bombay: Oxford University Press.

_____ 2004. The Republic of Hunger. *Social Scientist* 33: 9/10, 9-35.

_____ 2010. The Tendulkar Committee Report on Poverty Estimation. *People's Democracy* 34: 1, 1-4.

_____ 2011a. Unbalanced Growth, Tertiarisation of the Indian Economy and Implications for Mass Living Standards. In *Progressive Fiscal Policy in India* (ed.) P. Jha, 299-325. New Delhi: SAGE.

_____ 2011b. Imperialism, Resources, and Food Security, with Reference to the Indian Experience. In *India's New Economic Policy: A Critical Analysis* (ed.) W. Ahmed, A. Kundu & R. Peet, 217-39. New York: Routledge.

People's March. 1999. *30 years of Naxalbari – An Epic of Heroic Struggle and Sacrifice* (available on-line at: http://www.bannedthought.net/India/PeoplesMarch/PM19 99-2006/publications/30%20years/contents.htm, accessed 24 July 2015).

Rao, R. S. 1990. In Search of the Capitalist Farmer: A Comment. *Economic and Political Weekly* 5: 51, 2055-2056.

Rao, R. S. & M. Bharathi 2010. A Comprehensive Study of Land and Poverty. In *In Search of Method: Collection of Articles* (ed.) M. Bharathi, 323-367. Hyderabad: Centre for Documentation, Research and Communication.

Research Unit for Political Economy. 2006. Why the United States Promotes India's Great-Power Ambitions. *Monthly Review* 57: 10 (available on-line at: http://monthlyreview.org/2006/03/01/why-the-united-states-promotes-indias-great-power-ambitions, accessed 24 July 2015)

Shetty, S. L. 2011. Growing Inequality: A Serious Challenge to the Indian Society and Polity. In *Progressive Fiscal Policy in India* (ed.) P. Jha, 86-147. New Delhi: SAGE.

Sweezy, P. 1985. What is Marxism? *Monthly Review* 36: 10, 1-6.

Vijay, R. 2012. Structural Retrogression and Rise of 'New Landlords' in Indian Agriculture: An Empirical Exercise. *Economic and Political Weekly* 47: 5, 37-45.

Young, G. 1980. On the Mass Line. *Modern China* 5: 2, 225-40.

Unpublished Sources

CPI(Maoist). 2004a. *Hold High the Banner of Marxism-Leninism-Maoism* (available online at: http://www.bannedthought.net/India/CPI-Maoist-Docs/#Founding_Documents, accessed 24 July 2015).

_____ 2004b. *Strategy and Tactics of the Indian Revolution* (available on-line at: http://www.bannedthought.net/India/CPI-Maoist-Docs/#Founding_Documents, accessed 24 July 2015).

_____ 2004c. *Party Programme* (available on-line at: http://www.bannedthought.net/India/CPI-Maoist-Docs/#Founding_Documents, accessed 24 July 2015).

_____ 2007a. *Strategy and Tactics of the Indian Revolution* (available on-line at http://www.satp.org/satporgtp/countries/india/maoist/documents/papers/strategy.htm, accessed 24 July 2015).

_____ 2007b. *Party Programme*. Unpublished.

Part 2

Armed movements in Latin America and the Philippines

Chapter 4

THE FARC-EP AND CONSEQUENTIAL MARXISM IN COLOMBIA

James J. Brittain

Abstract *The Revolutionary Armed Forces of Colombia-People's Army (FARC-EP) has maintained its base among small-holders including coca farmers and expanded its struggle through a local interpretation of Marxism and Leninism. This chapter reviews current accounts of its history and contemporary presence. The author then provides his own analysis of their strategy, namely that they have successfully pursued a gradual expansion of a separate power base and economy from that of the state and its capitalist economy, a situation that Lenin described as 'dual power', or, as Gramsci elaborated, a challenge to the hegemony of the ruling bloc. His visits and interviews and two recent documentary films in the FARC-EP areas show that the economy under FARC leadership, while taxing and controlling the processing and selling of coca, is still one of private small-holders. Many farmers grow coca as their main crop but all to some extent diversify into subsistence crops. This is a successful preparation for eventual state power of a completely different kind under which the economy will be socialised.*

For a half century the Revolutionary Armed Forces of Colombia-People's Army (Fuerzas Armadas Revolucionarias Colombianas-Ejército del Pueblo, FARC-EP) have played a key role in organising, sustaining, and leading revolutionary activity within the Latin American country of Colombia. Displaying a unique application of Marxism-Leninism this insurgency has demonstrated the capacity to achieve power throughout various sectors of the country due, in part, to the movement's distinct commitment toward radical societal change. Dating back to the 1960s, the FARC-EP, in conjunction with the Colombian Communist Party (Partido Comunista Colombiano, PCC), began working with several thousand rural civilians to organise networks of cooperation and security in response to expanding capitalist interests and state-induced repression. In the face of extreme political and military coercion,[1] the movement established itself as a goal-orientated defence-based peasant collective across the southern departments of Tolima, Huila, and Cauca and critiqued imperialist interference in Colombia while putting in place strategies addressing agrarian reform and alternative modes of development via worker-peasant alliances (Peace and Socialism 1966: 12-18). In those early days, attempts were made to construct an uncorrupted stable society based on local control and a new approach to countering repressive centralised state power through the construction of self-defence communities in various rural areas of the southwest.[2]

While many romantic accounts of these peasant-based communities exist, virtually all fall short of recognising the movement's militant construction and political goal. Describing her recollection of the self-defence groups, Maria Ovidia Díaz stated, 'the campesino self-defence groups were an organization that sought to address the daily needs of the farmers. In its origins these campesino self-defence groups were organized to protect the well-being of the community' (as quoted in Obando and Velásqeuz 2004). Far from docile these sociopolitical collectives sought a peace-filled existence through mechanisms that would defend their alternative development projects from reaction. Rather than existing as autonomous non-violent social organisations, as some have suggested,[3] the self-defence groups understood the need for objective security in response to dominant class-interests. Alberto Gomez (1972: 253), in particular, documented how in addition to establishing programmes of human development the collectives had an 'overall policy of preparing for guerrilla action' (a policy subsequently pursued in other zones as well).[4] The success of said communities led sectors of the dominant class to see 'a threat in the existence of the self-defence zones. It realized that they were not a sign of relative equilibrium in the class balance, but a manifestation of class struggle' (Gomez 1972: 251; see also Sánchez and Meertens 2001: 178-184). Their formation signified a growing peril for the rural elite and a potential time bomb for the state,[5] as the communities – arranged in a localised *dual strategy* of socioeconomic political-cultural development *and* defensive measures to sustain alternatives erected – did not promote a non-militant individualised existence but rather demonstrated an organised Communist ideology that was part of a larger struggle vying for a revolutionary shift in the social relations of production.

A Unique Praxis

Officially formed in 1964, the FARC-EP is one of the longest established insurgencies in the world. One of the most distinct features of this insurgency is that it has been shaped, organised, and remains prominently led by the peasantry.[6] Outside the FARC-EP, there has never been a peasant-founded, structured, sustained, or directed revolutionary organisation within Central and South American society (Richani 2002: 60; Veltmeyer and Petras 2002: 82; Wickham-Crowley 1992: 18, 26). This is not to imply that peasants have been uninvolved in past attempts of self-emancipation within Latin American struggles, of which there have been many. Nor does it suggest that Colombia's middle and upper economic strata, urban-based unionists, liberation-theologians or others sectors of society are not in the ranks of, or associated with, the guerrillas – for they most assuredly are. What the above does signify is that the FARC-EP depicts an alternative example of a Latin American insurgency via leadership, tactical ambition, and ideology application(s). For example, the guerrilla's organisational structure is based on a hierarchical chain of command made up of a multi-person leadership deeply connected to the countryside. The highest level of leadership is the Secretariat of the Central High Command, composed of seven members (Pastor Alape, Bertulfo Álvarez, Pablo Catatumbo, Joaquín Gómez, Mauricio Jaramillo, Timoleón Jiménez, and Iván Márquez).[7] Of those within the Secretariat each has some personal tie to the countryside, as do 'most of the commanders of the fronts and columns' (Weinstein 2007: 289).[8] The rank-and-file also deviate from many guerrilla groups in the region (including others in Colombia), as the majority, at all levels, have some historic and contemporary connection to a bucolic territory (Weinstein 2007: 289; de la Peña 1998: 353). This is not to say that the FARC-EP remains confined to the countryside, however.[9] The past four decades have seen significant changes for Colombian society due to the political-economic climate and so too has the guerrilla army developed into a complex and organised movement far outside rurality.[10] Today, membership has grown to incorporate indigenous populations, afro-Colombians, the displaced, landless rural-labourers, intellectuals, unionists, teachers, professionals, doctors, lawyers, priests, and sectors of the urban workforce (Brittain 2010b). Roughly 65% continue to come from the countryside or rural-based municipalities – 12% to 13% composed of various indigenous groups[11] – and the remaining 35% from urban sectors.[12]

Steeped in Communist ideology, the FARC-EP has held onto a Marxist-Leninist strategy to procure revolution that distinguishes it from other socialist powers in history both regionally and globally. Regionally, the FARC-EP was one of the only Latin America insurgencies that did not support a Cuban model of *foco* theory for the Colombian situation.[13] Apart from following any form of *foco* theory that H. Michael Erisman and John M. Kirk (2006: 162) presented, the FARC-EP has, in fact, never been strongly influenced by Havana at all (see also Maullin 1973; Gott 1970). They have rather opted to follow a model by which local power is amassed through the establishment of broad support over long periods. According to Alfredo Schulte-Bockholt (2006: 111), 'the FARC doctrine proclaimed that revolutionary conditions developed over time,' not, as dictated through a Guevara-derived model where the guerrillas would induce or create such revolutionary conditions in and of themselves. For James Petras (1999: 30), the FARC-EP 'has built its power base patiently over time with a precise strategic plan: the accumulation of local power.'[14] Globally, the FARC-EP objectively and subjectively disassociated itself from the USSR well before its collapse (see FARC-EP 1999: 47-48). Maintaining a distinct domestic ambition and peasant-based leadership – which depicts a revolutionary dual power strategy from below – may offer answers as to how the FARC-EP, unlike other Latin American insurgencies, did not derive any significant material loss upon the fall of Soviet communism.[15] Abiding by a contextual interpretation of Marxist-Leninist revolution 'saved us when the Berlin Wall fell,' according to one Comandante (as quoted in Lévy 2004: 80). After interviewing Iván Ríos, a former member of the Secretariat, and other members of the insurgency, philosopher Bernard-Henri Lévy (2004: 82) noted the distinctiveness of the FARC-EP's political ideology: '[T]here is something in this Marxism-Leninism that, despite its irreproachable rhetoric, resembles nothing I have ever heard or seen elsewhere ... this is an impeccable Communism; along with Cuba, this is the last Communism in Latin America and, certainly, the most powerful.' Hugh O'Shaughnessy and Sue Branford (2005: 25) have also concluded that the FARC-EP is shaped by a unique 'form of Marxism-Leninism' (see also Cala 2000: 59).

Unlike 'new' social movements or post-modern 'insurgencies,' the FARC-EP have committed themselves to a more classically-orientated yet contemporary Marxism-Leninism (see Goff 2004: 39-41). It has even been suggested that the FARC-EP not only has the potential to be victorious but that they are, in some aspects, succeeding in their revolutionary struggle[16] so that the FARC-EP may be 'the first leftist guerrilla movement to achieve success in the post-cold war era' (Cala 2000: 56).[17]

Continuity in Power and Form

The last twenty years have witnessed the guerrilla movement expand social, economic, political, and cultural programs while escalating security measures against state reactionism (Brittain 2010a). The FARC-EP has been able to do this since it has become 'more sophisticated, shifting from small guerrilla units using hit and run tactics to "mobile warfare," employing a large number of combatants (battalion-strength) and targeting well-armed garrisons in peripheral cities' (Richani 2005: 84, 95). In these areas, the FARC-EP has moved beyond mere guerrilla combat and matured to a place of partial politico-military control over select territories (González, Bolivar, and Vázquez 2002: 54).[18] Even with severe blows experienced in recent years, the insurgency has been able not only to stabilise campaigns toward designated targets but to increase activities on an annual basis.

For much of the 2000s the FARC-EP modestly amplified armed campaigns (949 [2004], 1,008 [2005], 1,026 [2006], 1,057 [2007]) against state forces. Subsequent years, however, witnessed a considerable jump in operations. In 2008, claimed by the state as a year of decline for the FARC-EP, the guerrilla deployed a total of 1,353 attacks, while 2009 saw the number of military attacks engaged by the insurgency average over five per day [1,614] (Ávila Martínez 2010). It is no surprise, when one examines this data, that journalist Adriaan Alsema (2009) concluded, 'despite nearly eight years of an aggressive military offensive against the guerrillas, the FARC are far from beaten but appear to be on the rebound. According to [one] report, the guerrillas increased their military attacks by 30% in 2009.' By 2010 significant events transpired that led many to believe the

FARC-EP may be 'on the ropes' with the death of long-time Comandante (and military mastermind) Jorge Briceño. Nevertheless, attacks increased. While some estimated these campaigns at 1,800,[19] the actual numbers by the end of the year exceeded 1,947 (Valencia and Ávila Martínez 2011; Valencia 2011). Not only was the greatest number of insurgent-based attacks against state forces in fifteen years mounted, but 2010 bore witness to the highest number of casualties suffered by state forces in a decade. Tensions increased in 2011 with the death of the guerrilla's Commander-in-Chief Alfonso Cano in a state-led operation. Far from discouraged, the guerrillas bettered their military conquests as FARC-EP attacks showed more than a 10% increase when compared to the preceding year (Valencia and Ávila Martínez 2011; Mannon 2011). Conservative estimates suggested insurgent campaigns would likely add up to between 2,000 and 2,200 by the year's end (Valencia and Ávila Martínez 2011; Semana 2011; El Pais 2011). These assessments proved accurate when final reports highlighted the greatest expression of FARC-EP politico-military power in history, as 2,148 attacks were successfully waged throughout the nation (Alsema 2012b). Such accounts not only highlight the insurgency's capacity to sustain tactics but it emphasises renewed consolidation of control over various sections of the country.

With 2011 witnessing an average of seven campaigns per day, 2012 had an even more devastating effect on the state's control of the country. During the first 20 days of 2012 alone, the FARC-EP deployed over 132 attacks against security forces in a plethora of locations across the country (Radio Caracol 2012). As the year went on, the guerrillas demonstrated a capacity to fully consolidate control over of territory in numerous departments (Putumayo, Caquetá, Choco, etc.) thereby preventing multinational resource production and extraction, trade and intervention (Barrett 2012; Leonard 2012; Parkinson 2012). Apart from the scope of force being raised, so too had the numerical scale of campaigns grown. Attacks were noted to last longer and include larger numbers of armed guerrillas when compared to the 'hit and run strategy' earlier (Alsema 2012a). By the middle of the year, the FARC-EP was launching, on average, three hundred politico-military campaigns per month (Petterrson 2013c, 2013d).

Recognizing the insecure realities ahead, the administration of Juan Manuel Santos Calderón [2010-2014] agreed to begin an arduous series of peace negotiations with the FARC-EP to reduce the insurgency's momentum.[20] During the catalytic phase of the peace talks in September 2012, FARC-EP attacks dropped precipitously by seventy percent with an overall decrease of eighty percent once negotiations had begun, thus illustrating the fluid communications and manoeuvring of the insurgency's chain of command throughout the country (Pettersson 2013b, 2013d, 2013e).[21] While some measure of stability has occurred, it must be understood within the context of the civil war; a precarious political moment of negotiation when the insurgency has chosen to reserve operations outside the normalcy of national violence. Acknowledgment of this insecurity is shown by the fact that in the first quarter of 2013 the FARC-EP averaged fifty-seven political-military campaigns per month – in departments all over the country (Pettersson 2013a).

Not witnessed since the mid-1990s, the FARC-EP has amassed power not simply in the historic enclaves of its traditional support but in regions thought to have no guerrilla influence. While areas such as Caquetá, Cauca, Huila, Nariño, Tolima, Putumayo, and Meta are largely predisposed, it has been noted widely that the departments of Antioquia, Arauca, and Norte de Santander now have adequate levels of support for the FARC-EP (Valencia and Ávila Martinez 2011; The Economist 2011). This illustrates the guerrillas' revolutionary vitality, commitment, and broad support to respond even during periods of tribulation such as the loss of significant leaders (Chernick 2007: 69).

Theorising The FARC-EP's Revolutionary Strategy

In *Dual Power*, Lenin (1964: 38-39) demonstrated that a true revolution does not occur from above through the consolidation of power via pre-existing sociopolitical class structures but rather from below though an alternative class-based construct (both governing and militarily prepared), which exists beyond the conventional system. Some have tried to define dual power as the existence of 'two or more political blocs (including, typically, extant state officials and their allies), both or all of which claim to be the legitimate state, and both or all of which may possess significant means of coercion' (Goodwin 2001: 12). According to Charles Tilly (1978: 191-193), the situation of dual power, or what he labels 'multiple sovereignty,' occurs when contending groups vie for authority over a given population, thereby weakening one 'state' power in favour of another.[22] However, this is not what Lenin was pointing to. He argued that an alternative state must exist in dismissal of, not competition with, the existing model. In such a situation people 'set up their own organized power without having achieved political independence' (Lenin 1969: 401). Dual power then promotes a provisional state formed from and supported by the most exploited (in arms) through an entirely different form of self-governance whereby the people emancipate themselves and their class apart from the capitalist model (Lenin 1964: 38-40). Ernest Mandel (1994: 194 [italics added]) offered a more recent account of dual power as 'reflecting a territorial division of the country into liberated zones, in which a new state is *emerging*,' while other segments of the country remain entangled in the structure of the old (see also Bookchin 1996: 9-10). In time, new states consolidate more of the population as the once exploited establish additional zones apart from the previous system (see Wickham-Crowley, 1992: 155).

For Lenin, dual power does not come from those at the bottom *joining* external political groups that compete against the conventional political-economic order but rather *construct their own* alternative sociopolitical, economic, and culturally distinct state. This dual power is not continuity of competition between those seeking power but an evolutionary progression within distinct regions whereby emancipatory conditions have been *made by those from below* and *outside* the capitalist political-economic model.[23] The provisional state refrains from claiming legitimacy beside the capitalist state, for that which exists from below does not regard, nor does it associate with, the conventions of a capitalist system. Those from below grasp their newly emancipated provisional state (and actions) as an evolved sociopolitical, economic, and cultural formation existing apart from capitalism, not in competition with it. Created outside pre-existing elite control the new state alters class-dynamics of sociopolitical and economic relations (Petras and Veltmeyer 2005: 224). This form of revolution repudiates reassigning power through capitalist politics but substantively takes power from below.

Taking power is not only imperative for emancipation from inequitable social conditions but it is the most realistic method through which social change can remain a consistent reality in a given country. Yet, the taking of state power and the creation of a revolution can, and arguably must, assume different forms from those offered in popular approaches. Rather than utilising imposed models that emphasise the existing state structure as the ideal primary trajectory for change, via existing political processes (i.e., electoral politics), or more extreme strategies by which power is taken from existing governing bodies (i.e., *coup d'état*) (see Diagram 1), dual power facilitates revolution 'from below.' Instead of creating changes from the top-down, a change can begin through the creation of a war of position while the emancipation of localised conditions remain ongoing. This strategy can facilitate a situation of dual power created at levels of local support and territory. Conventional state structures become inundated as more and more municipalities *take power over the state rather than through existing conventional structures* (See

Diagram 2). Such a strategy creates a noose-like effect that strangles the existing capitalist (political-economic) power structure from outside, consequently taking state power.

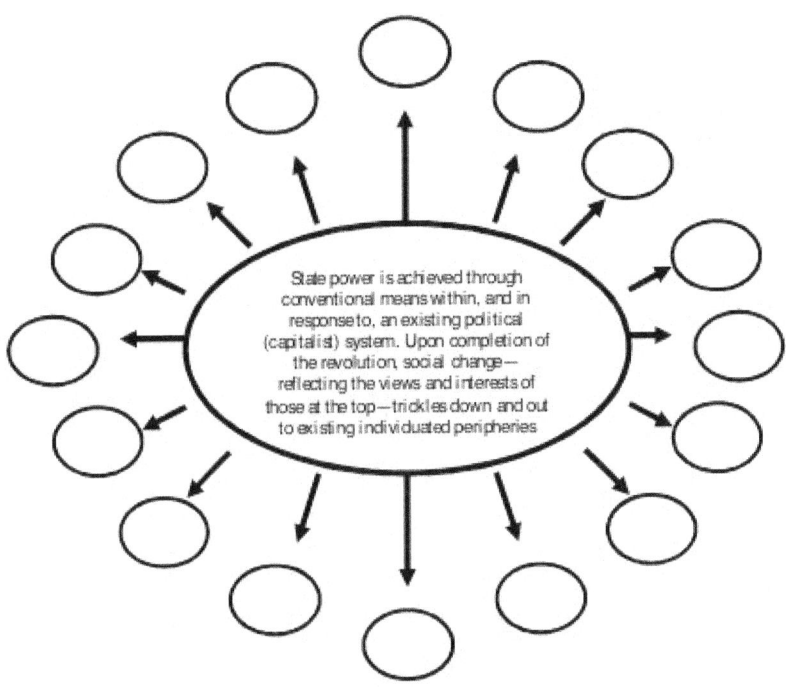

State power is achieved through conventional means within, and in response to, an existing political (capitalist) system. Upon completion of the revolution, social change— reflecting the views and interests of those at the top—trickles down and out to existing individuated peripheries

Diagram 1: Top-Down (State-Centred) Approach

Social change from below is important for it looks at revolution beyond the confines of politics. The crumbling of a political form, in and of itself, does not, in fact, constitute a revolution but rather a window of opportunity for the next most dominant political faction to usurp power. Understanding this, Marxists are not overly concerned with the 'conception of the state, as such, but the relation between this conception and

Marx's attitude to the proletariat (or, rather, to "the poor" ...)' (Löwy 2005a: 29). Revolutions, by their very nature, cannot come through those already empowered but are made real only through the conscious and organised action of the disempowered. Hence, revolutions can best be defined by the extent to which those exploited under the dominant paradigm of capitalism are emancipated (Löwy 2005b: 24). Marxism-Leninism then emphasises the potential power of the powerless to respond to the contradictory social relations of productions as *the* important factor concerning revolution.

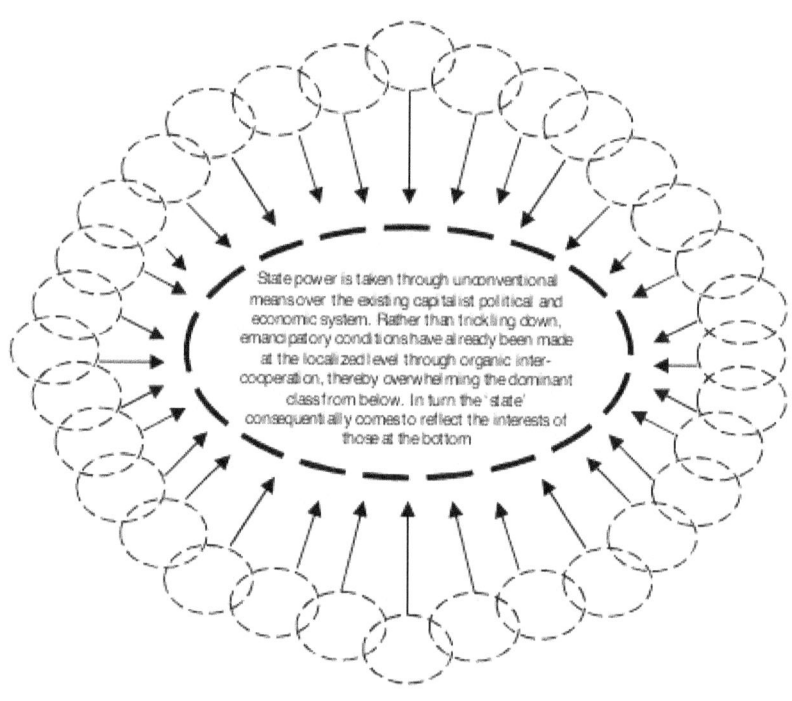

State power is taken through unconventional means over the existing capitalist political and economic system. Rather than trickling down, emancipatory conditions have already been made at the localized level through organic inter-cooperation, thereby overwhelming the dominant class from below. In turn the 'state' consequentially comes to reflect the interests of those at the bottom

Diagram 2: From Below (Dual Power)

For going on two decades, the FARC-EP demonstrated

a tangible change in political-military positioning when it 'began to move away from the rigid top-down bureaucracy to one more dependent on a system of regional blocs and fronts operating throughout the country' (Murillo and Avirama 2004: 75). Emphasising a 'local power' strategy of regional linkages increased acceptance and support in various localities (both rural and urban). In these regions – most of which were/are impoverished – various socio-political, economic, and cultural alternatives were grounded. One explicit alternative strategy through which dual power can be expressed is through the FARC-EP's (pre)revolutionary tactics toward coca (the principle ingredient related to the processing and production of cocaine).

Coca and the FARC-EP

Countless state-based reports, scholastic papers, popular media scripts, and even some subscribing to a 'progressive' social justice mentality have, to a point of uninformed acceptance, highlighted the FARC-EP's direct involvement with Colombia's coca-industry. This observation is sadly fascinating since it has materialised without any kernel of evidence from critical academic inquiry, field research, participant observation, and so on. Ironically, those of us who have engaged in such fieldwork have found that, rather than displaying any direct involvement (i.e., cultivation, processing, production, trafficking, etc.), the FARC-EP has created strategies to strengthen sociopolitical and economic conditions for people in Colombia's peripheries, weakening the industry's stranglehold over them.

The FARC-EP has never promoted the production of coca. For decades the guerrillas have sought alternative development strategies to alleviate small producers' dependence on coca (see Coghlan 2004: 207; Livingstone 2003: 130; Richani 2002: 99; Gamboa 2001: 100; Ruiz 2001: 62). They have worked tirelessly to discourage farmers, *campesinos*, semi-proletarians, etc. from succumbing to coca cultivation and/or to limit the narco-economy from completely taking over rural sections of the country (Holmes, Amin Gutiérrez de Piñeres and Curtin 2006; Glenn, 2003; Stokes 2002). Historically, they did this by fighting land concentration and the political sway of emerging primary drug cartels (Camacho Guizado and López Restrepo 2007: 80; Labrousse 2005: 177; Felbab-Brown 2005: 113; Dudley 2004: 57, 102; Gutiérrez Sanín 2004: 282; Rochlin 2003: 107; Clawson and Lee III 1998: 52, 58, 180). Several years ago, the insurgency even worked alongside the United Nations (UN) in a series of projects related to crop substitution in zones under their control (Labrousse 2005: 175; see also Ahmad 2006; Schulte-Bockholt 2006; Labrousse 2005; Glenn 2003).

Realising that an anti-coca position could be interpreted as anti-peasant – thereby eroding their support-base – the FARC-EP shifted its policy during the early-mid 1990s. In short, as a revolutionary movement, the guerrillas opted to stand beside those marginalised and was 'compelled to accept the peasants' shift to illicit crop plantations as a supplementary income' (Richani 2002: 71; see also Molano 2005: 32).[24] Rather than dictating and remaining in ideological opposition to those marginalised under capitalistic material conditions, the 'People's Army' chose to 'accept' the peasantries' need to grow coca as a means of survival. This acceptance was not, however, on the basis of directly becoming involved in the industry but rather indirectly through a complex class-based model of taxation of specific sectors of the rural economy (which included the coca-industry).

For over a decade the FARC-EP has established a series of tax platforms for select persons and corporations throughout regions where they hold power.[25] The levies imposed by the insurgency are based on a person's relation to the means of production. The FARC-EP's class-based taxation model imposes an intricate system of levies and tariffs on sectors of the coca industry, as it does on much corporate or economic activity in the periphery (i.e., oil production, lumber, bananas, or any other commodity/service). The taxes obtained are collected but not spent by the FARC-EP. In many cases, they are forwarded to a locally elected neighbourhood council, which implements social programmes such as education centres, health-care provisions and/or services, and infrastructure. Such activities show how the FARC-EP is not aligned with the drug economy but rather heavily involved in overseeing *all* aspects of class-based production in areas under their control (see Kirk 2003: 227-228). In other words 'the guerrillas do not constitute another "cartel." Their role in the drug trade is in extorting a percentage of the commercial transaction of coca and coca paste, just as they do with many other commercial products in the areas which they operate, be it cattle, petroleum, or coffee (Chernick 1996).

The class-based taxation model has created off-shoots that have enabled the peasantry to secure 'a stable economic base for the colonos and small peasants by regulating the market relations and prices and by providing financial and technical assistance to the peasants and protection of the colonos' (Richani 2002: 70; see also Kenney 2007: 230). Exempting the producers from any form of levy, the guerrilla has forced the middle and upper-echelons of the industry consistently to pay peasants and rural wage-labourers the going market price for coca leaves, coupled by an additional expense for labour power spent by the workers (Rochlin 2003: 136; Richani 2002: 70). The FARC-EP regulates what an equitable and fair return would be and makes certain that middlemen abide by the set wage (Peceny and Durnan 2006: 107; Labrousse 2005: 172; Stokes 2005: 86). As the insurgency ensures that the buyers pay the coca growers a fair price, the class-based taxation model has translated into better wages for peasants in FARC-EP-controlled areas (International Action Center 2001: 3). There is proof of this: 'areas in which the guerrillas' presence is weak or nonexistent, the price of labor is lower than in areas where it has a strong military presence' (Richani 2002: 110; see also Felbab-Brown 2005: 109). While this in no way suggests an economic boom for the peasants, it does provide them a guaranteed income that is not based on speculation, as traditional crops would be, but on guaranteed returns (Castaño 2006; Felbab-Brown 2005: 108; Villalón 2004a, 2004b).

Through this strategy the insurgency has proven its credibility not only by supporting local rural populations' efforts to benefit themselves and their community but also by legitimising the guerrillas' capacity to act within an ethical economic framework. O'Shaughnessy and Branford (2005: 27-28) acknowledge that 'although large sums of money are involved, there is little personal corruption' in the FARC-EP, on any level. 'There is no evidence,' according to Marc Chernick (2007: 73) 'that leaders or fighters in the FARC are accumulating individual wealth.' Very much ideologically-based in their actions, the insurgency has demonstrated collective versus individual motivation, especially concerning the tremendous sums obtained (Gutiérrez Sanín 2004: 268-269; see also Weinstein, 2007: 292, 294). Supporting such a claim, Francisco Gutiérrez Sanín (2008: 13) has noted that 'looting for individual benefit is nearly inconceivable.' After reviewing hundreds of cases of guerrillas in several separate databases, he found that cases of corruption are 'relatively rare, especially taking into account the magnitude of the sums handled by the guerrillas' and 'indeed, I am not aware of any reports of individualistic looting by the FARC; all the goods coming from military or illegal economic activities go to the organization' (Gutiérrez Sanín 2008: 13-14). He added that no evidence suggests Comandantes are involved in personal enrichment (Gutiérrez Sanín 2004: 268-269). Such untarnished practices have more than 'facilitated the accountability of the FARC' (Stokes 2005: 86).[26]

Regardless of the paradigm that a nation finds for itself, monocrop production leads to an unsustainable arrangement and outcome for a given society. As Harry E. Vanden and Gary Prevost (2006: 153) noted, 'by making the entire economy dependent on one primary product, the nation's economic health becomes heavily tied to the fortunes of that product on the international market. Devastating busts often follow boom periods.' In light of this, the FARC-EP has shown opposition toward monoculture while supporting crop substitution and the restoration of cultural traditions using agricultural practices. Yet, if all sectors in FARC-EP territory supported and maintained a simple systemic formula of crop substitution, moving to the next most lucrative crop, then a cyclical effect would occur due to the nature of capitalist expansionism. Such a reality is important for it exemplifies how mere reformist measures cannot be sustained over extended periods in a profit-driven environment. Even if a peasant successfully replaced their illegal product with another that is legal, it would be only a matter of time before the restrictions of capital drove the commodity to be devalued domestically and globally. In short, the primary problem facing rural Colombia(ns) is the capitalist model itself.

While substituting legal crops for illegal ones is important it does not address the negative consequences specifically resulting from the domestic capitalist framework. For the greater part of the past twenty years, three specific outcomes have resulted for peasants who moved away from coca cultivation. First, as numerous peasants adopted crop substitution an influx of a few specific crops arose in the same region, thus driving down prices of produced goods. This subsequently caused a cyclical effect of poverty. Once more rural producers fell back into the coca-industry as a means of survival. The second dilemma saw peasants, who agreed to state-imposed crop substitution, not receive promised incomes from the state, development agencies, or NGOs. Suffering from a lack of capital, producers were forced to return to coca, as no other means of subsistence was available. Lastly, peasants who once refrained from growing coca saw legal crops sprayed with poisonous defoliants during Colombian/US anti-narcotic campaigns. This left many peasants with little option but to leave for the city or ironically move to coca to cover their losses (O'Shaughnessy and Branford 2005: 13-14, 112).[27] These are some of the common realities that have been witnessed throughout Colombia as a result of so-called alternative crop substitution projects within the confines of a capitalist paradigm. To relieve such quandaries, the FARC-EP has prepared a more efficient program to slowly transform an individuated capitalist model to a socialised system.

An interesting policy concerning coca in insurgent-held territory is one whereby the FARC-EP 'urges peasants to dedicate parts of their parcels for foodstuff production and to retain only a part for coca growing' (Richani 2002: 70; see also Schulte-Bockholt 2006: 133-134; Pearce 1990: 33). Although it is not well known, a cultivation programme was established whereby peasants, who chose to grow coca, devoted a certain percentage of lands for alternative crop production (Brittain 2007; see also Villalón 2004a, 2004b; Labrousse 2005: 172; Leech 2000).

In consultation with small producers and local community-based political councils, the FARC-EP's program has seen producers allocate a percentage of their cultivation to agriculture, be it in the form of 1) subsistence crops; 2) traditional Colombian harvests; or 3) crops for regional barter. As I witnessed on two different occasions with a peasant-based coca-cultivator and a FARC-EP member, the mission aims to prepare the rural sector for a smoother transition from a capitalist mode of production to one based on socialised cooperatives. The method behind this process has been in the works for over two decades in selected regions under FARC-EP control but has been increasingly implemented across much of the insurgency's territory. Dating back to the 1980s, 'the FARC guerrillas ... encouraged the peasants in the coca growing areas they control to grow food crops as well as coca' (Pearce 1990: 33). This strategy continued throughout the 1990s when the FARC-EP compelled 'farmers to grow foodstuffs in addition to coca' (Schulte-Bockholt 2006: 133-134). In 2004, Carlos Villalón, made a documentary film entitled *Cocaine Country*, which recognized how the FARC-EP has increasingly instituted this programme. Within regions visited by Villalón (2004b), all peasants who chose to grow coca were required to devote a minimum of 3 acres of land to alternative crop production in proportion to every 7 acres of coca. In 2005, much higher percentages were seen by Alain Labrousse, who documented how the FARC-EP encouraged a 75% share of subsistence crops with only a quarter of the harvest allotted for coca (2005: 172). During discussions with both FARC-EP members and civilians it was noted that the alternative crop ratio programme anticipates future crop substitution strategies in the event of the insurgency seizing central state power.

The political-economic reality of coca cultivation and production is a by-product of necessity. The peasant's sole purpose for harvesting coca is because it is the only means by which they can procure some level of stability. In recognition of this, the drug industry is directly correlated with the deteriorated economy. If a large-scale socialised economy were provided – education, health-care, redistribution of land, etc. – peasants, having their social requirements met, would have little need for individual wealth. Consequently, vast segments of the rural sector could then dismiss coca cultivation because necessities were satisfied. This potentially results in a large proportion of the rural population, once dependent on growing coca, working with the FARC-EP to shift production to traditional agriculture, providing growth in caloric intake and nutritional sustenance for the population.

Another benefit from the alternative crop ratio model can be seen through a sociological examination of rural Colombia in the context of neoliberalism. By the 1970s, subsistence-based agriculture was largely abandoned in the south. At this time the cartels slowly started to gain momentum. With the 'opening' of the Colombian economy in the 1980s and full neoliberal policies being implemented during the 1990s, many in the south shifted to coca cultivation as a means of survival. The sociological result is that contemporary southern Colombia has a second and third generation of coca growers. Yet, unlike those that came out of the 1950s-1970s, present generations have never known an alternative model of agricultural production. The elder generation, once experienced in traditional crop production (coffee, yucca, lemons, maize, etc.), were forced to turn to coca as a result of land centralisation, state-based coercion, and neoliberal economic policies. The current generation does not share this cultural history nor do they relate to another model of crop production. Many of the rural producers I interviewed under the age of thirty-four acknowledged that they had little experience of crop diversification. They did, however, have considerable knowledge concerning highly advanced methods of cultivating coca – such as genetically modified strands of coca resistant to aerial fumigation. The ratio-programme helps them to become reacquainted with classical crop cultivation and production that will be much needed in the event of a FARC-EP victory.

Continuing to support a nationally-applied model of partial/complete crop substitution coupled with the class-based taxation system, the FARC-EP is actively involved in de-linking capitalist processes in sectors of Colombian society. If the insurgency is to assist the creation of a socialist society, based on Marxist-Leninist principles, then they must dissociate trade from profit-based models. This will not be sudden, but by using strategies that assist human development a structure can begin to acquaint Colombians with the benefits of an alternative non-capitalist method of subsistence, communal models that reinvigorate cultural methods of production, and socialist practices that confer domestic benefits. The above demonstrates how the FARC-EP are preparing to act as a legitimate government within a socialist Colombia not only for themselves but they are readying the population for a post-capitalist society not dependent monetarily on the coca-industry. Such conditions are disconcerting to the higher levels of the drug-trade, which derive extensive profits from the informal economy. More troubling to these individuals is the evidence of a clear pre-revolutionary project implemented from below that has been and continues to be successful in select areas of the country.

Conclusion

There cannot then be a *rigid* blueprint for socialist transformation based on the scale of various conditions that will, and must, lead to alternative corresponding relations of emancipation. A variety of revolutionary identities are to be realised in the conscious and active deconstruction of (pre)existing domestic conditions of oppression, as those in struggle begin to establish roots for social transformation (see Harnecker 1986: 128). Concretely, no revolution can be copied from elsewhere, since radical social change is based on immediate sociopolitical and economic conditions, not on an encoded or symmetrical outline. In lieu of this, the FARC-EP has avoided taking central state power through an immediate win over the governing apparatus or a series of revolutionary pushes aimed at the capital. By extending its influence through a slow, realistic, ideologically motivated programme, the FARC-EP continues to create a distinct counter-hegemony via 'the accumulation of local power' (Petras 1999: 30). While largely in (but not exclusively to) rural territories, the guerrillas have erected a 'system of dual power in several regions of the country' by offering an alternative to conventional state power (Petras 2003: 25). This reflects the reality of socialism as a process -- an intermediate and evolving series of developments for the betterment of a given society; a 'continuous and systematic revolution of a people,' not merely based on taking state power but 'a continuous process of formation and superseding of unstable equilibria,' always in response to the societal conditions of a revolutionary epoch (Gramsci 1977: 55, 1971: 182).[28] I have provided a glimpse of how the FARC-EP continues to contribute theoretically to conditions of revolutionary social change in Colombia through, of, and with those from below. Creating a platform on which radical measures are being created alongside concurrent revolutionary projects throughout parts of the country, the FARC-EP's unique Marxist-Leninist approach towards substantive change demonstrates how an insurgency can work closely with local communities to create a dual power revolutionary perspective. The insurgency has employed a model of transformation that not only obstructs the conventional state without taking central power but also continues to hamper existing pillars of capitalist political economy from further exploitation. Only time will tell if this will lead to an all-encompassing revolutionary transformation for the country and peoples of Colombia coming to fruition or if further shifts in response to internal conditions will be necessary.

Notes

1. While the military was directly involved in coercive activity against the rural population the government was virtually inactive in providing the majority of the populace with a lengthy list of social services such as education and healthcare.

2. The progression and expansion of these networks was rampant, with over sixteen being established by 1964.

3. See LeGrand (1986: 163); Walton (1984: 94, 99); Feder (1971: 189).

4. It has been suggested that the struggle for change in the countryside left few options than organizing into 'self-defence units by the Communist Party ... to avoid extermination' (Simons 2004: 41).

5. See Crandall (2008: 53).

6. This proves an exception to (accurate) assessments that numerous Latin American guerrilla leaders came from the middle economic strata (Castañeda 1994: 78; Calvert 1999: 112). The FARC-EP differs from many movements that were, are, or appear to be 'fundamentally the creation of' a singular person, military officer, or post-secondary educated individual (Castañeda 1994: 127).

7. Other essential figures associated with the Secretariat over the past quarter-century include Jacobo Arenas, Jorge

Briceño, Alfonso Cano, Efraín Guzmán, Manuel Marulanda Vélez, Raúl Reyes, and Iván Ríos

8. See also Richani (2007: 414-415, 2002: 63); Wickham-Crowley (1992: 331); CISLAC (2001).

9. There are essentially two distinct periods of importance concerning the FARC-EP's historical development; the post-1964 period, when a movement of militant subsistence agriculturists lived in relatively underdeveloped regions of the southwest and a post-1982 period when the *Ejército del Pueblo* (People's Army) was organized.

10. Both Admiral Edgar Cely and president Juan Manuel Santos Calderón [2010-2014] have acknowledged the FARC-EP's powerbase in numerous cities (Alsema 2011; Heyden 2011).

11. This is a substantial number when we consider the size of Colombia's indigenous population. Mario A. Murillo and Jesus Rey Avirama (2004: 41) believed that indigenous people represented roughly 5% of the domestic populace; however, it is more accurate to say that Colombia's indigenous peoples constitute less than 2% (Palacios 2006: 251; Lakshmanan 2004; Livingstone 2003: 124). The large percentage of indigenous members could be due to several factors: the systemic assaults waged against native populations and their lands or possibly a growing shift in class-consciousness and revolutionary class struggle rather than politics of identity and autonomy (Brittain 2005). It is also important to note that 69% of the country's eighty-four indigenous groups exist within the department of Putumayo alone (Flounders 2003: 84). With the Putumayo being one of the FARC-EP's strongest areas, the above percentage suggests that a great deal of the indigenous groups within this department may support the FARC-EP.

12. With respect to leadership, the movement has paid particular attention to gender equality (Gibbs 2011; Botero 2006). While women such as Miryam Narváez and Judith Grisales have been instrumental in the guerrilla movement

since its inception, currently 50% of the membership is female with 30% to 55% of Comandantes being women, depending on the region (Gutiérrez Sanín 2008: 10; O'Shaughnessy and Branford 2005: 27; Galdos 2004; Richani 2002: 62). In the two Fronts the author studied, women actually outnumbered men in areas of mid-level leadership by 2:1. One of the most powerful military Fronts, formerly headed by Comandante Mono Jojoy (Jorge Briceño), is currently led by Tanja Nijmeijer (Snyder 2011).

13. Closely associated with Ché Guevara (2006), *foco* theory is largely a strategy generated by Régis Debray's belief that small groups could themselves create revolutionary conditions (Debray 1967).

14. Such insight is doubly important as the idea that guerrilla ideology is easily shaped in time and space by dominant or charismatic authorities (see Wilkinson 1971: 139) is over-generalised, yet the FARC-EP has never displayed these characteristics (Gott 2008; Hylton 2008).

15. For context refer to Castañeda (1994: 240-241).

16. See Brittain (2010a); Goff (2004: 44, 47); Petras and Veltmeyer (2005: 126); Röhl (2004: 2).

17. In recognition of the above, some have demonstrated a lack of political and social theory or knowledge of the insurgency by stating that the FARC-EP 'espouse a dogmatic Marxist ideology' (Sweig and McCarthy 2005: 18).

18. This does not, however, suggest that the insurgency refrains from such methods, as it frequently adapts 'its military to offset the government's air power advantage by re-employing guerrilla warfare tactics, moving in small units, and dispersing its forces into larger areas' (Richani 2005: 89).

19. See Leech (2011).

20. Immediately, a divergence in military operations aimed at state and multinational targets occurred. This is a most

compelling expression of the FARC-EP's continued power, for they displayed a uniform capacity to cease (or implement) politico-military campaigns when the peace process arose.

21. In the midst of this calm, the guerrillas were still very much operative and capable to reengage operations. During a brief period following a bilateral cease-fire, the FARC-EP responded to state aggression by carrying out forty-eight campaigns throughout the country in the last ten days of January 2013 alone (Pettersson, 2013d).

22. For Tilly, those from below do not directly construct authority but come to be a part of it through their external support. In reference to the Colombian situation (see Wickham-Crowley 1991: 39).

23. Examples closer to this account of dual power can be recognised in Bookchin's work (1998: 114-115, 217).

24. While extended throughout the country only a minority of regions under FARC-EP control house a vibrant coca-industry (Rochlin 2003: 100, 137; Clawson and Lee III 1998: 179). Furthermore, numerous analysts have detailed how a clear number of Comandantes have tangibly rejected the coca-industry and refuse to have anything to do with its activities (Holmes, Amin Gutiérrez de Piñeres and Curtin 2006: 167; Rangel Suárez 1998; Craig 1987: 29).

25. The model has been incredibly effective and able to withstand state attempts to disrupt it. Even in areas where the FARC-EP was temporarily expelled by state or paramilitary forces, the tax system stayed intact due to the insurgency's counter-hegemony. MNCs and individuals knew the insurgency would in time retake the territory and re-implement the tax and/or respond to those who periodically stopped payment (see Ortiz 2006: 216-217).

26. Making sure funds are used for their intended social purpose local officials are contacted by the FARC-EP via secret meetings and 'are lectured and threatened for

stealing community funds and for other forms of corruption'
(Taussig 2004: 143; see also FARC-EP 2000).

27. One US official admitted the goal of fumigation was to
displace peasants structurally in order to increase cheap
labour in the cities while privately centralising rural
resources (Barstow and Driver 2003).

28. Gramsci approached revolutionary change as a constant
evolution and progression, not as a simple reality when the
proletariat seizes power (see also Lebowitz 2011).

References

Ahmad, A. 2006. Colombia's Lethal Concoction. *Frontline*
23: 6, 59-65.

Alsema, A. 2009. FARC is on the rebound: study.
Columbia Reports, 26 November, (available on-line at:
http://colombiareports.com/farc-is-on-the-rebound-study/,
accessed 19 August 2015).

_____ 2011. FARC returning to Colombian cities: armed
forces. *Columbia Reports*, 7 June (available on-line at:
*http://colombiareports.com/farc-returning-to-colombian-
cities-army/*, accessed 19 August 2015).

_____ 2012a. Number of FARC attacks highest in 15
years: Think tank. *Columbia Reports*, 24 January
(available on-line at: http://colombiareports.com/number-
of-farc-attacks-highest-in-15-years-thank-tank/, accessed
19 August 2015).

_____ 2012b. FARC attack southwest Colombia army
base; 3 killed, 18 injured. *Colombia Reports*, 11 February
(available on-line at: http://colombiareports.com/farc-
attack-southwest-colombia-army-base-3-dead-18-injured/,
accessed 19 August 2015).

Ávila Martínez, A. F. 2010. *La Guerra Contra Las FARC y*

La Guerra de Las FARC. Bogotá: Corporación Nuevo Arco Isis.

Barrett, B. 2012. Oil transporters refuse to work in dangerous southern Colombia. *Columbia Reports*, 14 March (available on-line at: http://colombiareports.com/oil-operations-suspended-for-security-reasons-in-southern-colombia/, accessed 19 August 2015).

Barstow, A & T. Driver 2003. *Colombians Speak Out about Violence and U.S. Policy*. Lanham, MD: National Film Network.

Bookchin, M. 1996. *The Third Revolution: Popular movements in the revolutionary era*. London: Cassell.

_____ 1998. *The Third Revolution: Popular movements in the revolutionary era Vol. 2*. London: Cassell.

Botero, J. E. 2006. *Últimas Noticias de la Guerra*. Bogotá: Testimonio.

Brittain, J. 2010a. *Revolutionary Social Change in Colombia: The origin and direction of the FARC-EP*. London: Pluto Press.

_____ 2010b. *Continued Insecurity: Documenting the permanence of the FARC-EP within the context of Colombia's civil war*. Ottawa: IRB.

_____ 2007. Formas de Desarrollo Poco Convencionales e Ilícitas: La compleja industria del narcotráfico en Colombia. *Cuadernos de Sociología* 4, 13-68.

_____ 2005. Run, Fight or Die in Colombia. *Counterpunch*, 12 March (available on-line at: http://www.counterpunch.org/brittain03122005.html, accessed 19 August 2015).

Cala, A. 2000. The Enigmatic Guerrilla: FARC's Manuel Marulanda. *Current History* 99: 634, 56-59.

Calvert, P. 1999. Guerrilla Movements. In *Developments in Latin American Political Economy: Status, markets and actors* (eds) J. Buxton & N. Ohillips, 112-130. Manchester: Manchester University Press.

Camacho Guizado, Á & A. López Restrepo 2007. From Smugglers to Drug Lords to Traquetos. In *Peace, Democracy, and Human Rights in Colombia* (eds) C. Welna & G. Gallón, 60-89. Notre Dame, ID: University of Notre Dame Press.

Castañeda, J. 1994. *Utopia Unarmed: The Latin American Left after the Cold War*. New York, NY: Vintage Books.

Casta, J. 2006. *Colombia: Why do small farmers cultivate coca*? (available on-line at: http://www.cpt.org/cptnet/2006/12/30/colombia-why-do-small-farmers-cultivate-coca, accessed 19 August 2015).

Chernick, M. 2007. FARC-EP: From Liberal guerrillas to Marxist rebels to post-cold war insurgents. In *Terror, Insurgency, and the State: Ending protracted conflicts* (eds) M. Heiberg, B. O'Leary & J. Tirman, 51-82. Philadelphia, PA: University of Pennsylvania Press.

United States, Congress, House, Committee on Foreign Relations. 1996. *Overall U.S. counter-narcotics policy toward Colombia: Hearing before the Committee on International Relations. Washington: House of Representatives*. Washington, DC: U.S. G.P.O.

O'Casey, A. 2000. *Colombia: Peace at What Price?* Sydney: Committee in Solidarity with Central America and the Caribbean.

Clawson, P & W. Rensselaer 1998. *The Andean Cocaine*

Industry. New York, NY: St. Martin's Griffin.

Coghlan, N. 2004. *The Saddest Country: On assignment in Colombia.* Montreal: McGill-Queen's University Press.

Craig, R. 1987. Illicit Drug Traffic: Implications for South American source countries. *Journal of Interamerican Studies and World Affairs* 29: 2, 1-34.

Crandall, R. 2008. *Driven by Drugs: U.S policy toward Colombia.* Boulder, CO: Lynne Rienner.

Debray, R. 1967. *Revolution in the Revolution? Armed struggle and political struggle in Latin America.* London: Penguin.

Economist, The. 2011. Never-Ending: The FARC is not finished yet. 7 July (available on-line at: http://www.economist.com/node/18928504, accessed 19 August 2015).

El Pais. 2011. *Suroccidente, el nuevo centro de operaciones de las Farc.* 18 July (available on-line at: http://www.elpais.com.co/elpais/judicial/suroccidente-nuevo-centro-operaciones-farc, accessed 19 August 2015).

Erisman, M. H & J. M. Kirk 2006. *Redefining Cuban Foreign Policy: The impact of the "Special Period".* Gainesville, FL: University of Florida.

FARC-EP. 1999. *FARC-EP Historical Outline.* Toronto: International Commission.

_____ 2000. *Law 003, About Administrative Corruption.* Mountains of Colombia: The Central General Staff of the FARC-EP.

Feder, E. 1971. *The Rape of the Peasantry: Latin*

America's landholding system. New York, NY: Anchor Books.

Felbab-Brown, V. 2005. The Coca Connection: Conflict and drugs in Colombia and Peru. *Journal of Conflict Studies* 25: 2, 104-128.

Flounders, S. 2003. Defoliation is Depopulation. In *War in Colombia: Made in the U.S.A.* (eds) R. Toledo, T. Gutierrez, S. Flounders & A. McInerney, 83-89. New York, NY: International Action Centre.

Galdos, G. 2004. Eliana Gonzales. *BBC News* (available on-line at: http://news.bbc.co.uk/1/shared/spl/hi/programmes/this_world/one_day_of_war/html/12.stm, accessed 19 August 2015).

Gamboa, M. 2001. Democratic Discourse and the Conflict in Colombia. *Latin American Perspectives* 28: 1, 93-109.

Gibbs, T. 2011. Voices from the Colombian Left: Women and the struggle for social transformation. *Labour, Capital and Society*, 43: 2, 57-84.

Glenn, C. 2003. Soldiers for the Banks: Paramilitaries in Colombia. In *War in Colombia: Made in the U.S.A* (eds) R. Toledo, T. Gutierrez, S. Flounders & A. McInerney, 71-76. New York: International Action Centre.

Goff, S. 2004. *Full Spectrum Disorder: The military in the new American century*. New York: Soft Skull Press.

Gomez, A. 1972. Perspectives of the Revolutionary Armed Forces of Colombia (FARC). In *National Liberation Fronts 1960/1970: Essays, documents, interviews* (eds) D. H. Hodges & R. E. Abu Shanab, 248-256. New York, NY: William Morrow & Company.

González, F., Bolivar, I., & T. Vázquez 2002. *Violencia Politica en Colombia: De la nación fragmentada a la construcción del Estado*. Bogotá: Centro de Investigación y Educación Popular.

Goddwin, J. 2001. *No Other Way Out: States and revolutionary movements, 1945-1991*. Cambridge: Cambridge University Press.

Gott, R. 2008. Uribe's Illegal Cross-Border Raid: Colombian Deaths in Ecuador. *Counterpunch*, 3 March (available on-line at: http://joun.leb.net/gott03042008.html, accessed 19 August 2015).

_____ 1970. *Guerrilla Movements in Latin American*. New York: Nelson.

Gramsci, A. 1971. *Selections from the Prison Notebooks of Antonio Gramsci*. New York, NY: International Publishers.

_____ 1977. *Selections from Political Writings, 1910-1920*. New York, NY0: International Publishers.

Guevara, E. 2006. *Guerrilla Warfare*. Melbourne: Ocean Books.

Gutiérrez, S. 2004. Criminal Rebels? A discussion of civil war and criminality from the Colombian experience. *Politics & Society* 32: 2, 257-285.

_____ 2008. Telling the Difference: Guerrillas and paramilitaries in the Colombia war. *Politics & Society* 36: 1, 3-34.

Harnecker, M. 1986. *Reflexiónes acerca del problema de la transición al sociliasmo*. Managua: Nueva Nicaragua.

Heyden, T. 2011. FARC increasingly moving operations to Colombian cities: Santos. *Columbian Reports*, 15 June (available on-line at: http://colombiareports.com/farc-increasingly-moving-operations-to-colombian-cities-santos/, accessed 19 August 2015).

Holmes, J., Gutiérrez de Piñeres, S., & K. Curtin. 2006. Drugs, Violence, and Development in Colombia: A departmental-level analysis'. *Latin American Politics & Society* 48: 3, 157-184.

Hylton, F. 2008. Colombia's Cornered President: High Stakes in the Andes. *NACLA* (available on-line at: http://news.nacla.org/2008/03/05/colombia%e2%80%99s-cornered-president-raises-the-stakes, accessed 19 August 2015).

International Action Center. 2001. *Fact Sheet – Colombia: The pentagon's new target in Latin America*. New York, NY: IAC.

Johnson, K. 2012. Los meses más violentos. *Semana*, 6 February (available on-line at: http://www.semana.com/opinion/articulo/los-meses-mas-violentos/253021-3, accessed 19 August 2015).

Kenney, M. 2007. *From Pablo to Osama: Trafficking and terrorist networks, government bureaucracies, and competitive adaptation*. University Park, PA: The Pennsylvania State University Press.

Kirk, R. 2003. *More Terrible Than Death: Massacres, drugs, and America's war in Colombia*. New York: Public Affairs.

Lakshmanan, I. 2004. Battling for Survival: Indigenous Colombians Caught Between Factions. *The Boston Globe*, 16 November (available on-line at: http://www.boston.com/news/world/articles/2004/11/16/st

ill_battling_for_survival_indigenous, accessed 19 August 2015).

Lebowitz, M. 2011. Reinventing Socialism and Recovering Marx. In *21st Century Socialism: Reinventing the project* (ed.) H. Veltmeyer, 33-47. Halifax, NS: Fernwood Publishing.

Leech, G. 2000. An Interview with FARC Commander Simón Trinidad. *Columbia Journal*, 25 June (available on-line at: http://www.colombiajournal.org/colombia15.htm, accessed 19 August 2015).

_____ 2011. The Hunt for FARC Commander Alfonso Cano. *Columbia Journal*, 17 January (available on-line at: http://colombiajournal.org/the-hunt-for-farc-commander-alfonso-cano.htm, accessed 19 August 2015).

LeGrand, C. 1986. *Frontier Expansion and Peasant Protest in Colombia, 1850-1936*. Albuquerque, NM: The University of New Mexico Press.

Lenin, V.1964. Dual Power. In *Collected Works 24: April-June 1917*, 38-41. Moscow, USSR: Progress Publishers.

_____ 1969. Report on the Present Situation and the Attitude towards the Provisional Government, April 14 (27). In *Collected Works Volume 41: 1896-October 1917*, 400-402. Moscow, USSR: Progress Publishers.

Leonard, C. 2012. Emerald Energy suspends operations in southern Colombia followingrebel attacks. Columbia Reports, 6 March (available on-line at: http://colombiareports.com/emerald-energy-suspends-operations-due-to-farc-attacks/, accessed 19 August 2015).

Lévy, B.H. 2004. *War, Evil, and the End of History*. Hoboken, NJ: Melville House Publishing.

Livingstone, G. 2003. *Inside Colombia: Drugs, democracy and war*. London: Latin American Bureau.

Löwy, M. 2005a. *The Theory of Revolution in the Young Marx*. Chicago, IL: Haymarket Books.

_____ 2005b. To change the world we need revolutionary democracy. *Capital & Class* 85: 22-24.

Mandel, E. 1994. *Revolutionary Marxism and Social Reality in the 20th century: Collected essays*. Atlantic Highlands, NJ: Humanities Press.

Mannon, T. 2011. Rise in FARC violence not due to Santos' security policy: Report. *Columbia Reports*, 18 July (available on-line at: http://colombiareports.com/colombia-news/news/17727-rise-in-farc-violence-not-due-to-santos-security-policy-report.html, accessed 19 August 2015).

Maullin, R. 1973. *Soldiers, Guerrillas, and Politics in Colombia*. Lexington, KY: Lexington Books.

Molano, A. 2005. *The Dispossessed: Chronicles of the desterrados of Colombia*. Chicago, IL: Haymarket Books.

Murillo, M & J. Avirama 2004. *Colombia and the United States: War, unrest and destabilization*. New York, NY: Seven Stories Press.

O'Shaughnessy, H & S. Branford 2005. *Chemical Warfare in Colombia: The costs of coca fumigation*. London: Latin American Bureau.

Obando, L & L. Velásqeuz 2004. *Tras Las Huellas de la Resistencia* (available on-line at: https://www.youtube.com/watch?t=108&v=p3LE50hD7mo, accessed 19 August 2015).

Ortiz, R. 2006. Renew to Last: Innovation and strategy of the Revolutionary Armed Forces of Colombia (FARC). In *Teaching Terror: Strategic and tactical learning in the terrorist world* (ed.) J. J.F. Forest, 205-222. Boulder, CO: Rowman & Littlefield Publishers.

Palacios, M. 2006. *Between Legitimacy and Violence: A history of Colombia, 1875-2002*. Durham, NC: Duke University Press.

Parkinson, C. 2012. Authorities fail to prevent FARC 'armed strike' in west Colombia. *Columbia Reports,* 2 March (available on-line at: http://colombiareports.com/colombia-news/news/22570-colombian-authorities-fail-to-prevent-farc-armed-strike.html, accessed 19 August 2015).

Peace and Socialism.1966. *Colombia: An embattled land*. Prague: Peace and Socialism Publishers.

Pearce, J. 1990. *Colombia: The drug war*. New York, NY: Aladdin Books.

Peceny, M & M. Durnan 2006. The FARC's Best Friend: U.S. anti-drug policies and the deepening of Colombia's civil war in the 1990s. *Latin American Politics & Society* 48: 2, 95-116.

de la Peña, G. 1998. Rural Mobilizations in Latin America since *c.* 1920. In *Latin America: Politics and society since 1930* (ed.) L. Bethell, 291-394. Cambridge: Cambridge University Press.

Petras, J. 1999. *The Left Strikes Back: Class conflict in the age of neoliberalism*. Boulder, CO: Westview Press.

_____ 2003. *The New Development Politics: The age of empire building and new social movements*. Hampshire: Ashgate.

Petras, J & H. Veltmeyer 2005. *Social Movements and State Power: Argentina, Brazil, Bolivia, Ecuador*. London: Pluto Press.

Pettersson, O. 2013a. FARC attacks decrease as peace talks progress. *Columbia Reports*, 2 May (available on-line at: http://colombiareports.com/farc-attacks-decrease-amid-colombia-peace-talks, accessed 19 August 2015).

_____ 2013b. ELN-related violence peaks, FARC attacks fall in March. *Columbia Reports*, 2 April (available on-line at: http://colombiareports.com/colombia-news/news/28771-eln-related-violence-peaks-farc-attacks-fall-in-march.html, accessed 19 August 2015).

_____ 2013c. FARC strongholds shift to Colombia's periphery: NGO. *Columbia Reports*, 7 March (available on-line at: http://colombiareports.com/colombia-news/news/28435-farc-strongholds-shift-to-colombias-periphery-ngo-html, accessed 19 August 2015).

_____ 2013d. Colombia rebels carry out more than 60 attacks in January. *Columbia Reports*, 3 February (available on-line at: http://colombiareports.com/colombia-news/news/27972-colombia-rebels-carry-out-more-than-60-attacks-in-january.html, accessed 19 August 2015).

_____ 2013e. FARC violence diminished 80%: NGO. *Columbia Reports,* 8 January (available on-line at: http://colombiareports.com/colombia-news/news/27600-farc-violence-diminished-80-ngo.html, accessed 19 August 2015).

Radio Caracol. 2012. *En 20 días las Farc han cometido 132 atentados a la Fuerza Pública*. 24 january (available on-line at: http://caracol.com.co/radio/2012/01/24/nacional/1327373

220_611081.html, accessed 19 August 2015).

Rangel Suárez, A 1998. *Colombia: Guerra en el Fin de Siglo.* Bogotá: Tercer Mundo.

Richani, N. 2002. *Systems of Violence: The political economy of war and peace in Colombia.* New York, NY: SUNY.

_____ 2005. Third Parties, War System's Inertia and Conflict Termination: The doomed peace process in Colombia, 1998-2002. *Journal of Conflict Studies* 25: 2, 75-103.

_____ 2007. Caudillos and the Crisis of the Colombian State: Fragmented sovereignty, the war system and the privatisation of the counterinsurgency in Colombia. *Third World Quarterly* 28: 2, 403-417.

Rochlin, J. 2003. *Vanguard Revolutionaries in Latin America: Peru, Colombia, Mexico.* London: Lynne Reinner Publishers.

Röhl, K. 2004. *Greed or Governance: Why does the FARC keep fighting* (available on-line at: http://www.monitor.upeace.org/Colombia.pdf, accessed 19 August 2015).

Ruiz, B. 2001. *The Colombian Civil War.* Jefferson, NC: McFarland & Company, Inc.

Sánchez, Gand & D. Meertens 2001. *Bandits, Peasants and Politics: The case of "La Violencia" in Colombia.* Austin, TX: The University of Texas.

Schulte-Bockholt, A. 2006. *The Politics of Organized Crime and the Organized Crime of Politics: A study in criminal power.* Lanham, MD: Lexington Books.

Semana. 2011. *A un año de la muerte de 'Jojoy', ¿qué ha pasado con las FARC.* 21 September (available on-line at: http://www.semana.com/nacion/articulo/ano-muerte-jojoy-que-ha-pasado-farc/246757-3, accessed 19 August 2015).

Simons, G. 2004. *Colombia: A brutal history.* London: SAQI.

Snyder, M. 2011. Dutch Guerrilla Leading FARC Forces: Activist. *Columbia Reports,* 4 July (available on-line at: http://colombiareports.com/colombia-news/news/17386-dutch-guerrilla-leading-farc-forces-activist.html, accessed 19 August 2015).

Stokes, D. 2002. Perception Management and the US Terror War in Colombia. *Znet,* 7 June (available on-line at: https://zcomm.org/znetarticle/perception-management-and-the-us-terror-war-in-colombia-by-doug-stokes/, accessed 19 August 2015).

_____ 2005. *America's Other War: Terrorizing Colombia.* London: Zed Books.

Sweig, J. & M. McCarthy 2005. Colombia: Starving off partial collapse. In *The Andes in Focus: Security, democracy & economic reform* (eds) R. Crandall, G. Paz & R. Roett, 11-43. Boulder, CO: Lynne Rienner.

Taussig, M. 2004. *My Cocaine Museum.* Chicago, IL: The University of Chicago Press.

Tilly, C. 1978. *From Mobilization to Revolution.* Reading, MA: Addison-Wesley.

Valencia, L. 2011. ¿Está desmoralizado el Ejército? *Semana,* 16 July (available on-line at: http://www.semana.com/opinion/articulo/esta-desmoralizado-ejercito/243104-3, accessed 19 August 2015).

Valencia, L. & A. Ávila Martinez. 2011. La nueva realidad de las Farc. *El Tiempo*, 16 July (available on-line at: http://www.eltiempo.com/archivo/documento/CMS-9927204, accessed 19 August 2015).

Vanden, H. E. & G. Prevost 2006. *The Politics of Latin America: The power game*. New York: Oxford University Press.

Veltmeyer, H. & J. Petras 2002. The Social Dynamics of Brazil's Rural Landless Workers' Movement: Ten hypotheses on successful leadership. *The Canadian Review of Sociology and Anthropology* 39: 1, 79-96.

Villalón, C. 2004a. Cocaine Country. *National Geographic* 206: 1, 34-55.

_____ 2004b. Cocaine Country. *National Geographic* (available on-line at http://ngm.nationalgeographic.com/ngm/0407/sights_n_sounds/media2.html, accessed 19 August 2015).

Walton, J. 1984. *Reluctant Rebels: Comparative studies of revolution and underdevelopment*. New York, NY: Colombia University Press.

Weinstein, J. 2007. *Inside Rebellion: The politics of insurgent violence*. London: Cambridge University Press.

Wickham-Crowley, T. 1991. *Exploring Revolution: Essays on Latin America insurgency and revolutionary theory*. New York, NY: M.E. Sharpe Inc.

_____1992. *Guerrillas and Revolution in Latin America: A comparative study of insurgents and regimes since 1956*. Princeton, NJ: Princeton University.

Wilkinson, P. 1971. *Social Movement*. London: Macmillan Press.

Chapter 5

UPS AND DOWNS OF A CONTEMPORARY MAOIST MOVEMENT: SHIFTING TACTICS, MOVING TARGETS AND (UN)ORTHODOX STRATEGY: THE PHILIPPINE REVOLUTION IN PERSPECTIVE

Dominique Caouette

Abstract *The Communist Party of the Philippines (CPP) combines organized social movements in the cities and plains with mountain-based armed insurgency and has sustained both despite severe tensions between engaging in electoral politics and maintaining itself as a revolutionary movement. Like the Indian Maoists, it has based its analyses on Mao's characterisation of China as semi-feudal and semi-colonial. Yet in the case of the CPP this has not been dogmatic. Indeed, the CPP leadership has been very flexible in its analysis of and adaptation to changing economic and political circumstances. It has been able to form alliances with other liberation movements and their organisations. On the basis of documents and interviews with leaders of the CPP, the chapter relates the successes and failures of engagement, the internal schisms and yet survival of the CPP as a revolutionary movement. This is related to revolutionary movements outside the Philippines, including those described in this book, by singling out key issues that they all have to address.*

Introduction

In an era of 'neoliberal globalisation,' and global resistance in the form of a multiplicity of alter-/anti-globalization movements, the persistence of an armed Maoist revolutionary communist movement in the Philippines may seem to be an anachronism. Today, the Communist Party of the Philippines (CPP), established in 1968 at the height of Mao's Cultural Revolution and student protests in the West, continues its struggle for state power. Understanding the persistence of this armed Maoist revolutionary struggle is the puzzle that this chapter seeks to elucidate. It is particularly fascinating given the major domestic and international changes that have occurred since the Party was first established a half century ago. At the domestic level, the Philippines experienced a partial democratic transition following the ousting of the Marcos dictatorship in 1986, a return to regular electoral contests, some limited economic growth and various unevenly successful attempts at social reforms, along with an expanding space for NGOs, legal political activities and greater press freedom (Caouette 2009). Internationally, we have seen the demise of Eastern European communist regimes, the temporary suspension of East-West conflict, the capitalist orientation of the Chinese communist party state, US closure of its army bases in the Philippines, and the emerging alter-globalisation movement largely organised outside the confines of a single ideological party. All of these changes would seem to make an armed communist revolution a hard-sell. Such persistence is all the more puzzling given that the CPP missed a key opportunity to seize power (or at least a share of it) with the toppling of the Marcos dictatorship, underwent bloody and traumatic internal purges and survived a major internal schism in the early 1990s.

This persistence is also surprising given that the Philippine Armed Forces have been trying for several decades now to annihilate the CPP with substantial American financial and military support. Following the events of September 11th, 2001 and the American 'war on terror,' the CPP was designated as a 'foreign terrorist organization' (FTO) by the US State Department on August 9, 2002. Officially, the CPP is not the primary target of a government campaign against 'terrorists,' the main targets are rather the small bandit group, Abu Sayaf, and the Moro Islamic Liberation Front. However, it is clear that the Philippine Army has also intensified its repression campaign against the CPP.[1]

The Philippine revolutionary movement constitutes a rich case revealing the interplay between domestic and global change and revolutionary collective action. Its trajectory offers a number of significant insights into how a Marxist-Leninist-Maoist revolutionary movement evolved through time and in particular how radical collective action and social protest are organised and can be channelled in a range of forms and modalities according to changing domestic and international contexts. In reviewing the CPP's trajectory, my aim is to show that the CPP armed revolutionary movement has persisted over time despite domestic and international change because it has the defining elements of a social movement. With the formation of the Communist Party of the Philippines (CPP), a new armed revolutionary movement with its own repertoire of collective action emerged. On the one hand, this communist revolutionary movement needed to distinguish itself from the Partido Komunista ng Pilipinas (PKP), and on the other hand, it sought to bring a new syntax and grammar of revolutionary struggle to the Philippines. The formative years of the revolutionary movement were crucial on four counts: 1) a particular 'repertoire of collective action' was gradually created as a syncretic mixture of various forms of protest; 2) the self-defined identity of a 'national-democratic activist' was constructed; 3) a body of relatively accessible ideological and theoretical writings was developed that could be easily communicated to others; and 4) a particular organisational form of revolutionary movement, comprising a vanguard political party, a guerrilla organisation and a set of social movement organisations, was established.

Over the years, the CPP-led revolutionary movement demonstrated both skilful understanding of political opportunities and struggles combined with a highly instrumentalist approach to social mobilisation (Putzel 1995; Abinales 1996; Rutten 2008). In fact, it responds to political opportunities in a way that ensures its survival. Contrary to arguments that the movement has been dogmatic (Reid 2000; Magno 1998), a review of its past shows that it has been very flexible, not only in terms of its tactics, as many have already pointed out (Jones 1989; Rocamora 1994), but also in its interpretation of Maoist revolutionary theory. The broad and abstract analytical categories and rhetoric of the CPP have been treated so elastically that almost any change domestically and internationally can be explained and located within the grand narrative of revolution. Its frame of action is both interpretative (explaining reality) and action-oriented (it offers a way to act). It is highly voluntaristic and presents itself as *infallible*. Through a series of protocols and courses that can be mass reproduced and easily understood, but also witnessed on the guerrilla battlefield, the revolutionary movement generates a collective identity, the 'national democrat.' New urban-based recruits or international solidarity activists make 'field visits' to the guerrilla zones during vacations or take 'exposure tours.'

Since the early 2000s, the ideologically orthodox CPP has ventured into new experiments such as electoral participation and setting up several legal electoral parties, including Bayan Muna, Anakpawis, Gabriela, Migrante, COURAGE, ACT, and Katribu. More recently, the CPP through its legal mass organisations has successfully inserted itself into the anti-globalisation movement while continuing to be rooted in rural areas, given its Maoist strategic line, with the New People's Army (NPA) launching tactical offensives from time to time. In the sections that follow I review the history of the CPP highlighting key moments and features that reveal the interplay between its interpretative and action-oriented dimensions.

Re-establishment and Drawing the Revolutionary Line

The 're-establishment' of the Communist Party of the Philippines (CPP) in late 1968 came as a result of a party split within the PKP (Partido Komunista ng Pilipinas).[2] It initially began when members of the PKP, dissatisfied with its orientation, strategy and positions decided to challenge the aging leadership. Tension between these ambitious young revolutionaries and the old guard of the PKP became most intense when the former requested that a review of the PKP's history be written in preparation for an upcoming congress. One of these young cadres, Amado Guerrero (José Maria Sison's first *nom de guerre*), an English literature professor at the University of the Philippines, volunteered and wrote a critical analysis underlining the series of mistakes committed by the PKP leadership. This document began a spiralling process wherein debates around the appropriate revolutionary strategy, the appropriate combination of armed struggle and mass movement, and theoretical understanding of the Philippine political economy all became intertwined. The process would eventually come to an end with the formation of the CPP in 1968.

Making Sense of Favourable Conditions

By the time of the 1969 election, there were growing tensions within the ruling elites (Anderson 1988: 18). At the same time, electoral competition had become more and more expensive essentially because of the practice of vote buying and increasing violence.[3] There was also growing discontent among the middle class who were starting to demand greater political participation and social reforms.

A key event in the emergence of a new revolutionary movement had been the founding of the Kabataang Makabayan (KM or Patriotic Youth) on November 30, 1964. PKP Youth Section Secretary Sison, along with other student leaders, played a central role in organising and leading KM. The youth organisation formed and trained a new generation of activists.[4] At the time, Mao Tse-tung's writings and the Chinese Cultural Revolution held the greatest interest for this new generation of activists. In fact, the Filipino professor of Asian Studies Armando Malay explains:

> As in the Western countries, a certain amount of faddist ostentation attended the gestative period of Maoism in the Philippines. Mao jackets, caps, and badges became status symbols, worn as so many political statements denoting either adherence to Marxism-Leninism-Mao Tse-tung Thought, or a recent visit to the People's Republic, or better yet, both. (Malay 1984: 48)

The Vietnam War, which had direct connections with the American military bases in the Philippines, played a key role in symbolising 'imperial power' (Abinales 1988: Chapter 3, 1984: 28; Chapman 1987: 74).

Equipped with what they took to be the most advanced 'theoretical tools', KM leaders, including Sison, were able to develop an 'organisational package' that had the power of linking the present with the past, creating a new and attractive path to channel the energies of the radicalised students (Sison 1967: 4).

While fighting the PKP and trying to secure control of legal institutions and mass organisations, Sison was revising his draft review of the PKP's history. This document entitled 'Rectify Errors and Rebuild the Party' was to be discussed during a founding congress for the 're-establishment' of the Communist Party of the Philippines. By mid-1968, Sison and his followers felt that they had gathered enough momentum to plan this Congress.

Founding Congress

The Congress for the Re-establishment was quite modest. Many have recalled how fourteen young urban activists and intellectuals gathered in a barrio about four hours from Manila, in Pangasinan, Central Luzon to re-establish the Communist Party of the Philippines.[5] The group decided to use December 26, 1968, Mao Tse-tung's birthday as the founding date, to mark clearly their connection with Mao's thought.

The Congress itself did not last very long and consisted mostly in adopting a series of documents probably already discussed in the few months preceding the Pangasinan Congress (Nemenzo 1984a: 64, 1984b: 80). All of those who participated in the discussions became Central Committee members and several were elected officers, including Sison who was elected as Chairman. A first executive committee and a political bureau were constituted. At that point, the newly re-established CPP did not yet have a real armed force, but it was only a matter of weeks before it did. In January 1969, Sison and the CPP forged an alliance with one of the remaining units of the Huk army led by Dante Buscayno and planned to establish the New People's Army (NPA) (Nemenzo 1984b: 80).

The official date for the formation of the new insurgent army was March 29, 1969, the 27th anniversary of the Hukbong Bayan Laban saHapon (or the People's Army against Japan, also referred to as the Huk army).[6] When it was established, the NPA consisted of about 65 fighters with only 35 firearms between them, of which only nine were automatic rifles (Sison with Werning 1989: 60).[7] The NPA helped give a degree of credibility to Sison's 'master plan' for an armed revolution in the Philippines.

On May 12-13, 1969, the CPP held its first Central Committee Plenum. The Plenum was held in a small barrio Sta. Rita in Tarlac, the same barrio where the NPA had been founded two months earlier and now the 'secret party headquarters' (Sison with Werning 1989: 64). The

Central Committee expanded to 22 members with the inclusion of Dante Buscayno and seven other NPA commanders and peasant leaders. The Plenum adopted resolutions aimed at intensifying party rebuilding and the armed revolution (CPP 1965: 5). Not long after, on June 9, 1969, the Philippine Army (AFP) raided the small CPP/NPA's headquarters located in a tunnel in Barrio Sta. Rita. The raid turned out to be a fortuitous event for the fledging revolutionaries. Hoping to alert the population and deter followers, the AFP (1970) published a series of pamphlets entitled 'So People May Know.' By doing so, the AFP failed to understand the popular appeal that the new movement would gather.

The First Quarter Storm

In the context of the later 1960s – early 1970s, the CPP/NPA political programme appeared particularly attractive. There was a growing wave of social protest in Manila. Calls ranged from demands for greater democracy and clean elections, constitutional reform, and national democratic revolution. Politically heterogeneous demonstrators included students, peasants and workers and some sectors of the middle class. However, it was the students and the youth who were the most vocal and started to demonstrate regularly in the streets of Manila.

The so-called First Quarter Storm was a turning point in student and mass protest in the Philippines. It began on January 26, 1970 when an anti-Marcos demonstration was violently dispersed. In the morning, mass organisations from various political formations (Christian Left, PKP-led and CPP-led organisations) held public rallies in different locations. In the afternoon, they marched and converged on the Philippine Congress where Marcos was to address both the Congress and Senate to deliver his 'State of the Nation' address. When Marcos and his wife Imelda were about to leave Congress, the angry students tried to approach them. But the police moved the demonstrators on. The largest riot since Independence was followed the next day by another demonstration in front of the American Embassy. These five days of rallies marked the beginning of the 'First Quarter Storm.' During the next three months, protest rallies and teach-ins were organised on various university campuses, including the famous barricade and seizure of the University of the Philippines campus, renamed for the occasion, the Diliman Commune. Twice during this period, Marcos invoked the possibility of Martial Law.

The period between January 1970 and September 1972 was particularly important because it saw an increasing polarisation of the student movement and intense struggles among various factions within it. During this process of greater student radicalisation, NPA guerrillas became folk heroes to many students.

Seizing the Momentum

The First Quarter Storm (FQS) was also significant because it was the juncture when 'the CPP seized the initiative from the blundering PKP and absorbed the new radical forces that spontaneously emerged' (Nemenzo 1984a: 67). Whereas the PKP was very cautious and made its existence as 'discreet' as possible, the CPP was very open about its plan to carry out and win a 'people's war.' Following the FQS, the CPP rapidly expanded its network of mass organisations, especially among students.

While mass organisations were being organised and protests were increasingly frequent, the NPA was becoming progressively more popular both in the countryside and in urban areas.[8] In Manila, especially in university and college campuses, NPA commander Dante Buscayno and other NPA commanders were becoming local heroes and legends. Scores of activists of the First Quarter Storm would eventually join the NPA and the CPP and live underground (Sison with Werning 1987: 63). At that time, however, the NPA remained relatively small in terms of fighting capacity.[9]

Underground activities were still on-going and the

Party held its Second Plenum in mid-1971. On January 25, 1972, a united front organisation, the National Democratic Front Preparatory Commission, was established with the goals of: a) popularising the National Democratic line; and b) winning over the middle forces and isolating the enemy diehards.

Philippine Revolution 101

To understand how the incipient CPP and NPA eventually became a genuine threat to the Philippine state in the early 1980s, we must review the key CPP document, 'Philippine Society and Revolution' (hereafter referred to as PSR) written by Amado Guerrero (Sison's *nom de guerre*). PSR accomplished two fundamental things: first, it set out the CPP armed revolution as a continuation and heir of the Philippine nationalist and revolutionary tradition, and second, it 'organised' and 'explained' Philippine contemporary reality in such a way that it made sense to revolt. In a way, this document more than any other, was able to capture the imagination of a large and heterogeneous following made up of students, religious leaders and intellectuals as well as peasants, agricultural labourers, workers and the urban poor.

PSR needs to be seen in the context of Sison's gradual emergence as the chief entrepreneur of the new revolutionary movement, the 'national democratic movement' (informally referred to, until now, as the 'nat-dem' movement). Sison's 'framework' derived its strength from ability to invent its own genealogy from four sources: the Philippine nationalist movement of the late 19th century; Philippine economic nationalism of the 1950s; the early Philippine communist movement; and, the international revolutionary movements, especially those with a Maoist revolutionary perspective (Weekley 1996: 23).

In fact, PSR is best seen as a textbook on Philippine revolution. Organised into three main chapters, 'Review of Philippine History,' 'Basic Problems of the Filipino People' and 'People's Democratic Revolution,' PSR follows a didactic logic.[10] First, it surveys Philippine history in a way that leads to the second chapter detailing the three basic ills of the Philippine society - US imperialism, feudalism and bureaucratic-capitalism. Having understood Philippine history and the basic ills of a semi-feudal and semi-colonial society, PSR proposes a model of collective action, the people's democratic revolution.[11]

With PSR, Sison was able to 'order reality' and infuse it with historical meaning. At the same time, he was also fighting for the leadership of this wave of student protest that was much larger than the KM and other CPP-linked mass organisations. PSR's publication had an immense impact on the expansion and development of the CPP and played a crucial role in assisting it to recruit and transform student activists into 'national-democratic' activists and party members.

PSR had the advantage of following a 'successful revolutionary model' that is, the Chinese revolution.[12] It is built similarly on Mao Tse-Tung's works 'Chinese Revolution and the Chinese Communist Party' completed in December 1939 (1967: 305-334). As with the Chinese revolution, PSR argues that the Philippine revolution needs to be under the class leadership of the proletariat while its main force is the peasantry, which constitutes the 'largest mass force in a semi-colonial and semi-feudal society' (Guerrero 1979: 158). The revolution can only succeed if it has the peasants' support. By adapting the successful Chinese formula and its 'theoretical lexicon,' Sison and Guerrero established the grounds for debates and theoretical exchanges to take place within the Party.

Fulfilling Prophecy: Marcos' Declaration of Martial Law and Institutionalizing the Revolutionary Work

The declaration of Martial Law in 1972 by President Marcos fulfilled the prophecy of PSR. As Sison/Guerrero wrote: '[F]ascism is on the rise precisely because the revolutionary mass movement is surging forward and the split among the reactionaries is becoming more violent'

(Guerrero 1979: 125). As channels for reformist political change seemed to go nowhere and political space for legal protests was being closed, the more did the revolutionary alternative appeal to already mobilised students, as well as to some elements among the workers and middle-classes, including the Church sector.

In the early 1970s, the newly established CPP and NPA were at most a secondary threat to the Marcos regime compared to broader efforts from other political groups and political oligarchs. At the time, the CPP was trying to capitalise on the ongoing social protests to accelerate its expansion (Guerrero 1979: 161). Central Committee members were deployed in various regions of the country with the task of initiating and building both underground and legal organisations. By 1970, organising efforts were going on in various provinces of Central Luzon, Negros Oriental and Occidental, other parts of the Visayas and Mindanao.[13]

While Martial Law was anticipated by the CPP/NPA, it nonetheless had an impact on the revolutionary movement. The impact was most severe in the urban areas, especially in Manila, where there was a slowing down in the expansion and heightening of CPP revolutionary activities.[14] First, a number of urban-based party cadres and activists were arrested in the days following the Declaration of Martial Law.[15] Second, several lines of communications within the party were lost. Third, many CPP members and sympathisers underground were forced to leave the cities for rural areas (Guerrero 1974).[16] And fourth, it cut off some support from sympathisers and allies because now that it was significantly more dangerous, the 'cost' of supporting the movement became much higher (Rocamora 1983: 16).

Because many key CPP cadres and members were forced to leave the urban areas, various CPP bureaus stagnated or were dismantled. Communications among departments, regional party committees and the national leadership were also made more difficult. The rural bases of the guerrilla movement played an important role in the early years of Martial Law as 'sanctuaries' for party cadres, members and mass activists who were forced to leave the city and live 'underground.' Many in fact would end up joining the NPA (Chapman 1987: 97-104).

Mass arrests, widespread repression and a growing realisation that Marcos had his own interests in mind in the so-called 'New Society' combined to make the revolutionary alternative quite attractive by the mid-1970s.[17] The Party showed considerable creativity and adaptive skills in adjusting to the changing context. Within two years, legal mass organisations began to resume open protests.[18] One key factor for the resurgence of these open protests was the role of the Preparatory Commission of the National Democratic Front. Seven months after the Declaration of Martial Law, the NDF was established on April 24, 1973.[19] Initially, it tried with relative success to enlist the members of various organisations that were part of the Movement for a Democratic Philippines (MDP), banned under Martial Law, including the Christians for National Liberation (CNL).[20] The Church played a courageous and determining role in initially protecting and later mobilising urban poor communities.

Fine-Tuning the Revolution: Codifying and Structuring the Revolutionary Movement

The relative lull in the revolutionary movement's expansion, especially in the urban areas, lasted approximately until mid-1975. These were important years for learning and assessing how to take the revolution forward. Both theoretically and organisationally, the first two years helped synthesise and establish methodologies that would serve the movement well under the Martial Law regime. Two key documents marked the early period of Martial Law; the first was 'Specific Characteristics of Our People's War' completed in December 1974 and the second was 'Our Urgent Tasks' completed in 1976 following discussions held during the 3rd Plenum held in December 1975 (Sison with Werning 1989: 83).[21] These documents were key for adjusting the armed revolution to Philippines conditions and laying down a concrete program of action.

For some analysts, 'Specific Characteristics' represents the first true departure from the Maoist model and Sison's original attempt to adapt armed revolution to the Philippine context (Abinales 1992: 35).[22] The 1974 document introduces new categories that depart from Mao's writings. One innovation was to talk of 'pink areas,' somehow located between white areas (unorganised, usually urban areas) and red areas (organised and consolidated areas, usually guerrilla bases). A second novelty was to talk about 'semi-legal' activities, described as being between legal and illegal activities (Guerrero 1974: 5-7). This creative conceptual stretching would prove to be quite useful, because it permitted description and naming of a broader set of situations and tactics. Given the complexity of launching a people's war in a vast archipelago, notably different from the Chinese context, and having learned from the past four years, Sison suggested adjustments to the organisational framework of the NPA. The main ones outlined in the document were: 1) '... to adopt and carry out the policy of centralised leadership and decentralised operations;' 2) 'The development of the central revolutionary base somewhere in Luzon will decisively favour and be favoured by the development of many smaller bases in Luzon, Visayas and Mindanao;' 3) '... take the policy of 'a few major islands first, then the other islands later;' 4) '... develop self-reliance; maintain our guerrilla units within a radius that is limited at a given time to avoid dissipation of our efforts but wide enough for manoeuvre; and advance wave upon wave, always expanding on the basis of consolidation;' 5) 'Each regional Party organization should see to it that at the present stage it develops only one, two or three armed fronts;' 6) 'The regional executive committee of the Party should be based in the main front;' 7) '... Mountains are usually the natural boundaries of provinces. Thus, we can maintain influence in several provinces even if we were to operate from only one mountainous border area'

(Guerrero 1974: 6-7).

'Specific Characteristics' was also significant because it identified specific tactics for how to actually conduct the armed revolution. Given the balance of forces, Sison argued that it was necessary for the guerrilla movement to launch a 'protracted war' in multiple locations at the same time.[23] It was important to concentrate on building up and securing mass support. Such mass support could help the NPA acquire more weapons but would also increase security in facing the Philippine military. The main forms of attack should be 'raids' or 'ambushes' on small 'enemy' forces and only when the NPA could be sure of wiping it out. A great deal of flexibility, timeliness, and quick decisions were also required to balance between tactical offensives, organising rural communities and propaganda work.

Almost five years after its Second Plenum (held in January-February 1971), and a little more than three years after the imposition of Martial Law, the Party held its Third Plenum in December 1975. Martial Law had revealed that the structures and methodologies developed during the Second Plenum in 1971 were inadequate to deal with the new context (CPP 1972: 7). The Third Plenum was important in defining concrete measures and methodologies to combine legal and illegal tactics, and to reach out, organise, and mobilise mass and underground organisations. An important item of the Third Plenum was discussion of the document 'Our Urgent Tasks' (OUT) that Sison/Guerrero had drafted. After having adapted the Maoist protracted people's revolutionary war to the Philippines context with its specific peculiarities and having defined protocols to strengthen the party organisationally, the next major contribution of OUT was a programme of action for the coming years, more specifically a systematic listing of procedures to build the revolutionary mass movements in rural and urban areas, expand and strengthen the New People's Army, and bring about a broad united front.

The strategic line remained 'to encircle the cities from

the countryside' until such time that the NPA would be 'capable of moving on the cities from stable revolutionary bases in the countryside' (CPP 1972: 18). To complement the development of the mass movement and the NPA in rural areas, OUT prescribed an expansion of the urban revolutionary mass movement. Economic strikes could be transformed into political strikes and demonstrations. In urban poor communities, OUT suggested that it was best to rely primarily on organised workers and the urban poor to conduct the work of organization rather than send youth activists as before.

Taken together, these documents and discussions from the Third Plenum contributed significantly to systematising and codifying a series of step-by-step protocols aimed at expanding and consolidating the armed revolution. The conceptual toolbox was a double-edged sword. On the one hand, it helped party cadres and NPA commanders define a program of action. On the other hand, it acted as a 'mental jail' because it forced upon them a series of concepts and definitions to wrestle with while trying to understand the political and revolutionary situation, especially when 'unexpected' or 'un-theorised' events happened (Rocamora 1994: 21, 23). If the pre-Martial Law years saw the emergence of a specific syntax and lexicon for the CPP, the years following Martial Law served to establish the rules and protocols of the revolutionary 'grammar.'

A New Momentum

Following its Third Plenum and when the various adjustments proposed in OUT were circulated, the revolutionary movement experienced its greatest momentum (1976-1985). It began expanding at a faster rate across the archipelago and there were clear indications that legal mass organisations were able once again to launch protest activities in urban areas. By 1978, it had become clear for increasingly large segments of the population, including parts of the Philippine bourgeoisie and nationalist elite, that Martial Law was evolving into a patrimonial regime centered on the Marcos couple and their retinue of cronies. With growing social discontent, the revolutionary movement became increasingly acceptable to middle forces, including large sections of Church workers.[24]

When Marcos declared a snap presidential election in 1985, the national democratic movement under the leadership of the Communist Party of the Philippines had become the dominant and most powerful leftist political force in the country. One observer estimated that it possibly represented as much as 80% of organised leftist activists.[25] By 1985, the CPP claimed that its guerrilla army, the New People's Army (NPA), included 15,000 full-time and 20,000 part-time armed combatants. A year later, the United States estimated that there were about 22,500 full-time and 15,000 part-time armed combatants.[26] The CPP/NPA controlled about 18% of all *barangays* (the smallest local government administrative entity), and was active in 59 provinces out of a total of 73.

Weeks after Marcos' unexpected announcement of a presidential election to be held in February 1986, the CPP's Executive Committee called for a boycott of the election without convening a special meeting of the Executive Committee or a meeting of the Politburo. The elections and especially the vote counting turned out to be quite fraudulent. Soon after, on February 16, presidential contender Corazon Aquino, the widow of political opposition figure, Benigno 'Ninoy' Aquino (assassinated in August 1983 on his arrival in the Philippines from exile in the United States), organised a popular rally and, declaring herself the winner of the election, spearheaded a people's disobedience campaign. In the end, Marcos's dictatorship was ousted by a combination of military coup and a popular uprising in Metro-Manila, later baptized the EDSA Revolution.[27]

During the EDSA revolt, the revolutionary movement was significantly marginalized as it was side-stepped by an odd alliance between reform-oriented groups, the hierarchy of the Catholic Church, and factions of the military and opposition elites gathered around the figure of Corazon Aquino (Anderson 1988: 24). This massive mobilisation combined with diplomatic pressure from the United States eventually forced the Marcos couple to leave the country without the revolutionary movement having been a key player or present in the events.

Many within the CPP argued that the revolutionary movement was not able to seize the political opportunity provided by the snap election and people's revolt. Critics pointed out that the revolutionary movement found itself in the position of being a mere observer. The Party later assessed its boycott position as a 'tactical blunder.'[28] The decision also led to an important questioning of the Party leadership and the eventual demotion of then CPP chairman, Rodolfo 'Rudy' Salas who had led the Party since José Maria Sison, the founding party chairman, was arrested in 1977.

Electoral Boycott: A Tactical Blunder or Missing Out on a Key Juncture?

During the next two years, the Party leadership seemed quite disarticulated and undertook several initiatives (ceasefire, peace negotiations, electoral participation, etc.) without a clear sense of where these would lead. Three different processes seem to have marked those confusing years (1985-1987). The first was a significant claim for autonomy from some party organs and units that was rooted in scepticism towards the Party central leadership. A second was the emergence of dissenting voices within the Party and the growing importance of party-associated non-government organisations (NGOs). The third was a growing impatience to achieve political and military gains pushed by factions of the New People's Army at a time when the party membership and militancy were declining.

While the Party seemed to be going in several directions, the Aquino regime managed to survive a series of coup d'état attempts and was able to launch a massive counter-insurgency campaign. With financial and military assistance from the USA, this campaign was nationwide. After an initial opening to negotiations with the movement and the release of political prisoners, Aquino gradually aligned herself with the more conservative elements in her regime. By March 1987, the Aquino government announced its 'Total War Policy' against the revolutionaries. Several leaders of mass organisations were threatened if not killed. Aquino's counter-insurgency campaign also combined socio-economic work and community organising with massive military operations.

The period starting with EDSA brought into the open dilemmas that had been simmering since the CPP's early days: the role and place of legal work and mass organisations, electoral politics, and how to react to political opportunities while maintaining ideological leadership. Internal party dynamics, numerous arrests and a high turn-over of staff, hindered the revolutionary movement's ability to learn from the range of new experiences it was confronting with the Aquino regime. In addition, the upsurge of the first half of the 1980s and the clear momentum for mass organising, as well as the time pressure to 'act' swiftly as 'victory' seemed close by, created a younger generation of cadres who did not have the same theoretical and revolutionary experience as the founders. Although protocols and organising techniques, developed in the 1970s under Martial Law, continued to provide models, these younger activists and party cadres saw themselves more as 'doers' than 'thinkers,' more pragmatic than theoretical.

Adjustment to the new context was made all the more difficult by a series of traumatic internal purges that added to the party's misfortune. A few months before EDSA, the revolutionary movement experienced some of its darkest moments with a massive and extremely costly (in terms of human lives) anti-infiltration campaign in Mindanao. The Mindanao and other internal purges profoundly damaged moral and social norms and trust within the revolutionary movement. They undermined the precious and essential social network solidarity that had previously existed and had provided much safety and cohesion.[29] The combination of the EDSA debacle and the internal purges brought the morale of revolutionary leaders to a low point.

On top of this, there were other dynamics at work. One symptom that threatened the more militant character of the Party was gradual bureaucratisation and the tendency for 'revolutionary apparatchiks' to dominate the organisation.[30] Another trend that became increasingly pronounced in the late 1980s was questioning the adequacy of the Party leadership's analysis. Third, in late 1989, the problem of recruitment for full-time cadres in the underground became more pronounced, especially in Manila.[31] The availability of funds and jobs within above-ground NGOs also created a set of dilemmas for revolutionary work. NGOs were not new to the revolutionary movement but their numbers increased rapidly after EDSA. Two different processes were at work. One was an attempt to seize the financial opportunities provided by all the agencies and funds that started to flow into the Philippines following the demise of the Marcos dictatorship. The other was that NGOs involved in development work became a way for many cadres to remain part of the movement while at the same time having a legal status and enjoying some of the benefits of more open political space.

Internal Implosion and Persistence in a Different World

During the years of the Aquino regime, from 1986 to 1992, the revolutionary movement was never able to regain its momentum. Six years after the 1986 'tactical blunder,' political analysts, and former and current revolutionary movement personalities, estimated that the party had experienced a 40% drop in its armed combatants, the same in terms of controlled territory (Bello 1992), a decline of 15% in party membership, and a massive drop of 60% in the 'mass base' or popular support (CPP 1993: 5).

The years from 1989 to 1992 contained moments of lively effervescence in terms of theoretical and strategic debates within the CPP. This was a time when multiple pathways existed and were hotly discussed internally until a faction of the Party leadership reacted and closed down the debate. This decision became a point of no return. This daring move sought to stop the debate by *reaffirming* the basic orientation and principles of the Party as well as the strategy of protracted people's war.

In 1991, the exiled founding CPP chairman, José Maria Sison writing under his second pseudonym, 'Armando Liwanag,'[32] launched a rectification campaign that sought to reaffirm the basic principles Amado Guerrero (his first *nom de guerre*) had outlined more than twenty years earlier in his paradigmatic *Philippine Society and Revolution*. In late 1991, the first version of 'Reaffirm our Basic Principles and Rectify Errors' began to circulate in Europe and the Philippines. The 'Reaffirm and Rectify' document, along with a 'General Review of Important Events and Decisions from 1980 to 1991,'[33] were later slightly revised and approved during the 10th Plenum of the Central Committee held in July 1992.[34] The 'rectification process' rapidly turned into a bitter dispute because many party cadres and members who differed with Sison's assessment and felt that he was trying to shift the blame to some individuals and re-assert his leadership. The accused replied that, in reality, the so-called deviations had had the collective approval of the highest authorities of the party.

Internal tensions reached a climax when the dispute broke into the open in what became known as the 'fax attacks' (Magno 1992: 1). In December 1992, Sison began sending faxes to a leading Philippine newspaper, identifying specific party cadres and charging them with being agents of the state and traitors to the revolution. This was the breaking point. Following this, not only did debates and splits become public and exposed in the mass media, but also new political blocs began to emerge while the Rectification campaign imposed tight discipline on members who chose to stay with the Party.[35]

Rescuing an Orthodox Revolutionary Movement with Unorthodox Tactics

By late 1994, most of the tension and stress due to the division and break up of underground organisations and the fight over legal institutions, had significantly diminished.[36] The *Reaffirm* CPP bloc (RAs) had established its bases and was undergoing an ideological consolidation whereas the main lines of division between the various factions of the *Rejectionists* (those who rejected Sison/Liwanag's 'Rectify and Reaffirm' paper, and referred to as RJs) were becoming increasingly clear. As time passed, each of these blocs experienced further divisions. However, comparatively speaking, the Reaffirm bloc remained the least fractured.

Having gained a more consolidated position within the Philippine Left by the late 1990s, the ideologically orthodox CPP ventured into new territory such as electoral participation, successfully inserted itself within the anti-globalisation movement while continuing to be rooted in rural areas, upholding the strategic line, with the New People's Army launching from time to time tactical offensives. As early as 1998, Sison recognised that there was potential to be explored within the party list.[37] This project of Party List participation (a portion of the seats in the Philippine Congress are elected using a proportional system) materialised in 2001, when CPP-led organisations in the Philippines put up a political party, Bayan Muna! (Nation First).

Twenty years after launching the Rectification movement, the multiplication of political blocs, experiments with the formation of electoral political parties of the Left, tensions between new social movements and older ones, and fights among and between NGOs and popular organisations aligned with certain political factions, are still on-going. This might or might not be part of the unfinished process of reconfiguration of the Philippine Left.

Conclusion: Philippine Revolutionary Movement: An Anomalous Persistence?

The CPP is still a very long way from the day it can seize power in Manila. Yet, its persistence and ability to bounce back after major internal schisms are worth discussing. Three features emerge. One is the movement's capacity to learn from the past, while remaining clear about the strategic line of revolution at the rhetorical level, a capacity to deploy and use a range of unorthodox tactics. Another feature is the second coming of José Maria Sison as the central figure of the movement, as ideologue, strategist and tactician. A third feature is that Rectification simplified the revolutionary movement's structures and organisations, which has meant more cohesion and a reduction of the institutional autonomy that marked the past. There has been a return to clear protocols and modular action prescribing very detailed lines of conduct and objectives. The Party has used its international experience and skills to connect with various anti-globalisation movements, making it possible for the revolution to appear quite contemporary and yet remain Maoist at its core. With Sison's exile in Europe and the support of some European Maoist Parties, the revolutionary movement has also been able to maintain a wide network of solidarity groups within the Philippine diaspora covering a vast array of issues (migrant workers, youth, women, union and labour issues, human rights, international solidarity with people's struggles, etc.). These groups contribute directly and indirectly to the revolutionary movement with finance, logistics and through organising abroad,.

The Philippine revolutionary collective action frame might persist for several years because it gives meaning to action and rebellion more than it explains reality. Over the years, a number of scholars have sought to challenge the description of Philippine society as semi-feudal and semi-colonial as presented in *Philippine Society and Revolution*, but they have not managed to reduce its appeal and capacity to organise reality, so that it helps people understand or rationalise why they engage in such high risk activism. This indicates that there is more going on than just an academic exercise; people engage in violent collective action because it makes sense to them in the circumstances. Another reason for expecting the CPP revolution to persist is the demographic availability of new members, meaning that there are many potential recruits, mostly in rural areas where the CPP has focused its efforts since the beginning of its 'Second Rectification Campaign.' While the first generation of CPP cadres came from the student movement, there is now recognition that the largest number of members and guerrilla fighters are from peasant and worker (urban poor) origins.[38]

Other leftist political parties, who find it hard to work together and constitute a potential alternative to the CPP's control of the radical left agenda, are also helping the CPP maintain its credibility. Even if the anti-globalisation movement offers potential for non-Maoist leftist groups to connect to international progressive movements beyond the limited circle of Maoist communist parties, the revolutionary movement, despite an orthodox Marxist-Leninist-Maoist rhetoric, has always been extremely responsive to political opportunities.

Given all this, the CPP and its armed revolution are likely to persist for many more years without ever winning, because of its ability to maintain vibrant and active international links and creative political engagements in the legal arena while maintaining an armed insurgency that can capture the imaginations of peasants and the urban poor living in economically marginal areas as well as activists and diaspora members who are exposed to and feel connected to a living revolutionary movement 'at home.'

Notes

1. This has been particularly evident in the increasing and alarming number of extra-judicial killings carried out against suspected sympathisers of the CPP between 2001

and 2008. See Philip Alston's report (2007).

2. The term 're-establishment' was used by those who split from the PKP to indicate that the new CPP represented the true heir of the original Communist Party of the Philippines established on November 7, 1930. See Richardson (1984); Hoeksema (1956); Allen (1985).

3. Bonner reports that the 1969 election 'cost Marcos a staggering $50 million, which was $16 million more than Nixon had raised for his successful presidential bid the year before' (1987: 76).

4. Some of the elected members of the first KM national council would eventually become key personalities and members of the Central Committee of the re-established Communist Party of the Philippines, among them: José Maria Sison, Nilo Tayag, and Carlos del Rosario. See Katabaang Makabayan (1965: back cover).

5. See Chapman (1987: 77); Jones (1989: 18-19); Nemenzo (1984a: 62-63); Weekley (1996: 28-30).

6. As Jones has written: 'Sison had purposely selected the date – the twenty-seventh anniversary of the founding of the World War II Hukbalahap communist guerrilla organization – to formally launch the reconstituted communist army, the New People's Army' (1989: 31). There are many accounts of the Hukbalahap, for some of the more useful see Kerkvliet (1979: 61-109); Lachica (1971); Taruc (1953).

7. See also Chapman (1987: 79); Jones (1989: 32).

8. These new guerrillas were mostly urban activists coming from universities in contrast with the HMB, which recruited primarily from the peasantry. See Nemenzo (1984b: 81).

9. Based on his interviews with leaders of the CPP and rank-and-file members, Jones affirms that by 1970, the NPA could only field around 300 lightly armed guerrillas, mostly concentrated in Central Luzon (Jones 1989: 45). On the eve of Martial Law, the US estimated the number of armed

guerrillas between 1,000 to 2,000 (Niksch and United States, Senate, Congress, Committee on Foreign Relations, Library of Congress, Foreign Affairs and National Defense Division 1985: 21).

10. As Weekley notes: 'The evidence and arguments are presented in tight, logical fashion – minimising the room for doubt in the mind of the reader – and in simple, often simplistic terms' (1996: 53).

11. Abinales makes a similar observation (1992: 31).

12. Written under the pseudonym of Amado Guerrero (1979), PSR's scholarly qualities have been regularly challenged, see Kathleen Weekley (1996: 53-104); Reid (2000: chapters 6 and 7).

13. CPP (1972: 8,); CPP, Regional Committee – Western Visayas (circa 1981: 3).

14. An internal Party document entitled 'Philippine Situation' produced around 1977 explained that: 'After the declaration of martial law, our work in the countryside expanded (1973-74). But during the time also our work in the cities weakened ...' (CPP circa 1977a: 3).

15. CPP (circa 1977b: 1).

16. As Chapman wrote, these activists 'are called today the 'martial law babies,' those hundreds of young students for whom Marcos' proclamation in 1972 was the signal to flee into the communist underground' (1987: 97).

17. Martial Law contributed to the radicalisation of a number of organisations and former reformist student leaders. See Pimentel Jr. (1989: 109-167).

18. For example, around 1974, the SDK (Samahang Demokratiko ng Kabataan) released a document on legal organising under Martial Law. See Samahang Demokratiko ng Kabataan (SDK) (1974).

19. See Rocamora (1978: 2-6). When it was formed, the NDF encompassed several sectoral organisations: Kapisanan ng mga Gurong Makabayan (KAGUMA or Association of Patriotic Teachers), Kabataang Makabayan (KM or Patriotic Youth), Katipunan ng mga Samahang Manggagawa (KASAMA or Federation of Labor Union), Makabayang Kilusan ng Bagong Kababaihan (MAKIBAKA or Free Movement of New Women), Pambansang Katipunan ng mga Magbubukid (PKM or National Association of Peasants), and the Christians for National Liberation (CNL).

20. The initial Preparatory Commission of the NDF included church radicals and members of Movement for Democratic Philippines (MDP). See Abinales (1992: 34); Sison with Werning (1989: 77).

21. See also Guerrero (1974); CPP (1976).

22. See also Magno (1988); Malay Jr. (1982, 1984b: 51); Francisco Nemenzo (1984: 90-91).

23. For a large part, the rest of the document follows Mao Tse-Tung's writings, especially 'On Protracted War' (1969: 113-194).

24. For the Church sector, see Youngblood (1993: especially Chapter 4, 65-100). On the 'middle-forces,' see Pimentel Jr (1989: 171-181). See also Timberman (1991: 98-116); Wurfel (1988: 124-127).

25. See Rocamora (1994: 5). Kathleen Weekley adds that the CPP 'won the hegemonic place in the Philippine left ...' (1996: 2).

26. See Porter (1987); United States Senate, Congress, Senate, Committee on Foreign Relations (1984).

27. EDSA (Epifanio De Los Santos Avenue) is the large avenue in Manila, where people had gathered to block the loyal army troops that sought to crush the military rebellion.

28. This was the expression used in the Central Committee's

publication, Ang Bayan (1986: 1-3).

29. Author's interview with 'Maude,' September 26, 1995. Author's interviews with 'Pierrot,' Manila, April 10, 1995; and 'Fidel Vinzon,' Manila, October 11, 1995. In fact, there were two parallel campaigns, one called Operation Missing Link (OPML) that affected mostly Southern Tagalog region, and a second called Operation Olympia that was conducted in Manila and focused on the Party central units.

30. Author's interview with 'Joey,' February 17, 1996.

31. According to a leading member of the Party: 'Fewer and fewer people wanted full-time work with the underground or to be transferred from Manila.' Author's interview with 'Joey,' February 17, 1996.

32. Although Sison himself would not officially confirm this for safety reasons, it is widely assumed that Armando Liwanag (meaning more of less loading/arming radiance/light) was Sison's second *nom de guerre*.

33. See CPP 1993: 1-63.

34. The amended and approved version during the 10th Plenum was later published in Rebolusyon. See Communist Party of the Philippines, Central Committee (1993: 1-82).

35. Rocamora, one of those accused by Sison, describes these tight organizational policies imposed by the Rectification movement as follows 'Only "Reaffirm" and other documents approved by the leadership can be discussed by Party Units. Criticism and self-criticism can be done only within Party units' (Rocamora 1994: 111).

36. This was in contrast to early 1994, when there were still open threats made publicly and a significant number of personal attacks (author's interview with Joey, Manila, February 5, 1995).

37. Sison, interview with author, Utrecht, April 17, 1998.

38. 'Alfonso,' interview with author, Utrecht, April 16, 1998.

References

Abinales, P. N. 1984. *Building the Parliament of the Streets: The Birth, Hegemony, and Crisis of the Philippine Student Movement.* Unpublished mimeograph. Diliman: Third World Studies Center, University of the Philippines.

_____ 1986. *Philippine Student Movement: Creating a Parliament of the Streets Final Draft.* Mimeograph. Diliman: Third World Studies Center, University of the Philippines.

_____1988. *Radicals and Activists: Birth, Hegemony and Crisis of the Philippines Student Movement.* Unpublished mimeograph. Diliman: Third World Studies Center, University of the Philippines.

_____ 1992. Jose Maria Sison and the Philippine Revolution: A Critique of an Interface. *Kasarinlan: A Philippine Quarterly of Third World Studies* 8: 11, 7-81.

Allen, J. S. 1985. *The Radical Left on the Eve of War: A Political Memoir.* Quezon City: Foundation for National Studies.

Alston, P. 2010. *Report of the Special Rapporteur on extra-judicial, summary or arbitrary executions: Study on targeted killings.* UN doc A/HRC/14/24/Add.6, 28 May (available online at: http://www2.ohchr.org/english/bodies/hrcouncil/docs/14session/A.HRC.14.24.Add6.pdf, accessed 25 August 2015).

Anderson, B. 1988. Cacique Democracy in the Philippines: Origins and Dreams. *New Left Review* 169, 3-33.

Armed Forces of the Philippines. 1970. *So People May*

Know. Quezon City: Armed Forces of the Philippines.

Bello, W. 1992. The Philippine Progressive Movement Today: A Preliminary Report on the State of the Left. *Philippine Alternatives* 1: 2, 3-6.

Bonner, R. 1987. *Waltzing with a Dictator: The Marcoses and the Making of American Policy*. New York, NY: Times Book.

Canoy, R. R. 1984. *The Counterfeit Revolution: The Philippines from Martial Law to the Aquino Assassination*. Manila: Philippine Editions.

Chapman, W. 1987. *Inside the Philippine Revolution*. New York, NY: W. W. Norton & Company.

Communist Party of the Philippines Central Committee. 1966. *Rectify Errors and Rebuild the Party* (available on-line at: http://www.philippinerevolution.net/documents/rectify-errors-rebuild-the-party, accessed 25 August 2015).

_____ circa 1977a. *Philippine Situation*. Unpublished.

_____ circa 1977b. *Filipino Women in the Struggle Against Martial Law*. Unpublished.

_____ 1970. On the January 26th Demonstration. *Ang Bayan* (available on-line at https://fqslibrary.wordpress.com/2010/01/29/on-the-january-30-31-demonstration/, accessed on 25 August 2015).

_____ 1972. *Summing Up Our Experience: First Three Years*. Unpublished document.

_____ 1976. Our Urgent Tasks. *Rebolusyon: Theoretical and Political Journal of the Central Committee of the*

Communist Party of the Philippines 1: 1, 1-33.

_____ 1986. Party Conducts Assessment Says Boycott Policy Was Wrong. *Ang Bayan* 18: 3, 1-3.

_____ 1992. *General Review of Important Events and Decisions from 1980 to 1981* (available on-line at: http://www.philippinerevolution.net/documents/general-review-of-important-events-and-decisions-1980-to-1991, accessed on 25 August 2015).

_____ 1993. Reaffirm our Basic Principles and Rectify Errors. *Rebolusyon: Theoretical and Political Journal of the Central Committee of the Communist Party of the Philippines* 1, 1-80.

_____ 2013. *Advance the national-democratic revolution through people's war amid the worsening global and domestic crisis* (available on-line at http://www.philippinerevolution.net/statements/20131226_advance-the-national-democratic-revolution-through-people-s-war-amid-the-worsening-global-and-domestic-crisis, accessed on 25 August 2015).

Communist Party of the Philippines Regional Executive Committee. 1979. *Party Situation and Policies in the Mindanao Region*. Unpublished.

Communist Party of the Philippines Regional Committee – Western Visayas. 1981. *Isang Dekadang Pagpupunyagisa Rebolusyonaryong Pakikibakasa Kanlurang Kabisayaan*. Unpublished.

Guerrero, A. 1974. *Specific Characteristics of Our People's War* (available on-line at http://bannedthought.net/Philippines/CPP/1970s/SpecificCharacteristicsPW-Riple-1974.pdf, accessed on 25 August 2015).

_____ 1979. *Philippine Society and Revolution.* Oakland, CA: International Association of Filipino Patriots (IAFP).

Hawes, G. 1990. Theories of Peasant Revolution: A Critique and Contribution from the Philippines. *World Politics* 42: 2, 261-298.

Hoeksema, R. L. 1956. *Communism in the Philippines: A Historical and Analytical Study of Communism and the Communist Party of the Philippines and its Relations to Communist Movements Abroad.* PhD, Harvard University.

Hutchcroft, P. D. 1998. *Booty Capitalism: The Politics of Banking in the Philippines.* Quezon City: Ateneo de Manila University Press.

Jones, G. R. 1989. *Red Revolution: Inside the Philippine Guerrilla Movement.* Boulder, CO: Westview Press.

Kabataang Makabayan National Secretariat. 1965. *Kabataang Makabayan Handbook.* Manila: Progressive Publications.

Kerkvliet, B. 1979. *The Huk Rebellion: A Study of Peasant Revolt in the Philippines.* Quezon City: New Day Publishers.

Lachica, E. 1971. *Huk: Philippine Agrarian Society in Revolt.* Manila: Solidaridad.

Lopez, A. 1994. Running a Revolution: The Life and Times of the Philippines Most Formidable Guerrilla Chief. *Asiaweek*, 28-41.

Magno, A. R. 1988. The Filipino Left at the Crossroads: Current Debates on Strategy and Revolution. In *Marxism in the Philippines* (ed.) Third World Studies Center, 79-65. Quezon City: Third World Studies Center, University of the Philippines.

_____ 1992. Critical Juncture for the Left. *Kasarinlan: A Philippine Quarterly of Third World Studies* 8: 2, 1-2.

Malay, Armando Jr. 1982. The 'Legal vs. Illegal' Problem in CPP-ML Strategy and Tactics. *Asian Studies* 20, 122-142.

_____ 1984a. Some Random Reflections on Marxism and Maoism in the Philippines. In *Marxism in the Philippines: Marx Centennial* (ed.) Third World Studies Center, 45-67. Quezon City: Third World Studies Centre, University of the Philippines.

_____ 1984b. The Influence of Mao Zedong Thought on the Communist Party of the Philippines Marxist-Leninist. In *China and Southeast Asia: Contemporary Politics and Economics* (ed.) T. C. Cariño, 42-59. Manila: De La Salle University Press.

Mao Zedong. 1967. Selected Works of Mao Tse-Tung Volume I-IV. Peking: Foreign Language Press.

Nemenzo, F. 1984a. An Irrepressible Revolution: The Decline and Resurgence of the Philippines Communist Movement. Work in Progress Seminar, Research School of Pacific Studies, Australia National University, November, Canberra.

_____ 1984b. Rectification Process in the Philippine Communist Movement. In *Armed Communist Movements in Southeast Asia* (eds) L. Joo-Jock with S. Vani, 69-101. Singapore: Institute of Southeast Asian Studies.

Niksch, L. A & United States, Senate, Congress, Committee on Foreign Relations, Library of Congress, Foreign Affairs and National Defense Division 1985. *Insurgency And Counterinsurgency In the Philippines.* Washington: U.S. G.P.O.

Pimentel Jr., B. 1989. *The Unusual Journey of Edgar Jopson.* Quezon City: Ken Inc.

Porter, G. 1987. *The Politics of Counterinsurgency in the Philippines: Military and Political Options.* Honolulu: Center for Philippine Studies, University of Hawaii.

Project Ploughshares, Institute of Peace and Conflict Studies. 2002. *Armed Conflicts Report 2002 – Philippines-CPP/NPA* (available online at: http://www.ploughshares.ca, accessed on 25 August 2014).

Reid, B. 2000. *Philippine Left: Political Crisis and Social Change.* Manila: Journal of Contemporary Asia Publishers.

Richardson, J. A. 1984. *The Genesis of the Philippine Communist Party.* PhD, School of Oriental and African Studies, University of London.

Rocamora, J. 1978. The United Front in the Philippines. *Southeast Asia Chronicle* 62, 2-6.

_____ 1983. *Imperialism and Revolution.* Giornate biennali di studio sul diritto e la liberazione dei popoli, 1-5 December, Rome.

_____ 1994. *Breaking Through: The Struggle of the Communist Party of the Philippines.* Manila: Anvil Publishing.

Samahang Demokratiko ng Kabataan (SDK). circa 1974. *Hinggilsa Legal ng Pakikibaka.* Unpublished document.

Schirmer, D. B. & S. R. Shalom (eds) 1987. *The Philippines Reader: A History of Colonialism, Neocolonialism, Dictatorship and Resistance.* Quezon City: Ken Inc.

Shalom, S. R. 1986. *The United States and the Philippines: A Study of Neocolonialism*. Quezon City: New Day Publishers

Sison, J. M. 1967. Report to the Second National Congress. In *Kabataang Makabayan: Documents of the Second National Congress* (ed.) Kabataang Makabayang. Manila: Kabataang Makabayan.

Sison, J. M. & R. Werning 1989. *The Philippine Revolution: The Leader's View*. New York, NY: Crane Russak.

Student Power Assembly. 1969. *The Diliman Declaration*. Unpublished

Taruc, L. 1953. *Born of the People*. New York, NY: International Publishers.

Timberman, D. G. 1991. *A Changeless Land: Continuity and Change in Philippine Politics*. Singapore: Institute of Southeast Asia Studies.

United States, Congress, Senate, Committee on Foreign Relations. 1984. *The Situation in the Philippines*. Washington: U.S. G.P.O.

Weekley, K. 1996. *From Vanguard to Rearguard: The Communist Party of the Philippines, 1968-1993*. PhD, University of Sidney.

Wurfel, D. 1988. *Filipino Politics: Development and Decay*. Quezon City: Ateneo de Manila University Press.

Youngblood, R. L. 1993. *Marcos Against the Church: Economic Development and Political Repression in the Philippines*. Quezon City: New Day Publishers.

Part 3

Armed Movements and State Formation in Nepal, Nicaragua and Mozambique

Chapter 6

IDENTITY POLITICS AND THE MAOIST PEOPLE'S WAR IN NEPAL

Anne de Sales

Abstract *This chapter explores the tensions between ethnic and class-based emancipation through an in-depth analysis of the Nepali case. The first section shows that cultural diversity was at first legally recognised but organised according to caste hierarchy. This was, in the course of the 20th century, contradicted by the individual equality of all citizens before the law. However, in both cases, cultural subordination was also economic and political. The second section shows, through observations made of one indigenous community, the Kham-Magars, how the Maoist movement acted in violation of their class analysis: both intentionally (through its tactic of alliance with ethnic fronts) and incidentally (following the failure of its cultural revolution) it politicised Kham-Magar ethnic identity. The chapter concludes that it is necessary to distinguish between the 'capacity for culture', involving healthy debates within a community, and conservative identity politics.*

Nepal's recent history has been marked by a movement for political emancipation, which took two intertwined, but often conflicting directions. There was first a Maoist struggle, based on a class analysis that succeeded in overthrowing an autocratic Hindu monarchy after 10 years of armed insurgency (1996-2006) and established a democratic republic. Second, there were claims for political and cultural recognition from a large component of the population[1] in quest of a federal constitution based on ethnic distinctions.

These conflicting tendencies in Nepal's recent emancipatory struggle have to be set in the historical context from which they developed. The ideal of modernity that came to dominate the world in the post-colonial 20th century was conceived, *mutatis mutandis*, as emancipation from local affiliations and particularisms inherited from an irrelevant past. The future was imagined as 'breaking the chains' of the past and local attachments (kin, regional) were synonymous with alienation. Autocrats and liberals alike shared a conviction that the modern nation state had to be centralised and unified under one dominant cultural model in order to promote economic and social progress. However, from the 1990s on this national policy, vigorously implemented in Nepal in the second half of the 20th century, was increasingly criticised by indigenous peoples as 'internal colonisation' by upper Hindu castes.

In contrast, the communist revolutionaries had the explicit aim of mobilising 'oppressed people,' including ethnic and Hindu groups of low status such as the Dalits, on the basis of their membership of an (international) socio-economic class. The communist revolutionaries saw membership of this international oppressed class as something to be nurtured among Dalits and indigenous groups above any other sort of local and ethnic sense of belonging. However, ethnic sentiment proved to be stronger than class solidarity as a basis for mobilisation during the insurgency. In this context, the revolutionary leaders had to resort to ethnic mobilisation tactics that potentially contradicted their ultimate and ideal goal of a communist society. Their vision of emancipation, based on a class perspective aimed at equal distribution of wealth, was not always compatible with one which valorised cultural or ethnic identity.[2]

This chapter explores the tensions between ethnic and class-based emancipation through an in-depth analysis of the Nepali case. It begins with a historical sketch of the legal and political treatment of ethnic and cultural diversity in Nepal from the founding of the kingdom, in the second half of the 18th century, to the Panchayat regime implemented in the early 1960s and ended by a popular uprising in 1990. The kingdom was initially designated as 'all countries ruled by the dynasty of Gorkha' (*gorkhā rāj bhar-muluk*), an expression that encapsulated the process of its own formation and recalls the structure of an empire: several 'countries' or principalities were conquered by one of them, the principality of Gorkha, while remaining differentiated from their conqueror who was more concerned with their submission to his authority than with their cultural assimilation. It was only in the middle of the 20th century that the kingdom was proclaimed a 'monarchical Hindu state' (*rājtantrātmak hindu rājya*) and defined as a 'nation' (*rāstra*) (Gaborieau 1982: 277). This chapter shows how the cultural diversity that was legally recognised but organised by caste hierarchy was then contradicted by the principle of individual equality of all citizens before the law.

The second part will try to clarify the position of the Communists towards ethnic groups through observations made of one community, the Kham-Magars, whose territory the Maoist leaders made the stronghold for their military insurrection. Were the villagers 'heroes or instruments' in the People's War, to quote the French historian Lucien Bianco on the role of the peasants in the Chinese Revolution (Bianco 2005)? Indeed, the Constituent Assembly's (formed after the Maoist People's War)[3] failure to come to terms with federalism in contemporary Nepal leads us to ask whether there was an overlap of interests between the minorities and the Maoists during the military insurrection, or was the minorities' need for recognition exploited (Lawoti 2003). Also did increasing ethnic and cultural hybridity resulting from economic emigration, changing life-styles, urbanisation and political disruption affect the supposed 'purity' of local cultures? Most important, how do the villagers envisage their own emancipation? I suggest that listening to the villagers may be the best way to prevent radical demands for recognition escalating into violent confrontation, and may help us to imagine other possible futures.

Nepali Ethnic and Cultural Politics: a History of Domination[4]

Nepal's formation: hierarchical cultural differences

Current claims of ethnic comunities for political and cultural recognition are based on the historical experience that they have of the various ways they have been integrated into the nation at different times. The distant past of ethnic groups in Nepal is poorly documented, and largely absent from school textbooks that are exclusively focused on the history of the Shah dynasty that ruled the country until 2008. However, local cultures convey certain conceptions of the relations that ethnic groups have had with the dominant groups. While not mistaking popular imagination for historical reality, rites and legends are part of this historical experience and should not be overlooked. We know that Hindu princes fleeing from Mughal India took refuge in Nepal and took over local chiefdoms that they incorporated into their new principalities. If the warrior princes fought the natives who resisted them violently, they also gave those who cooperated with them some ritual precedence, especially with regard to worship of local deities that they were anxious to appropriate. Moreover, these groups claimed to be riven by internal wars and in need of an outside leader of royal rank who might unite their clans and establish peace. This ancient immigration from India is popularly represented as colonisation, but a form of colonisation that remained quite distant and relatively respectful of or indifferent to local practices – and which may have been well received in places.

This historical experience varies by region, but it also

reveals common features beginning with the military conquest of the indigenous groups that lasted for half a century (1744-1790). Prithvi Narayan Shah, the ruler of a Hindu principality in the middle hills to the west of the country, embarked on unifying about eighty independent principalities. He and his successors allied themselves with a number of local communities that they enlisted in their army,and rewarded with land or exemption from slavery (Stiller 1973). This is how groups of Magars and Gurungs from western Nepal came to have a privileged relationship with the rulers. By contrast, indigenous groups in eastern Nepal, grouped under the ethnonym Kirat, developed highly conflictual relationships with the Shah dynasty, despite obtaining certain privileges, such as keeping their clan land. At the other extreme were communities, such as those who would come to be grouped under the ethnonym 'Tamang' in the early 20th century, who were dispossessed of their land in central Nepal. This is probably the ethnic group that presents the clearest case of a subaltern history of internal colonisation (Tamang 2009).

The Shahs' military conquest was accompanied by an effort to classify social and cultural diversity along the lines of the caste society of their homeland in central Nepal. Indigenous groups were included in the caste hierarchy and subjected to blanket laws such as the ban on killing cows, or marrying a woman of lower status, or for a man to marry the wife of his older brother should the latter die. If breaking rules was fined, certain customs rejected by the Hindus of central Nepal, such as matrilateral cross-cousin marriage could nonetheless be performed for a fee. Fines and taxes gradually instilled a new model of society while filling the coffers of the state (Lecomte-Tilouine 2009: 295-300).

This effort of classification was further systematised under the government of Prime Minister Jang Bahadur Rana (1847-1877), whose lawmakers drafted a civil code, the Muluki Ain, in order to fix and unify the country's laws. The idea of a civil code was innovative at that time in South Asia. The influence of the Napoleonic code may be detected, especially since the Muluki Ain followed a couple of years after Jang's journey to Paris and London. The content of the Nepalese code is, however, very different from its French counterpart: the caste hierarchy is re-affirmed, as is the primacy accorded to Hindus from the hills. Ethnic groups are given an intermediate position between the castes of the Twice-born[5] and the Untouchables, Dalits. Most of them belong to the Shudras, the lowest of the four pure varna, and therefore have no access to Vedic knowledge – a restriction that, at the time, meant no access to any form of literacy. Within this broad category of Shudras, each group was recognised as constituting a different caste (*jāt*), free to speak its language and follow its customs within certain limits. The code reveals a society based on legal recognition of cultural differences but also on their statutory ranking within a single model organised by the principles of Hinduism. This system initiated two opposite and complementary social dynamics: cultural hegemony on the one hand and the emergence of new ethnic groups (ethnogenesis) on the other.

Indeed, social prestige was clearly associated with the upper castes of the hills, and other ethnic groups felt encouraged to emulate their practices and embrace their values in the hope of enhancing their social status. This process of 'Sanskritisation' (Srinivas 1952) contributed to a certain social homogeneity. Brahmins and wandering yogis helped to spread the Hindu religion around the country while legitimating the social order and the political power of the upper castes. This system of social classification involved a simplification of the vast cultural complexity of a mountainous country where every valley boasts its own language, customs and ritual calendar – a complexity that the new rulers might have considered difficult to monitor. However, the allocation of rights and duties to *groups* rather than individuals made various identity strategies also possible. While some of these groups were tempted to move up the caste hierarchy by showing their strict adherence to Hindu rules of commensality and marriage and by inventing a past of being degraded Twice-born, others forged an altogether new identity in order to enjoy some privileges (Höfer 1979; Levine 1987).

A good example of this use of the Nepalese code is the emergence of a new group, the Chantyal, a community of former miners of diverse and dubious origins – the product of prohibited inter-caste marriages, former runaway slaves or landless peasants, among other categories – to whom the government gave land after closing the mines in the early 20th century. The former miners forged for themselves a past as Chetri, a Twice-born caste who, during a forced migration that pushed them to cold and inhospitable territories, were doomed to drinking alcohol and eating meat and subsequently lost their status. It seems that they first gave their daughters to landless in-laws from different origins, and then reversed their marriage strategy to one of strict group endogamy in search of a higher status under the assumed name of a Chetri clan, the Chantyal. However, this strategy of upward mobility in the Hindu hierarchy was challenged in the late 1980s by a new strategy that involved playing another card, that of ethnic identity. It was then that the Chantyal claimed to have a language and culture of their own in order to justify this new allegation (de Sales 1993). This process of ethnogenesis was carried through successfully and the Chantyal were duly registered in the 2001 census and recognised in this way as a collective entity.

In other words, the primary intention of the founder of the kingdom and his descendants to reduce culturally different groups to a manageable political entity, through formalisation of these differences in the Civil Code, led a version of identity politics that prefigures the current situation in some ways: the emergence of a multitude of new groups trying to use the new rules and opportunities to their advantage. However, reducing identity politics today to a straightforwardly pragmatic or instrumental dimension may be going a little too fast. The second part of this historical sketch will suggest that the Panchayat era transformed identity politics through the principle of equality of all citizens before the law.

The Panchayat era: equal and undifferentiated citizens

With the emergence of the Liberal Congress Party that was secretly born in India in 1947, Nepal entered a new period of its history and the first universal suffrage elections were held in 1959. Even if, under the pretext of restoring peace after the outbreaks of violence that followed this attempt at democracy, King Mahendra managed to quickly resume the reins of power and restore his autocratic rule, skillfully using new ideas. The modern views expressed in the new constitution of 1963 are striking for their radicalism. Gaborieau remarks that, while we might have expected a modernised but moderate interpretation of the caste system along Gandhi's line,[6] all reference to such a system was eradicated in the new text. Similarly, when we might have expected the denial of social classes, the unequal positions of the different segments of society were instead described in terms of the divergent and even contradictory class interests, as for instance between the peasants and the major landowners. However these concessions to Marxism were only on paper and the key concept of class *struggle* was categorically rejected. Classes had to be persuaded to abandon their interests in favour of the national interest. They were expected to stay in their place and live in harmony, like castes in the old system (Gaborieau 1982: 263-270).

This feature of the so-called 'guided democracy' of the Panchayat system eventually led the people to rise against the regime in 1990. The modernising attempt to mask social cleavages systematically by imposing a 'counterfeit reality' (Burghart 1993: 11), through brutal repression if necessary, led to unsustainable contradictions: on the one hand, a system of democratic representation (mostly indirect) was supposed to meet a growing popular desire for emancipation and political participation, while the king practiced autocratic rule backed up by a repressive system.

There was also a contradiction between claiming that

Nepal was the last Hindu kingdom and a conception of society that was almost entirely secular: Nepal was a nation and its inhabitants were citizens, equal before the law regardless of caste or ethnicity. With the new constitution, rights and duties were no longer allocated to groups as in the old Nepali code but to *individuals*. At the same time, the ethnic and cultural diversity legally recognised and ritually organised in the old system was now officially denied in the name of national unity and equality. The unifying model, however, remained that of the dominant ethnic group, the Indo-Nepalese from the hills (Parbatya). The Panchayat regime deployed all possible means of communication in support of this model, starting with the school apparatus extended throughout the country, and systematic learning of Nepali as the vernacular language. This effort of cultural homogenisation benefited from international development aid that in turn contributed to greater centralisation. Any ethnic claim was repressed as political subversion and an attempt to destabilise the state.

Ethnic associations were careful not to show any aspirations other than strictly cultural ones. At the same time they aimed to reform local traditions, criticising the 'bad habits' of indigenous groups: these included alcohol consumption that allegedly reduced the quantity of grain available for food; overspending on communal ceremonies, prestigious events in the life cycles of individuals and shamanistic rituals. The activists faced a paradox when seeking to eradicate practices at the heart of the collective life of the communities they claimed to defend (Pettigrew and Shah 2009). Similarly there was a huge gap between educated people living in the city and the majority of ordinary villagers. The former's concern for reform was intended to redress the stereotype of ethnic groups as being careless (because of their lack of education) and extravagant spenders – a stereotype that stood as the symmetrical opposite of the austere and parsimonious (literate) Brahmin. This was a recipe for alienation whereby the oppressed or colonised groups are doomed to adopt the values of those who want to

distinguish themselves from them. Two ideologies –
Hinduism and development – combined to stigmatise
peripheral populations and ethnic groups.

Ethnic groups had a position in the caste hierarchy
even if at the lowest rank. They were now considered not
only to be backward but also responsible for the
country's lack of economic development because of their
supposed blind attachment to ancestral practices. The
only choice open to individuals wishing to improve their
living conditions through social mobility was to accept
assimilation into the dominant society, that is, to follow
Hindu rules and join one of the patronage networks that
linked local communities with the political centre. At the
apex of these networks were 'big men' who all belonged
to upper castes. Furthermore, as Joanna Pfaff-Czarnecka
has pointed out, this process of assimilation was only
open to individual members of ethnic groups who had the
means of engaging with this process. The formation of
local privileged elites made the integrity of these groups
even more vulnerable (Pfaff-Czarnecka 1999: 58) and
further embittered those who felt left out.

I have suggested that the pre-national identity
dynamic might have been more pragmatic than
essentialist. Indeed, under the old law when the relevant
social unit was collective entities like ethnic communities
and castes, a group's identity rested on its *collective*
distinctiveness. Presumably changes in group identity did
not provoke existential angst in individual members of
the group, membership was not threatened. By shifting
the basic unit of society from the group to the individual,
the constitution of 1963 established a fundamental break
from the old system and we must try to understand
current ethnic claims in this context.

Ethnic demands made in Nepal today come after half a
century when individuals, all equal before the law and
undifferentiated, were encouraged to embrace their
national identity. In a sense Panchayat propaganda was
pushed to the limit by the revolutionary communists, who
asked citizens to die for their nation against the

imperialist enemy. The only intermediate groupings between individuals and the nation recognized by the new ideologies are classes: pseudo-classes introduced by the Panchayat were not intended to be effective[7] and the Maoists tried to mobilise classes in the Marxist sense for a revolutionary uprising. However, despite the official speeches made by revolutionary leaders in which class rhetoric was omnipresent, their propaganda was slow to convince the villagers. The 'class struggle' was translated into a simple and radical opposition between oppressors and oppressed, a formulation that was more effective for mobilising people.

Nepal's modern history was marked by two processes that neatly illustrate the general problem: how to reconcile recognition of cultural differences and the principle of legal equality for all. Legal recognition of cultural differences between social groups was a feature of the Hindu caste system, but it put ethnic groups at the bottom of the hierarchy. However, legal equality for all citizens led the groups in question to identify with other oppressed categories under the cultural hegemony of the high castes. One way or the other, this subordination was accompanied by economic and political subordination. The two different, and in many respects opposite, processes had a similar result, suggesting that the problem may not be the philosophical one of irreconcilable approaches focused on difference or equality, but a problem of governance.

Moreover, the dichotomy between oppressors and oppressed does not coincide with the opposition between castes and ethnic groups. Ethnic groups are not all oppressed to the same degree, for both historical and cultural reasons, as we have seen. Groups with a trading tradition, for instance, can adapt to the modern economy better than groups which live from farming alone. Similarly, caste members are far from all being privileged and the service castes are still heavily stigmatised by both higher castes and ethnic groups, who enjoy higher status than the Dalits. Finally, 'modern' Panchayat ideology, by shifting the legal social unit from groups to individuals, introduced a new sense of identity involving a *personal* or existential anxiety that found an expression in identity politics. A look at the Kham-Magar community below may help us to dissipate confusion concerning their involvement in the Maoist movement and to clarify their aspirations as an ethnic group.

The Maoists and the Need for Recognition of Ethnic Groups: a Case Study

According to the revolutionary epic, Prachanda, the leader of the Maoist movement, chose Kham-Magar country as where he would start 'his long march.' The role of being the 'crucible of the revolution' that this community played has given rise to the mistaken belief that the insurgency responded somehow to identity frustration. Yet closer examination reveals that mobilising the local population has gone through several stages; the Kham-Magars' ethnic claims grew out of the insurgency and the international context in which it took place rather than being its source. The particular history of this hill community reveals how the revolutionary movement went back and forth between theory and practice in dealing with the ethnic groups and the Kham-Magars in turn responded pragmatically to the insurgents'strategy and tactics.

An Underground and Local Communist presence: 1950-1990

The Kham-Magars are 40,000 to 50,000 people whose Tibeto-Burman language (*kham*) distinguishes them from the largest minority in Nepal, the Magars, who helped to conquer the country under the banner of the Shah Dynasty. The Kham-Magars are grouped together in the high valleys of two districts, Rolpa and Rukum, to the north and west of what was Magarant. Distinct from the Magars by their language, clan names, customs and a part of their history, at the time of the insurrection they formed a little-known minority within the Magar minority. Tucked away on their hilltops the Kham-Magars were what James Scott would call a 'non-state' people (Scott

2009): they are highland maize eaters not lowland rice-eaters; an important part of their diet and income consists of forest products; they were slash-and-burn cultivators in the past and are highly mobile today; their social organisation is egalitarian, in contrast with caste society, notably the relations between men and women; their exclusively oral tradition centres on shamanic practices and they generally mistrust outsiders. Until 20 years ago, their subsistence economy was based on high altitude agriculture and transhumant sheep herding. The shepherds go up to the Himalayan foothills with their flocks in summer and descend to the southern plains in winter. The local economy is no longer sufficient to support the population and emigration abroad provides vital additional resources. With no road until recently this region, like most of western Nepal, has been isolated and neglected by economic development. Individuals do however travel, and since the 1950s ideas have circulated from south to north through transhumance.

Unlike the Chantyal mentioned above, the Kham-Magars never sought recognition within the census and registered under the Magar ethnonym.[8] There were several reasons for this. Away from urban and political centers, the Kham-Magars have long been more interested in commenting on the differences between the customs and dialects of their respective valleys and villages than in any national ethnic policy. Ethnic activists, meanwhile, have shown little interest in this population: Gore Bahadur Khapangi, who founded the Nepal Magar Association in 1990, considered them to be insufficiently educated then and too backward to be mobilised for a national cause. Despite this initial lack of political awareness, their official membership of the Magar minority was an advantage for anyone who wanted to be recruited into the Gurkha regiments of the British army. For young men of certain ethnic minorities, soldiering had long been the only hope of escaping their condition as shepherds or farmers on poor mountainland while also offering the promise of a pension, if not a glorious future.

In the 1950s, the Congress Party led the opposition to the autocratic Rana regime. The Communists were present only in central Nepal and brought together a small minority of opponents who made up just 7% of the votes in the first parliamentary elections in 1959.[9] However, they were very active among the 'classes' of farmers and students, unlike the liberals who had neglected them. These social classes served as a cover for their political activity when, between 1952 and 1956, their party was banned.[10] At this time Barman Budha,[11] a young shepherd from the Kham-Magar village of Thabang (Rolpa District), was introduced to communism by Mohan Bikram Singh, the founding father of Nepali Maoism and a native of the neighboring district of Pyuthan.[12] The Communist cell of Thabang remained the only underground bridgehead in Rolpa of the Pyuthan group's activities for nearly thirty years, from 1956 to 1985.

In 1984, Mohan Bikram Singh and his party were signatories to the first convention of the Revolutionary International Movement (RIM), a (now defunct) international Communist organisation which upheld a version of Marxism-Leninism-Maoism. But he soon withdrew from the committee because he disagreed with the founder of the RIM, the American Bob Avakian: while in theory he presented himself as a defender of armed insurrection and against the parliamentary vote, he felt that 'the objective and subjective conditions' were not met to ensure the success of an armed struggle.[13] This break, like many other ruptures on points of doctrine, masked a personality clash between leaders which resulted in the village of Thabang following a new faction. In 1985, Mohan Baidya, a Brahman teacher from Rolpa, founded a new party that was later to become the CPN(Maoist). He was followed by Pushpa Kamal Dahal, the future Prachanda, and both were eager to start the armed struggle. They were encouraged by their affiliation to the RIM which offered Nepalese Maoists an international forum and boosted their confidence in starting the armed struggle. The role of epicentre of the insurgency that promoted the village of Thabang and the

Kham-Magar community had contrasting effects for the lives of the villagers and their perceptions of themselves.

The Kham-Magars, Heroes or Victims of the People's War?[14]

The Maoists started to prepare for the insurgency several years before the 1990 popular uprising, and were anxious to secure a base area for organising their guerrilla operations and to which they could retreat safely. They were fully aware of how jealous the Kham-Magar villages were of their autonomy and of the difficulty of bringing them together under one banner. In 1995, on the eve of launching the People's War, they organised the Sija campaign, named after the two mountains that dominate the Kham-Magar country, Sisne to the north and Jaljala to the south. The campaign was aimed at strengthening the solidarity of the cadres from different villages. Apart from doing some communal work (building latrines and helping to repair roads), the activists also collected homemade hunting weapons in preparation for the insurgency. In this way, they would also control their use by the villagers and discourage all resistance. There was no question of an ethnic claim in this first phase, but rather of class struggle in order to overturn the oppressors and establish a communist society. The way the 'Initiation day' of the People's War (February 25, 1996) was organised throughout the country illustrates this point.

Seven actions took place on that day at different locations in the country. They all aimed at symbolic rather than material gain. The policy of not killing anyone was respected and the militants made long speeches explaining their revolutionary political motives. In Gorkha, for instance, a large group of men and women stormed an office of the state-owned Agricultural Development Bank, and made a bonfire with all the loan documents. However the land registration certificates were kept safe and later returned to their respective owners. The 'initiation day' was therefore a carefully staged peasant rebellion aimed at convincing the local population of both the Party's good moral character and also of its potential power to act. It focused on the immediate problem that the majority of farmers had to face: the need for cash and their oppression by moneylenders. This focus on loans is a pragmatic way of expressing the abstract notion of class struggle; it is the great tradition of communism translated into the idiom of the little tradition of village communism – ideology in action (Scott 1979).

The first five years of the People's War were characterised by rigorous development of the Maoist forces that gradually transformed these initial demonstrations into a national insurrection. In this process the Kham-Magar country was one cog in an implacable machine focused on systematic mobilisation of the villagers. The Magars paid a particularly heavy toll in these early years: according to the Informal Sector Service Centre in Kathmandu, Magars accounted for nearly 20% of those killed by security forces between 1996 and 2001. The proportion of Magars killed by the Maoists (12, 5%) is also sizeable but less significant. Some ethnic activists, like Gore Bahadur Khapangi, did not miss the opportunity to point out that the Maoist leadership, who belonged mostly to the upper castes, were using the Magars as cannon fodder in the same way that Prithvi Narayan Shah had used them in his conquest of the country some 250 years earlier. To this accusation, however, Barman Budha would reply that 'only iron could cut iron.' The old Thabangi leader felt that high-caste people were indeed in the best position to abolish caste privileges and prejudices precisely because they were so dominant. He turned the argument of Magar exploitation on its head and restored to his fellow Kham-Magars the agency that had been denied to them by ethnic activists, while embracing the communist ideal of a classless and casteless society.

In 2001, the People's War entered a second phase: the king declared a state of emergency and sent the army against the rebels. The insurgency was growing into a civil war and the success (or failure) of guerrilla operations increasingly depended on the support of local populations, who were put to the test. It was therefore crucial to keep villagers on the rebels' side. As in the case of their Naxalite counterparts, it was only in this second phase of the insurgency that the Maoists confronted the ethnic issue and initiated a policy of alliance with the regional ethnic liberation fronts (Pahari 2010). In April 2002 the Party singled out a Kham-Magar territory for the honour of the title 'special district.' This new administrative unit was understood as a transitional formation pending the declaration of the Magarant Autonomous Region. This took place less than a year later, on 9 January 2004, in Thabang. The special district was then dissolved and Santos Budha, a native of the village, was elected president of Magarant.

It is ironic that the backward and marginal Kham-Magars were brought to front-line ethnic politics, even at the very heart of the historical Magarant, through the Maoists' success. Following the Marxist-Leninist approach to nationalities,[15] Santos Budha himself was clear about the transitional character not only of the special district but also of the autonomous region. The politics of autonomy were aimed at mobilising the minorities towards a goal known to satisfy their need for recognition and thereby to secure faithful supporters in the base areas for the protracted war. Ethnic interests were subordinated to the political and military conquests of the central power, and autonomous Magarant was dissolved in 2006 when the Maoists joined the government. This clearly instrumental use of ethnicity by the Party could not but increase the frustration that the Kham-Magars had begun to feel, notably in the cultural domain.

Indeed, the revolutionary ambitions of the Maoists aimed at a radical transformation of the self in accordance with universal principles borrowed from the European Enlightenment. Scientific arguments were evoked to distinguish between proven and indisputable truths on the one hand and, on the other, superstitions that should be eradicated to build a better world. Maoist cadres were taught that religion was in the hands of merchants of illusion in search of profit; they strove to impose new rules, banning the villagers from performing blood sacrifices. The brutality with which they imposed these rules might have reflected their own lack of familiarity with this new 'scientific' vision of the world. Local people were deeply offended by all this and were reluctant to change their habits, which in their view had little to do with the fight against oppressors or the justice to which they aspired. In the same way as the Kham-Magars would not hesitate sometimes to drive out of the village a Brahman priest, a representative of the dominant Hindu religion, they resisted this Maoist acculturation by secretly continuing to practice their rituals, or collectively expressing their dissatisfaction in the course of village festivals.[16] The Maoist so-called 'cultural revolution' was a failure in this area, and reinforced Kham-Magar perceptions of their 'traditional cultural identity' as something to be defended, even at the risk of reifying a culture that hitherto was anything but monolithic.

We have seen that Kham-Magar identity was not much politicised before the 1990s, but ethnic feeling gradually crystallised around the notion of territory through the experience of the insurgency. The Maoist base area, with its symbolic occupation of the Kham-Magar country throughout the Sija campaign, the creation of the 'special district' and finally the proclamation of Magarant could not but reinforce a general trend. Indeed the notion of territory became more and more essential to the definition of ethnic groups in general: initially designated as *jāti,* a term that distinguished them from Hindu *jāt,* ethnic groups became *janajāti* ('people's castes') after the 1990 popular uprising; *janajāti* was then translated into English by 'nationality,' an expression that was in turn translated into Nepali as *rāstra,* designating precisely a 'political territory' (Lecomte-Tilouine 2009). The territorial dimension of this conceptual evolution was attuned to the declaration of the decade of Indigenous Rights by the United Nations in 1993 and to the accompanying notion of autochthony. This historical process supported a multi-national and ethnic concept of nation, and raised the question of federalism as one of the main bones of contention in writing the constitution of the new Republic.

Following the great tradition of socialist propaganda, the Nepali Maoists made extensive use of the 'model' tactic. The village of Thabang was raised to this status, and the Kham-Magar community was given the privilege of representing the whole nation in the march towards a bright future. I would suggest that by virtue of being a 'model' for the nation, those chosen are given an opportunity to become national actors *through their very specificity*: the tactic includes its own potential subversion.

Observation of the annual village festival in honor of the local god offers a useful entry point, because the festival's stated aim is precisely to represent the community to its own members and to the outside world. In June 2010, in Thabang, the festival revealed how the revolutionary communist party then in power sought to control the authority that is the deity (and the underlying clan organisation) by reforming certain ritual procedures; these attempts resulted in heated debates between the different components of the population (older women, activists of the first hour, informed young villagers) whose metaphysical recognition by the local god was just as important as their political recognition within the Nepali nation. The fervour of these debates evoked the emotional charge involved in any attempt to redefine 'we.' Contrary to expectations, these debates about ancestral rites were less oriented towards the past than to the future. At stake was the image of their collective self that the villagers were trying to present to others and to themselves: a progressive community that aspires to be part of the outside world – thanks in part to tourism but also to its increasingly numerous links with foreign countries through emigration – without losing its specificity; that is to say, what makes the Kham-Magars feel unique and therefore irreplaceable. We can now answer the question concerning the role of this community in the insurrection: although they have been instruments of Maoist strategy, they have also been and still are – at times heroic – actors in history.

Conclusion

I chose to address the issue of political emancipation through the case study of the Kham-Magar minority because it was the geographical, political and symbolic center of the Maoist armed struggle, and because my familiarity with this community long predates the insurrection. However, it should be clear that all the Nepalese minorities, whether ethnic groups from the hills or castes from the plains, participated in the liberation of the country from the yoke of monarchy and the dominant culture of the Hindu hills. The underlying motivations of these minorities vary according to their own historical experience, but it was under the leadership of the Maoist movement that, for the first time in Nepal's history, they challenged the dominance of the upper-caste elite. The violent uprising of the people in the Tarai plains in 2007 imposed the multi-national model on the political field (ICG 2012).

The exemplary case of a small hill community, the 'crucible of the revolution,' has shown that ethnic frustration was not the reason why the Kham-Magars became involved in the Maoist movement. Their frustration was above all political and economic. Instead, the movement contributed both intentionally (through its tactic of allying itself with Nepal's ethnic fronts in the second phase of the war) and incidentally (following the failure of its cultural revolution) to forging Kham-Magar ethnicity; that is, politicising a cultural identity that used to be limited more or less to the confines of the village. Now, the villagers no longer follow their ancestral strategy of avoiding the outside world, which they used to perceive as a potential threat. They are instead engaged with the world in the hope of being a part of it on an equal footing, as long as they can imagine the future offering them new opportunities (schooling, urbanisation, migration, development). In this new positioning, their growing need to know about their culture and to debate its content in a world that they see as growing larger and providing more elements of comparison, needs to be taken seriously.

It is important, however, to follow Terence Turner in clearly distinguishing two very different conceptions of culture separated by only a fine line in political contexts where local communities come under stress. The village festival in which cultural issues were debated within the community showed that the 'capacity for culture is a collective power emergent in human social interaction' (Turner 1993: 426). This capacity needs to be nurtured and protected. In contrast, when culture is merged with ethnic identity, it is doomed to be haunted by 'repressive demands for communal conformity' and exclusion. Indeed, any claim for identity is, ultimately, a way of claiming power and status, without saying so explicitly.

The village of Thabang was the only one in the country that boycotted the elections for the new Constituent Assembly in November 2013 – an indication that villagers had withdrawn their trust from the Maoists in power. As in 1985, they followed Mohan Baidya's faction, which claimed to remain faithful to the revolution. For this small community of farmers, economic redistribution and cultural identity are two faces of the same coin, and therefore of the same fight for emancipation.

Notes

1. Over 37% of the population and 59 ethnic groups were registered in 1990.

2. It must be stressed, following Uradyn Bulag, that both class and ethnicity (and the accompanying notions of nation and nationality) are Western ideas that have been introduced into specific historical and cultural situations. These 'irreconcilable concepts' are ways of 'thinking the political' (Valentin-Yves Mudimbe quoted in Bulag 2000: 534) that came to dominate the contemporary debate. This reminder

does not necessarily imply that these concepts are irrelevant to an understanding of the Nepali situation, but aims rather to draw attention to the *historical experience* of the concerned social actors.

3. A couple of years after the end of the People's War, a Constituent Assembly was elected in 2008. The Maoist Party was the largest, with 220 seats out of 575, and its leader Prachanda was Prime Minister. Due to its failure to draft a new constitution, the Constituent Assembly was dissolved on 12 May 2012 after a tenure of 4 years.

4. A number of recent studies have traced the history of Nepal from the perspective of its ethnic diversity such as Pfaff-Czarnecka (1997, 1999); Gellner (2001, 2007); Lecomte-Tilouine (2009).

5. Traditional Hindu society is divided into four ranks or *varna* (Brahmins, Kshatriyas, Vaishyas and Shudras). The male members of the three higher varna undergo an initiation or spiritual rebirth, hence the expression 'Twice-born.'

6. After Indian independence, the law punished caste discrimination, but the caste system, seen as integral to Hinduism, was not abolished. In Nepal, by contrast, the caste system was officially abolished in 1963.

7. Eight 'classes' accounted for different age groups (children and youth), joint trainees (retired soldiers), gender (female) and socio-economic classes (peasants, workers, graduate students).

8. This is why their number can only be estimated.

9. Several publications retrace the political history of the communist movement since the 1950s. For a general overview see Welpton (2005). For a more specific study, see Ogura (2008)

10. The Communist Party of Nepal was founded in Calcutta April 29, 1949. It participated in the overthrow of the Rana regime in 1951 and was banned between 1952 and 1956,

then again during the Panchayat years (1962-1990).

11. For Barman's biography, see de Sales (2011).

12. For Mohan Bikram Singh's biography, see Cailmail (2008).

13. According to communist dogma, the given conditions of a society ('objective conditions') must be matched by the level of consciousness ('subjective conditions') that the oppressed classes have of their oppression.

14. This question is developed in de Sales (2013).

15. For Lenin, the democratic revolution includes national aspirations as one of its elements, but they are supported only insofar as they might contribute to the class struggle (Haupt and Lowy 1974).

16. I have given examples of such conflicts in two earlier articles. See de Sales (2009, 2010).

References

Bulag, U. E. 2000. From Inequality to Difference: Colonial Contradictions of Class and Ethnicity in 'Socialist' China. *Cultural Studies* 14: 3/4, 531-561.

Bianco, L. 2005. *Jaqueries et Revolution dans la Chine du XXème siècle*. Paris: Editions de la Martinière.

Burghart, R. 1993. The Political Culture of the Panchayat Democracy. In *Nepal in the Nineties* (ed.) M. Hutt, 1-13. Oxford: Oxford University Press.

Cailmail, B. 2008-9. A History of Maoism since its Foundation by Mohan Bikram Singh. *European Bulletin of Himalayan Research* 33:4, 11-38.

de Sales, A. 1993. When the miners came to light: the ethnogenesis of the Chantyal. In *Nepal Past and Present* (ed.) G. Toffin, 91-97. Delhi, Sterling.

_____ 2009. From Ancestral Conflicts to Local Empowerment: Two Narratives from a Nepalese Community. *Dialectical Anthropology* 33, 365-381.

_____ 2010. Pride and Prejudice: an Encounter between Shamans and Maoists. In *In Hope and in Fear* (eds) P. Manandhar & D. Seddon, 123-133. New Delhi: Adroit Publishers.

_____ 2013. Thabang: The Crucible of Revolution. In *Revolution in Nepal. History and anthropology of the Nepal People's War* (ed.) M. Lecomte-Tilouine, 164-210. New Delhi: SAGE.

Gaborieau, M. 1982. Les rapports de classe dans l'idéologie officielle du Népal. *Purushartha* 6, 251-290.

Gellner, D. 2001. From Group Rights to Individual Rights and Back: Nepalese Struggles with Culture and Equality. In *Culture and the Anthropology of Rights* (eds) J. Cowan, N. Dembour & R. Wilson, 177-200. Cambridge: Cambridge University Press.

_____ 2007. Caste, Ethnicity and Inequality in Nepal. *Economic and Political Weekly* 42: 20, 1823-1828.

Haupt, G. & M. Lowy 1974. *Les marxistes et la question nationale, 1848-1914*. Paris: Maspero.

International Crisis Group. 2011. *Nepal: Identity Politics and Federalism* (available on-line at: http://www.crisisgroup.org/~/media/Files/asia/south-asia/nepal/199%20Nepal%20-%20Identity%20Politics%20and%20Federalism.pdf, accessed 24 July 2015).

Höfer, A. 1979. *The Caste Hierarchy and the State in Nepal. A Study of the Muluki Ain of 1854*. Innsbruck: Universitätsverlag Wagners.

Lawoti, M. 2003. Maoists and Minorities: Overlap of Interests or the case of exploitation? *Studies in Nepali History and Society* 8: 1, 67-97.

Lecomte-Tilouine, M. 2009. Ruling Social Groups—From Species to Nations: Reflections on Changing Conceptualizations of Caste and Ethnicity in Nepal. In *Ethnic Activism and Civil Society in South Asia* (ed.) D. Gellner, 291-336.Thousand Oaks, CA: SAGE.

Levine, N. 1987. Caste, State and Ethnic Boundaries in Nepal. *Journal of Asian Studies* 46, 71-88.

Middleton, T. & Schneiderman, S 2008. Reservations, Federalism and the Politics of Recognition in Nepal. *Economic & Political Weekly*, 39-45.

Ogura, K. 2008. *Seeking State Power: The Communist Party of Nepal (maoist).* Berlin: Berghof series. Resistance/Liberation Movements and Transition to Politics (available on-line at: http://www.berghof-center.org/, accessed on 4 December 2012).

Pettigrew, J. & A. Shah 2009. Windows into a Revolution: Ethnographies of Maoisim in South Asia. *Dialectical Anthropology* 33: 3/4, 225-221.

Pfaff-Czarnecka, J. 1997. Vestiges and Visions: Cultural Change in the Process of Nation Building in Nepal. In *Nationalism and Ethnicity in a Hindu Kingdom* (eds) D. Gellner, J. Pfaff-Czarnecka & J. Welpton, 419-470. Amsterdam: Hardwood Academic Publishers.

_____ 1999. Debating the State of the Nation: Ethnicization of Politics in Nepal — A Position Paper. In *Ethnic Futures. The State and Identity Politics in Asia* (eds) J. Pfaff-Czarnecka et al., 41-98. Thousand Oaks, CA.: SAGE.

Pahari, A. K. 2010. Unequal Rebellions: the continuum of 'People's War' in Nepal and India. In *The Maoist Insurgency in Nepal* (eds) M. Lawoti and A. K. Pahari, 195-215. London and New York, NY: Routledge.

Srinivas, M. N. 1952. *Religion and Society Amongst the Coorgs of South Asia.* Oxford: Clarendon Press.

Scott, James. 1979. Revolution in the Revolution: Peasants and Commissars. *Theory and Society* 7: 1/2, 97-134.

_____ 2009. *The Art of Not Being Governed. An Anarachist History of Upland SouthEast Asia.* New Haven, CT: Yale University Press.

Stiller, L. F. 1973. *The Rise of the House of Gurkha.* Kathmandu: Ratna Pustak Bhandar.

Tamang, M. 2009. Tamang Activism, History, and Territorial Consciousness. In *Ethnic Activism and Civil Society in South Asia* (ed.) D. Gellner, 269-290.Thousand Oaks, CA: SAGE.

Turber, T. 1993. Anthropology and Multiculturalism. *Cultural Anthropology* 8: 4, 411-429.

Whelpton, J. 2005. *A History of Nepal.* Cambridge: Cambridge University Press.

Chapter 7

THE SANDINISTAS, ARMED STRUGGLE, PARTICIPATION, DEMOCRACY, VERTICALISM AND MASS MOVEMENTS IN NICARAGUA

Harry E. Vanden

Abstract *This chapter explores one of the most crucial tensions in the relationship between armed struggle, mass movements and democratic practices. The FSLN, or Sandinistas, who displaced the long-standing dictatorship of Somoza in Nicaragua in 1979, is the only revolutionary movement in Latin America to succeed after the Cuban revolution. It is analysed here by one of the movement's most committed critical observers. While mass mobilization was perhaps even more crucial than the armed struggle of a vanguard in the overthrow of Somoza, once in power the Sandinista government became more and more isolated from their mass base and fell into the trap of becoming an unresponsive hierarchy, as can occur in vanguard parties and movements. Opting for a form of Liberal representative democracy in the 1984 elections and after, as they fought the contras and battled pressure from Western capitalist democracies, they soon lost touch with their own base. The sad tale is told of how the Sandinista party became less revolutionary as it transformed its practice of substantive democracy and betrayed its founder Sandino's inspiration in the 1990s.*

After the Mexican and Bolshevik Revolutions, radical ideologies based on nationalism and Marxism began to inspire people and political movements throughout Latin America. In the wake of a revolution that turned Marxist – Cuba – there was a rash of revolutionary movements that thought they could seize power through armed struggle and install Marxist regimes. Yet only one Marxist movement was able to fight its way to power in Latin America – the FSLN, or the Sandinistas, in Nicaragua. The others failed, are still struggling on in some form (the FARC and ELN in Colombia) or achieved power after they laid down their arms (the FMLN in El Salvador). In this context a study of how and why the Sandinista revolutionaries were able to harness the power of the masses and take power through armed struggle in Nicaragua would seem justified for a systematic discussion of Marxist movements in the South.

The Genesis of Sandinismo

The Sandinista Revolution in Nicaragua did not emerge full blown in the politically charged atmosphere that characterised Latin America after the Cuban Revolution, but had its roots in the country's past. It relied on the ideological vehicle of Sandinismo, a popular vision of the national past based on the historic struggle of Augusto César Sandino in the late 1920s and early 1930s, that could be recaptured by the Nicaraguan masses and became a means of empowerment and mobilisation.

Sandinismo was inspired by and heavily influenced by the heroic guerrilla war of Sandino and his followers against the U.S. Marines and reactionary Nicaraguan forces, waged from 1925 to 1933, which became a popular national struggle. Sandino embraced an internationalist vision of popular revolutionary nationalism that was linked to other revolutionary movements throughout the world: 'It would not be strange for me and my army to find ourselves in any country of Latin America where the murderous invader had set his sights on conquest' (Sandino as cited in Escobar 1978, see also Fonseca Amador 1984). Sandino was not a communist, but he shared their desire to abolish exploitation and the capitalist system through a worldwide revolution of the oppressed. He was influenced by Mexico's revolutionary government, the Peruvian but Mexican-based American Popular Revolutionary Alliance (APRA), and the Communist International (Macaulay 1985: 157).

The struggle by the original Sandinistas was one of the first modern examples of what a guerrilla army with mass popular support could do against a technologically superior invader, even when the latter was supported by local quislings and the mercenary military forces at their disposal. Mobile guerrilla bands were the components of an egalitarian people's army, organising and acting politically as well as militarily, with close ties to the peasants, and, most importantly, general popular support and involvement. Such were the lessons to be learned from Sandino's people's war against imperialism.[1] These lessons were not forgotten by the leadership of the FSLN as they began their struggle in the 1960s.

Carlos Fonseca, the original Sandinista leader, studied Sandino and found great inspiration in his struggle against the Marines, his strong class consciousness and internationalism. Apparently Gregorio Selser's *Sandino, General de Hombres Libres* influenced Fonseca most (Borge 1985: 22). Later Fonseca met Santos López, a veteran of the Sandino struggle who was the living link between the revolutionary generations. Although enthralled by the revolutionary actions of the Nicaraguan people, Fonseca did not limit his study to Nicaraguan history. He was becoming a Marxist and an internationalist. In 1957 Fonseca travelled to the Soviet Union and wrote *A Nicaraguan in Moscow*, a positive, almost uncritical acceptance of the Soviet model of socialism (ibid: 24). By 1959, however, he began to be disillusioned with the reformist approaches of the Moscow-oriented Marxist Leninist Party, the Nicaraguan

Socialist Party (PSN), and sought a new vehicle for change based on the method of armed struggle. Fonseca's disenchantment with the PSN did not involve a rejection of Marxism but rather a belief that the PSN was abandoning the use of Marxism as a dynamic philosophy. Fonseca saw in the July 26th Movement in Cuba a playing out and renewal of the revolutionary traditions of Sandino, and Castro's triumph showed that victory was possible. Deported to Guatemala in April 1959 following student demonstrations in Leon, he went briefly to Cuba. Then, with advice from Che Guevara and practical assistance from the Cuban government, he joined up with the 'Rigoberto López Pérez' column in the Honduran border region, a group of 55 Nicaraguans, Cubans and other Latin Americans who were waging a struggle against the dictatorship of Anastacio Somoza that had emerged after the assassination of Augusto Sandino in 1933.

However, neglecting to consider carefully enough specific national conditions in Nicaragua, the column was surprised and massacred; Fonseca was wounded but made his way to Cuba for convalescence. By then Cuba was clearly becoming both the inspiration and the basis of practical assistance.

In many ways Fonseca was arriving at a broad and important theoretical break with the strategy of the PSN and with almost all Latin American Marxism at the time. The Nicaraguan PSN argued that in the absence of fully developed capitalism in Nicaragua and an industrial working class, the main task of the revolutionary party, outside of trade union work in the embryonic working class, was to seek alliances within the 'national bourgeoisie' in pursuit of a 'bourgeois-democratic' era in Nicaragua.[2] The way the PSN sought bourgeois allies led Fonseca to eventually break with it and the mainstream of Latin American Marxism at that time. Rejecting the sterile analysis of the PSN, Fonseca opted to return to Lenin's theory of continuing revolution and Trotsky's theory of permanent revolution (which also had a profoundly democratic basis) that had been taken up by

Che Guevara (Liss 1984: 258-259). As Lenin and Trotsky had done in Russia, Guevara and Fonseca rejected the idea that the bourgeoisie had any significant revolutionary role to play in twentieth century semi-colonial countries like Cuba and Nicaragua. Rather, they believed the key to achieving fundamental change lay in the creation of a revolution based in a working class and the peasantry committed to armed struggle. Here there is a definite convergence with the often quoted phrase from Sandino: 'Only the workers and the peasants will go to the end, only their organized force will attain victory' (Fonseca 1984: 99-100).

Another element crucial to the revolutionary philosophy of Fonseca and Guevara, in contrast to that of the PSN and Soviet Marxism, was its emphasis on the will and a belief that to some degree revolution could be made by creating subjective conditions. Fonseca and Guevara turned to the Peruvian Marxist José Carlos Mariátegui and the Italian Antonio Gramsci to craft a philosophy based on revolutionary action, the importance of the subjective factor in making revolution and the role of ideology in motivating the masses (Hodges 1986:182-184). Mariátegui believed that the revolution was motivated by a 'myth' and not any narrow personal interest -- a theme echoed often in the speeches of Guevara and Fidel. Mariátegui also believed that myth could be turned into revolutionary action through careful political education for a broad segment of the people.[3]

The example of the Cuban revolution had already helped to inspire some of the previously mentioned guerrilla activity in the late 1950s. As the Cuban revolutionaries responded to US pressures and threats by deepening social transformation on the island and openly adopting Marxist-Leninist ideas, their example became increasingly attractive to the young militants in Nicaragua. Like many young Latin American revolutionaries, they were much taken by Fidel Castro's 26th of July Movement and believed that guerrilla warfare – as outlined by Che Guevara (1969) – was the best method of implementing political change. Their sympathies thus moved from the Stalinist outlook of the PSN to the dynamic and revolutionary Marxism being developed by the Cuban leaders. Guevara's theory of rural guerrilla warfare had borrowed from Sandino. The Sandinistas would, in turn, borrow from the Cuban example to continue Sandino's struggle.

The effort made to create a type of Marxism in both Cuba and Nicaragua that was based on their own national conditions met with considerable resistance in Moscow. Che Guevara's ideas were labelled 'tropical communism' by Soviet ideologues and during the 1960's there was open (but virtual) warfare between the established Moscow-oriented Latin American Communist parties and the Cuban revolutionary leaders and their allies like the FSLN. When, at the end of 1959, the PSN again declared armed struggle to be premature, attacked the activities of the Rigoberto López Pérez column and reconfirmed its long-standing reformist position, Fonseca was prepared for a definitive break with it. This break came in 1960 following Fonseca's final attempt to influence the PSN's youth group, Patriotic Youth, to adopt a stance of revolutionary, armed struggle.

In July 1961 the Sandinista National Liberation Front was formally launched in Tegucigalpa, Honduras at a meeting attended by Tomás Borge, Carlos Fonseca, Silvio Mayorga and Noel Guerrero (who soon dropped out of the movement). At its foundation, the FSLN consisted of just twelve militants including Santos López, a veteran of the struggle against the U.S. Marines in the late 1920s, and Victor Tirado López, later one of the nine members of the FSLN's National Directorate, along with Tomás Borge. According to Borge's prison writings, the name of the organisation and its clear link to Sandino was suggested and fought for by Fonseca, who realised that the full force of creative Marxist thinkers could best be brought to bear if it were concretised in the national setting. To that end, the figure of Sandino was and continued to be a significant factor in the shaping of the FSLN's political philosophy.

Armed Struggle

The new generation of Sandinistas began a movement that was a continuation of the popular struggle of Augusto César Sandino's guerrilla army and of efforts by the Nicaraguan masses to assert their control. Drawing heavily on Cuba's revolutionary experience and the writings of Che Guevara and Fidel Castro, the Sandinistas had to reinterpret Sandino's original struggle in light of historic and ideological developments since his death. Even during his guerrilla war, Sandino had concluded that the Liberal and Conservative politicians were traitors and cowards and must be replaced by worker and peasant leaders (Sandino as cited in Ramírez 1982: 12). By studying their own fight for national identity and liberation in the light of similar struggles in Cuba, Vietnam, and elsewhere, the Sandinistas were able to build on Sandino's tactics and ideology and began to infuse their movement with a coherent ideology.

However, like other young Fidelistas throughout Latin America, they initially felt that launching rural guerrilla warfare was sufficient to convince the popular masses (beginning with the peasantry) to take up arms and join the guerrillas. In Nicaragua, as elsewhere in the region, this was a fundamental and very costly error. The FSLN's first attempts at guerrilla warfare (Rio Coco and Rio Bocay 1963) met with tragic defeat. The new Sandinistas had failed to do what their namesake had done so well – mobilise the local populace on the side of the guerrillas through well-planned political and organisational activity that was coordinated with and part of the armed struggle. Tomás Borge would later explain: 'We committed the error of moving into the zone without first undertaking preparatory political work, without knowing the terrain, and without creating supply lines' (Borge as cited in Waksman 1979: 21). Retiring from their guerrilla adventures in the inhospitable mountainous jungle of northern Nicaragua, most of the remaining Sandinistas began to engage in semi-legal political work in urban areas, in uneasy cooperation with the Nicaraguan Socialist Party.

The FSLN's early operations were focused on armed struggle, guided by a revolutionary praxis modelled on the Cuban revolution. They were not firmly grounded in an adequate understanding of the socio-political conditions of the masses and did not have a clear organisational plan for them that could mobilise them in the armed struggle necessary to wrest power from the Somoza dictatorship. Thus, these early operations largely failed and resulted in a loss of many of the original cadre of the movement. One reason that the FSLN survived and most guerrilla movements in Latin America did not was that the FSLN learned more quickly than other groups the limitations of the *foco* approach because of its neglect of political organising. Immediately after its military defeats and retreat into Honduras, the FSLN concentrated its efforts in the poor neighbourhoods of Managua and other cities. Drawing on old roots and ties, this urban work was carried out in collaboration with the PSN and helped to develop deep links for the party. Yet, once again the FSLN proved incapable of resisting the superior military power of the National Guard. They had not yet fully assimilated the lessons to be learned from popular struggles for national liberation like those led by Sandino, Mao, Ho Chi Minh, and Castro.

Significantly, in Nicaragua the historic gulf between Marxist and Christian forces was bridged by the FSLN not simply through a brief tactical alliance but through the integration of progressive Christians into the revolutionary party. The result of this merger was that the political philosophy of the FSLN, and in particular its attitude towards Christianity, was innovative among Latin American revolutionary parties with Marxist origins (Girardi 1987). Popular empowerment of the masses and the mobilisation of grass roots participants through Christian base communities, liberation theology and the growing popular church also injected strong democratising tendencies and helped to introduce ideas of direct democracy and less centralist views of governance into the Sandinista movement.

Tragically, some of the FSLN's best cadres were cut off and surrounded at Pancasán in mid-1967. Most were killed as the National Guard closed their trap on the guerrillas. Like the Fidelista guerrilla currents all over Latin America (Che Guevara for instance, was killed in Bolivia the same year) they suffered a disastrous military setback. However, while this was occurring in the countryside, things were even worse in the cities. The traditional opposition forces continued to demonstrate their ineptitude. In contrast, the tenacity of the resistance waged by the FSLN focused national attention on their struggle, and helped to turn a military defeat into a political victory. Beginning with the peasants and university students, the process of merging the vanguard and a mobilised people into a unified fighting force was slowly getting underway. The popular classes and enlightened members of other classes were beginning to stir for the first time since Sandino – a national reawakening was finally beginning. But there was still much to learn before the people could be fully mobilised. Unlike many other guerrilla movements in Latin America, the Sandinistas were able to learn from the mistakes they made in Rio Bocay and Pancasán. They demonstrated considerable capacity for self-criticism and were thus able to transcend their initial mistake of isolating themselves from the masses (Tirado López 1979 1980: 7). Through painful trial and error and an increasingly astute study of Sandino's thought and tactics, and those of other revolutionary movements throughout the world, they were able to fashion a strategy that would eventually unleash the full power of the Nicaraguan people against the Somoza dictatorship. The FSLN began to establish what it called 'intermediate organisations.' This changed 'the orientation of the Front' (Borge cited in Waksman Schinca: 21).

The Sandinistas' success in rallying peasants to their cause in the mountains alarmed Somoza and the U.S. embassy. Large-scale, brutal counter-insurgency operations were launched. Peasants suspected of collaborating with the FSLN 'disappeared,' were tortured, hurled out of helicopters or simply murdered.

This forced adoption of new strategies and tactics. While the Sandinistas developed their theory of mass struggle, progressive sectors within the Catholic Church became more and more concerned with the condition of the masses. Motivated by this concern and the growing 'Liberation Theology' movement, they began to intervene actively in the process of social change. The empowerment of the masses and the mobilisation of grass roots participants through Christian Base Communities and the growing Popular Church also injected strong democratising tendencies and helped to introduce into the Sandinista movement ideas of direct participatory democracy and less centralist views of governance.

In a similar vein, José Carlos Mariátegui, writing in the context of the fervent religious beliefs held by most Latin Americans, did not see a contradiction between religion and Marxism and thought that the inspirational nature of religion was similar to the revolutionary myth that was such an important force in mobilising the masses.[4] Although this is just one example of the flexibility of the FSLN as a revolutionary organisation, it is one of its important contributions to the theory and practice of revolutionary organisations throughout the world. The FSLN's awareness of the need to mobilise the masses was already apparent in Carlos Fonseca Amador's landmark article of 1968, 'Nicaragua Hora Cero.' Drawing up a balance sheet on the Pancasán period, Fonseca wrote that: 'Organized mass work (student, peasant, worker) was paralyzed. On the one hand the quantity of cadres necessary for this work was lacking, and on the other, the importance this activity could have in the course of the development of the armed struggle was underrated.' To overcome this weakness, Fonseca pointed to the need 'to pay attention to the habits the capitalist parties and their hangers-on have imposed on the mass of the people ...' Many, he said, sympathised with the armed struggle but did not show this in action. 'This leads to considering the need to properly train a broad number of individuals from among the people so that they will be capable of supporting the armed struggle. To seek the people is not enough – they must be trained to participate in the revolutionary war' (Fonseca 1984b: 32-34).

Three political tendencies (Prolonged Peoples' War, Proletarian and Tercerista/Third Way) emerged in the FSLN, but after some internal struggle they finally converged around the fresh tactical and strategic questions brought to the fore by the upsurge of mass struggle that began in late 1977 (Vanden and Prevost 1993: 45-46). As the urban masses moved into action after the murder of the popular Somoza critic Pedro Joaquin Chamorro in early 1978, the trend was for all three tendencies to learn from the masses and from each other. This process was facilitated by their mature handling of unification and willingness to learn from each other and work together even before the achievement of full unity in March 1979. All had success in mobilising and empowering segments of the people. The old divisions were then superseded by the historic victory of July 19, 1979. It was only after the armed struggle was put into a national context of political organisation and there was massive popular mobilisation that the FSLN was able to seize power.

Sandinistas in Power

Once they had defeated Somoza and his National Guard, the Sandinistas wanted to maximise popular participation in economic and political processes. The three Sandinistas who were part of the five person junta that initially governed the country were, like most of the Sandinista leadership, very much aware that liberal democracy had had its drawbacks in Latin America and that in countries like Bolivia and Mexico it seemed to have helped derail their revolutions (Walker 1982: 9). Thus they were sceptical of a narrow, bourgeois definition of democracy that minimised direct popular participation and did not include a social and economic dimension. They also wanted to make sure that the form of democracy implemented did not block necessary social and economic restructuring or facilitate foreign manipulation. 'Democracy neither begins nor ends with elections...' (Ortega as cited in Ruchwarger 1987: 3-4). 'Effective democracy, like we intend to practice in Nicaragua, consists of ample popular participation; a permanent dynamic of the people's participation in a variety of political and social tasks...' (Sergio Ramírez as cited in Ruchwarger 1987: 4).

What they envisioned was a popular democracy that would not just allow participation by the few (or domination by the upper classes), but would build democracy from below through the construction of neighbourhood, gender or functional grass-roots and mass organisations (Walker 1982: 9-10). These new mass organisations were to become the primary mechanism for popular empowerment and for the political education and guidance that the masses would need from the FSLN until they fully understood the importance and complexity of their political role and were ready to assume their dominant class position in the revolutionary process (having achieved full political consciousness). These organisations were also to be the direct communication link between the masses and the political leadership. They would inform the people of new political directions and channel popular demands through the party to the National Directorate of the FSLN.[5] To hold the victorious coalition together and transform society, some form of political representation was needed that would allow the participation of anti-Somoza elements from the upper and middle classes but would facilitate direct representation from the lower classes and the Sandinistas.

Rather than an elected assembly, an appointed assembly became the first representative institution in the new Nicaraguan state. The Council of State was to some extent a compromise between the representative and participatory conceptions of democracy. Different political and functional groups would directly designate their own representatives to a national council. This guaranteed that traditional parties would be represented and even representatives of private sector organisations were included in the eventual 51 seats. But, the mass organisations and the FSLN were even more heavily represented. Each of the seven other parties had one seat while the FSLN had six. The neighbourhood-based Sandinista Defence Committees (CDS's) had nine representatives while the Sandinista Workers Central (CST) had three and the Sandinista-linked Rural Workers Association (ATC) had two. Legislative powers were shared with the Junta, but much policy direction and initiative actually originated with the nine man Sandinista National Directorate (Booth 1986: 35-36). While some central control was exercised by the leadership of the FSLN, the mass organisations were not only engaged in grass roots democracy at the lowest level, but also had direct representation in the national policy-making process. The fact that the traditional parties and upper classes had only minimal representation in the evolving governmental structure, through the Council of State, occasioned some criticism from their leaders and led to the resignation of Alfonso Robelo from the Junta (ibid: 32). Representative democracy existed, but was infused with a form of popular democracy that provided for direct national representation. Also in place was a form of democratic centralism which guaranteed the National Directorate of the FSLN dominance in the party and a great deal of influence in government decisions.

Mass Organisations and Participation

Clearly the most vibrant form of democratic participation in Nicaragua, from July 1979 to the mid-eighties, was that practiced by the mass organisations. Indeed the new political leadership was seeking a daily democracy, not just one that took place every four years. And effective democracy consisted of ample popular participation. For the new leaders, 'democracy (was) not merely a formal model, but a continual process capable of giving the people that elect and participate in it the real possibility of transforming their living conditions; a democracy which establish(ed) justice and end(ed) exploitation' (Ramírez as cited in Ruchwarder 1987: 4).

Like the Parisians who formed their commune in 1871, the Nicaraguan masses had taken to the barricades and driven out the remnants of the *ancien régime*. Unlike their comrades in Paris, they had spread their struggle throughout the capital Managua and the nation and had bonded with the FSLN as an armed revolutionary group capable of protecting them and destroying elements of the National Guard. It should also be noted that the leadership of the FSLN often had to catch up with radical mobilisations of the masses in the later phases of the struggle. The mobilised masses were, in the words of one Sandinista observer, 'architects of their history' because they had demonstrated that they were 'the principal agents in the revolutionary transformation' and had been 'active and conscious agents of the revolution' (Augustín Lara as cited in Ruchwarger 1987: 139). Having felt the exhilaration and power that resulted from their direct involvement in this process, they were ready for a meaningful say in governing the nation (Ruchwarger 1987: 289). The theoretical inspiration for their empowerment could be found in the testimony of Karl Marx who, upon witnessing the Paris Commune, was so enthralled by the possibilities of liberation and actual rule by the demos that he wrote *The Civil War in France*. It could also be found in the direct democracy practiced in Paris almost a century later in 1968. In Nicaragua, the toiling masses – if not the people generally – had been mobilised to overthrow the tyrant. They were ready to be involved in government. But unlike Paris in 1871 and 1968, a national (and not just local) revolution and national political organisations headed by the FSLN led the revolt and made sure that the masses would continue to exercise their newfound political power. And it would be necessary for the national political leadership to deal with these new organisations in which the revolution had awakened a new consciousness. For the members of the mass organisations in particular it was the 'beginning of a revolution that they felt was very much their own' (Nuñez 1980: 10). The construction of these participatory organisations proved to be an excellent way of integrating thousands of isolated citizens into large collective structures (Lobel 1988: 879-880). By the mid-eighties, membership in all these mass organisations had increased dramatically.

Inside and outside the FSLN, most of the organisation that did exist had been constructed from the ground up in the late seventies and the Nicaraguan revolution had triumphed because the people had organised and fought not only at the national level, but at the neighbourhood or *barrio* level. Indeed, it was the neighbourhood uprising in the mostly Indian neighbourhood of Monimbó in February of 1978 that set off the first phase of the national uprising that later spread through much of the country in 1978 and was rekindled in 1979.[6] As was the case in much of the rest of the country, some of the fiercest fighting occurred at the *barrio* level as the people mobilised against the dictatorship. After the victory, revolutionary neighbourhood organisations that had grown up all over the country during the struggle soon coalesced into neighbourhood Sandinista Defence Committees. Other Sandinista-affiliated political organisations became mass organisations like the Sandinista Workers' Central (CST), the Association of Rural Workers (ATC), the Nicaraguan Association of Women Luisa Amanda Espinosa (AMNLAE), the National Union of (Small) Farmers and Ranchers (UNAG) and Sandinista Youth (Juventud Sandinista). The political mobilisation that had guaranteed the victory was now channelled into on-going participation through these organisations.

By structuring participation in such a way that the common people could meaningfully participate at the local level and be represented directly at the national level, the Sandinistas had broken new ground. They had come the closest to realising the vision of democracy that Marx glimpsed in the Paris Commune and which the most radical of the American revolutionists had contemplated. And there were few precedents for this in Marxist or Western democratic regimes. Although some mass organisations did exist in Eastern Europe, they were almost universally completely subordinate to the

Communist parties and lacked any substantial autonomy. In Eastern Europe only the workers' self-management movement in Yugoslavia could offer any basis for popular empowerment, and it was limited to the workplace. As suggested in our book *Democracy and Socialism in Sandinista Nicaragua* (Vanden and Prevost 1993), socialism had been weak in turning power over to the demos. The popular movement in Cuba came closest to granting power to the common citizens, but even here its successes were exclusively at the local level and most observers believed that the central party apparatus still exercised control over neighbourhood democracy and especially popular organisations. In the West, there were few participatory town meetings (save for those in New England) or other structures of popular empowerment (block meetings) that functioned regularly and effectively.

The project for mass organisations was in part informed by how Antonio Gramsci thought socialism would be constructed. He believed it would be achieved by a broad alliance of people from all subordinated sectors of the population (Cunningham 1987: 281). The mass organisations would give voice and power to precisely these groups: peasants and small_farmers, urban workers, rural labourers, women and youth. They would enable these hitherto disenfranchised groups to participate actively and effectively in the policy-making process in the new government so that they – and not the traditional elites – could decide their own future. As with other visions of democracy, participation would be the guarantee that the people were actually exercising their power in rule (Pateman 1970: 20). Yet it could be difficult to construct such a system in Nicaragua where the people had been marginalised from the political process by the Somoza dictatorship and were badly under-educated (at the time of the Sandinista victory the national literacy rate was barely above 50% and was much lower for the popular classes). There was not a well-established tradition of participation or democratic involvement.

Socialists have traditionally looked to the working

class to lead the people in building socialism. This would have been difficult in Nicaragua. In 1975 the urban working class was only 16-18 percent of the active population and was mostly scattered in small production units of less than 100 workers (Ruchwarger 1987: 43). Nor was it well-organised – only 10% of the labour force was unionised. And those in unions were scattered among five different federations, one of which was controlled by Somoza (ibid: 43). If rural unions were also taken into account, there were still only 27,000 union members in the entire country in July of 1979 (1% of the population) (Pérez Flores 1989: 15). 'At the time of the triumph, the FSLN found a union movement that was disorganised, weak, poorly developed qualitatively or quantitatively, and was eminently economist in character' (ibid: 13). In order to empower and mobilise the urban working class, the FSLN helped develop the Sandinista Workers' Central (CST), which would serve as a sympathetic national labour federation as well as a mass organisation for urban workers. Given the lack of organisational experience and organisers, FSLN militants were often placed in key positions to ensure that the organisation functioned well and pursued an enlightened political path. A similar strategy was pursued in the development of the Association of Rural Workers (ATC).

These emerging national organisations were to provide the masses with the proper tools for assuming their place in the construction of the new Nicaraguan nation. Eventually the masses would achieve the necessary political wisdom and maturity to realise their full potential.

The mass organisations, like the educational system, would contribute to the development of a new political consciousness (Gilbert 1988: 36). Once achieved, the control and guidance that the FSLN believed were necessary in an initial (less politically conscious) phase could be relaxed. Until the masses had their consciousness fully developed, the Sandinista leadership would, however, have to be very wary of how they were being manipulated by other political forces. They continued to be quite concerned that the bourgeoisie would gain control of the revolutionary process and drastically limit its scope to little more than the removal of Somoza (ibid: 37). Given the political history of Nicaragua (indeed of Central America generally), it would be very easy for Nicaragua to slip into a process of Western-style representative democracy where the elite competed for political office and the participation of the masses was limited to selecting among elite candidates every few years. As in American Federalist James Madison's view of government, the *demos* itself could not participate directly in government, rather others -who were more capable- would decide for them. In *Direct Democracy* Thomas Cronin suggests that this view of government stems directly from (elitist) opposition to 'widespread and public participation in the conduct of government' (Cronin 1989: 8). Such broad participation was precisely the long-term goal of the Sandinistas, who were informed by a belief in the common people found in Sandino, Marx and Jefferson and traceable back to Rousseau's benevolent view of human nature. Once in power they were able to implement this vision in the first years of the revolution through neighbourhood organisations (Sandinista Defence Committees), popular organisations and the Council of State which incorporated representatives from a wide spectrum of groups in society. As noted below, this approach was later modified.

The FSLN

Within the party, a rather traditional form of Democratic Centralism appeared to dominate. Certain tendencies need to be noted in this discussion. In fact, the internal functioning of the Sandinista Party appears to have been authoritarian and centralised. Cultural tendencies, and the influence of Soviet Leninism, were intensified initially by the guerrilla origins of the party and subsequently by the Contra War and the generalised low intensity conflict waged by the United States. The nine-man National Directorate was predominant (one observer even suggested it was the vanguard within the vanguard) (Gilbert 1977). Although a Sandinista Assembly with 104 members acted as a permanent advisory body, its function was to 'support the National Directorate in making the Revolution's most important decisions.' Further, 'It was not elected directly or indirectly, rather its members were representative cadres named by the National Directorate' (FSLN 1986). There were also base, zonal, and regional committees. But here too important positions were usually filled by appointments from above and the agenda for discussion was generally handed down. As suggested by a political slogan often voiced by Sandinista militants – 'the national directorate orders' – political values seemed less democratic within the party and it remains to be seen if it managed to free itself from the centralised, bureaucratic approach that had characterised many parties in the socialist world. Indeed, the lack of democratic experience in Nicaragua may have facilitated centralised decision-making structures and 'verticalism'. This not only meant that the party did not function democratically, but this same style of decision-making was sometimes projected onto the mass organisations and was at times employed in relations between them and the party and between the party and society.

The 1984 Elections: The Demise of Real Socialist Participation

On November 4th 1984, Nicaragua experienced a unique experiment in political participation. Guided by a nationalist ideology that was Marxist in orientation and a political movement that had incorporated some Leninist elements, the revolutionary government nonetheless held Western-style elections which invited the opposition parties to compete for power through the electoral process. The FSLN had succumbed to pressure from the Western democracies and similarly organised Latin American states like Venezuela to hold elections, institute representative governance and diminish the construction of direct, participatory democracy.

The Sandinistas garnered 62.9% of the votes for

President and Vice President and 62.3% of the National Assembly votes. The six opposition parties divided 33% of the vote, while blank or invalid ballots accounted for a little more than 6% of the votes cast. Many wondered if the interests of the masses were being served. In a 1986 paper on the real nature of democracy, the well-known Mexican political scientist Pablo González Casanova noted that democracy is only meaningful if real popular power lies below the form of representative democracy. Indeed, he asked, 'What democracy are we speaking about, and whom does it serve' (González Casanova as cited in Jonas and Stein 1990: 15). As the structure of the new legislative assembly was debated in the Council of State prior to the 1984 elections, the opposition parties were able to successfully remove any structures that would give the mass organisations a role in the new assembly. This ended strong direct participation of these popular organisations in the legislature and thus in the governmental structure as a whole (Lobel 1988: 868). The new political institutions facilitated and became increasingly responsive to middle class and bourgeois mobilisation as manifested in the opposition parties that gained seats in the National Assembly became less responsive to the lower-class constituencies of the mass organisations which no longer had seats in the legislative body.

As time went on and Nicaragua moved toward a new set of elections in 1990, the FSLN tried to encourage all opposition parties to participate in the political process. Meanwhile the mass organisations became less and less powerful as the traditional political groupings played an ever more important role in decision-making.

The 1990 Elections or How Capitalism and Western Democracy Stopped the Revolution

In 1990, the revolutionary, participatory, grassroots democracy that had been initially envisioned as part of the Sandinista programme rushed faster toward a system of representative democracy that the dominant group in the Sandinista leadership hoped would satisfy the United

States and its capitalist allies. From 1982 on, the United States had used military, diplomatic and economic means to try to impose its will on the Sandinista government.

Nicaragua experienced a contra war that cost 30,000 lives and in excess of 12 billion dollars in economic losses, a total U.S. economic embargo from 1985 on and a continual threat of direct US invasion. Responding to such pressures and the Central American Peace Process, the Nicaraguan government not only decided to go ahead with the elections previously scheduled for November 1990, it advanced the time table to February 1990. The Nicaraguan leadership also hoped to show definitively that Nicaragua could satisfy the most stringent Western (capitalist) standards for democracy and could hold a squeaky clean election that would satisfy even its most strident critics. There was also a desire to demonstrate that Western-style democracy could exist within a state guided by a Marxist party.

Although only six opposition parties had opposed the FSLN in the 1984 election, by the beginning of 1988 there were 14 of them plus a few opposition political groupings. The Reagan Administration had pushed for the military side of low-intensity conflict and discouraged parties from participating in 1984. As Bush took office, US policy began to emphasise an electoral challenge to the Sandinistas. With the support of the United States, the opposition parties pushed very hard for modifications in the electoral laws that would ensure maximum political space and political manoeuvrability for them. The Sandinistas made a large number of concessions to achieve widespread party participation. Realising the strength of traditional Nicaraguan political factionalism, the Bush administration pushed for a unified opposing coalition and strongly encouraged the selection of fresh opposition candidates who could serve as a symbol around which the opposition could rally. Although lacking political experience, Violeta Chamorro, the widow of a martyred opposition leader to Somoza, Pedro Joaquín Chamoro, filled this role very well and became the United Nicaraguan Opposition (UNO) candidate. The UNO coalition she headed was composed of 14 opposition parties, including two Communist parties – the Nicaraguan Socialist Party (PSN) and the Communist Party of Nicaragua (PC de N) (See Party Table in Vanden and Prevost 1993: 134-136).

In order to compete successfully against the US-supported UNO coalition, the Sandinista leadership had to devote its organisational and human resources to an expensive electoral contest that ate up more than 7 million dollars of already scarce funds. The Supreme Electoral Council alone, the independent governmental body responsible for overseeing and running the election, spent in excess of 15 million dollars (Estevez interview 1990).[7] Many at the base level felt they were being crucified on an economic cross wrought from the US-sponsored contra war, the trade embargo, lack of economic and administrative expertise on the part of the Nicaraguan government and international economic conditions that had driven most Latin American states to desperation and governmental change.

The Sandinista leadership knew that conditions were bad, but thought the base could endure a little longer while they employed the human and material resources at their disposal to win the election. They were no longer well-connected to their mass base and refused to grasp the message of discontent that was being widely voiced. Some use of government resources by the FSLN was also reported. The Sandinistas reasoned that such extravagant spending was necessary to win the election in order to secure their position and legitimise their political system in the eyes of the West. Down to the eve of the election most opinion polls suggested that the Nicaraguan people would ratify the socialist, mixed economy experiment and continue with Sandinista democracy. However, the Sandinistas' stunning defeat at the hands of the United Nicaraguan Opposition (UNO) suggested that the demos was not satisfied with Sandinista rule or the type of socialist democracy that was developing in Nicaragua (Vanden and Prevost 1993: 143-146).

After years of Somocismo, the civil war, followed by the contra war and the economic embargo, the masses just did not have anything more to give. Indeed the neighbourhood-based Sandinista Defence Committees (CDS) had stopped functioning for all practical purposes (La Ramée and Polakoff 1990). Furthermore, many felt that the Sandinista leaders were isolated from the hardship of the masses, and that their political position facilitated access to goods that the poor could no longer afford. Many were also angered by what they perceived as increasing bureaucratisation in government offices. They saw the formation of a bureaucratic class that was not particularly sympathetic to popular needs and benefitted from a disproportionate share of scarce resources. This created a considerable amount of resentment. Thus it seemed to many that the Vanguard Party had lost contact with the very people it was supposed to represent and consequently was not responding to their needs and feelings. Rather it had become an institution ruled from the top down ('the National Directorate commands') and had_established a set of interests that was not the same as those of the people. Nor were party leaders or cadres always open to criticism or opinions that contradicted their own. And after a while, some Nicaraguans felt they could no longer express contrary views.

As the election results trickled in, it soon became apparent that – believing they had been abandoned by the Sandinistas – the residents of many working class neighbourhoods in the capital (Julio Bultrago, Las Brisas and San Judas among them) had given UNO a majority. This was also the case in other urban areas as well as in much of the countryside. UNO gained 54.7% of the vote while the Sandinistas received only 40.8% (most polls had predicted a substantial Sandinista victory, the ABC/Washington Post Poll predicted 48% to 32%). For the FSLN, convinced that it would win easily, this was a particularly stunning defeat. Since it had been so strongly committed to the election, it would have been difficult and contradictory not to accept its outcome. As

Nicaragua slipped back into traditional elite rule with the parties representing the interests of the bourgeoisie at the expense of the masses, the Sandinista party became ever less revolutionary and soon became largely controlled by the strong political leader (*caudillo*) and former Sandinista President, Daniel Ortega. A much less radical FSLN was not able to take control of the government again until 2006, and then only after making a devil's pact with the corrupt former president Arnaldo Alemán, leader of the traditional bourgeois Constitutional Liberal Party (PLC).

Conclusion

The experiment with radical revolution and socialist participatory democracy in Nicaragua succeeded for a while and would have continued if the FSLN had remained true to its base and continued to trust in the participatory avenues of democracy that were developed immediately after the revolutionaries took power in 1979. Heeding how the masses were mobilising, political ideas empowering them and defining their role as agents of change were introduced into the current mix of Latin American politics and in varying degrees became part of political practice in Nicaragua and elsewhere in Latin America. If the popular participation (mass mobilisations) that cemented the popular victory could be carried forward, new structures to accommodate this participation might be constructed.

When a small revolutionary group engaged in armed struggle, as in the Sandinista case, a Gramscian consensus could be created among large segments of the masses proving that revolutionary struggle was practically the only remaining road to end political oppression, making it possible to guide and sometimes direct the power of the people. If the revolutionaries could organise, encourage and support this direct participation of the masses after the revolutionary triumph, they would move closer to the vision of participatory democracy envisioned by Marx and other radical thinkers. By empowering wide segments of the population in this way, these sectors (segments) solidified their power and guaranteed that their views would be heard and heeded. In turn, the revolutionary leadership would have a mobilised, effective base to support its radical vision of social and economic change in a post-revolutionary society. The revolutionary movement would not have to subordinate itself to conservative national sectors or to the influence of powerful capitalist states preaching the virtues of a representative democracy that disenfranchised more than it empowered the people. The same principles of political education and mass involvement that guided the revolutionary struggle could shape the construction of a revolutionary society and the on-going empowerment and involvement of the people.

Notes

1. Macaulay underlines the close ties Sandino's guerrilla fighters had with the local populace and notes that Sandino's tactics 'essentially were the same as the tactics of the People's Liberation Army in China, the National Liberation Front in Algeria, the 26th of July Movement in Cuba and the Viet Minh and Viet Cong in Vietnam' (1985: 10). All these struggles were premised on mass involvement in the armed struggle and looked to well-developed political awareness and very close organisational ties to the masses as essential ways of achieving such essential popular involvement and participation.

2. The PSN was founded in 1944 while Nicaragua was an ally of the Soviet Union as part of the Allied war effort. Thus the party initially enjoyed the tolerance of the government.

3. For a fuller treatment of the ideas of José Carlos Mariátegui, see Vanden (1986) and Mariátegui (2011).

4. Mariátegui's thought in this regard was instrumental in providing an intellectual basis for the development of liberation theology. Gustavo Gutiérez used and cited Mariátegui in his ground breaking work, *Theology of Liberation*.

5. See Gilbert (1988), particularly Chapter 3, 'The Party in the State and Mass Organizations.'

6. In February of 1978, this tightly knit, lower-class and mostly Indian community on the outskirts of Masaya took over the neighbourhoods and held off the National Guard for more than a week. They had few weapons that they had not manufactured themselves and only some Sandinista support several days into the uprising. Interviews by Harry E. Vanden with several Monimbó families, Monimbó, July 1980.

7. Dr. Mariano Fiallos (1990), the President of the Supreme Electoral Council, indicated that it would be difficult to estimate the total cost of running the election, but his organisation had a budget of $18 million.

References

Booth, J. 1986. The National Government System. In *Nicaragua: The First Five Years* (ed.) T. Walker, 29-44. New York, NY: Praeger.

Borge, T. 1984. *Carlos, the Dawn is No Longer Beyond Our Reach*. Vancouver: New Star Books.

Cronin, T. 1989. *Direct Democracy the Politics of Initiative, Referendum and Recall*. Cambridge: Harvard University Press.

Cunningham, F. 1987. *Democratic Theory and Socialism*. Cambridge, MA: Cambridge University Press.

Escobar, J. B. 1978. *Ideario Sandinista*. Managua: SENAPEP.

Estevez, R. 1990. Interviewed by Harry E. Vanden. Managua: February 24, 1990.

Fiallos, M. 1990. Interviewed by Harry E. Vanden. Managua: February 20, 1990.

Fonseca Amador, C. 1984. *Ideario Político de Augusto César Sandino*. Managua: Departamento de Propaganda y Educación Política del FSLN.

Fonseca, C. 1984a. *Long Live Sandino*. Managua: Departamento de Propaganda y Educación Política del FSLN.

_____ 1984b. *Nicaragua: hora cero*. Managua: Department of Propaganda and Education, FSLN.

Gilbert, D. 1988. *Sandinistas, the Party and the Revolution*. New York, NY: Basil Blackwell.

Girardi, G. 1987. *Sandinismo, Marxismo, Cristianismo: La confluencia*. Managua: Centro Antonio Valdivieso.

Jonas. S & N. Stein (1990). The Construction of Democracy in Nicaragua. In *Democracy in Latin America: Visions and Realities* (eds) S. Jonas & N. Stein, 13-52. Grandby, MA: Bergin and Garvey.

Guevara, C. 1969. *Guerrilla Warfare*. London: Penguin.

Hodges, D. 1986. *Intellectual Foundations of the Sandinista Revolution*. Austin, TX: University of Texas Press.

La Ramée, Pierre & E. Polakoff 1990. Transformation of the CDS's and the breakdown of grassroots democracy in revolutionary Nicaragua. *New Political Science* 9: 1/2, 103-123.

Liss, S. 1984. *Marxist Thought in Latin America*. Berkeley, CA: University of California Press.

Lobel, J. 1988. The Meaning of Democracy: Representative and Participatory Democracy in the New Nicaraguan Constitution. *University of Pittsburg Law*

Review 49, 879-880.

Mariátegui, J. C. 2011. *José Carlos Mariátegui: An Anthology of His Writings* (trans. and eds. H. E. Vanden & M. Becker). New York, NY: Monthly Review.

Monimbó families. 1980. Interviewed by Harry E. Vanden. Monimbó: July 1980.

Macaulay, N. 1985. *The Sandino Affair*. Durham, NC: Duke University Press.

Nuñez, C. 1980. *El papel de las organizaciones de masas en el proceso revolucionario*. Managua: SENAPEP, FSLN.

Pateman, C. 1970. *Participation and Democratic Theory*. Cambridge: Cambridge University Press.

Pérez Flores, X. 1989. *Notas sobre la participación de los trabajadores in la revolución Sandinista, caso de la ATC y CST*. 15th Congress of the Latin American Studies Association, 4-6 December, Miami.

Ramírez, S. 1980. El ideario político-social de Sandino y el Sandinismo. Análisis histórico social del Movimiento sandinista desde el origen hasta la maduración. *Encuentro: Revista Académica de la Universidad Centroamericana* 15, 10-20.

Ruchwarger, G. 1987. *People in Power*. Grandby, MA: Bergin and Garvey.

Tirado López, V. 1980. *El pensamiento político de Carlos Fonseca Amador*. Managua: Secretaría Nacional de Popagnada y Educación Política del FSLN.

Vanden, H. E. 1986. *José Carlos Mariátegui's Thought and Politics*. Boulder, CO: Lynne Rienner.

Vanden, H. E. & G. Prevost 1993. *Democracy and*

Socialism in Sandinista Nicaragua. Boulder, CO and London: Lynne Rienner.

Vanden, H. E. & M. Becker 2011. *José Carlos Mariátegui: An Anthology of His Writings* (trans. and eds. H. E. Vanden & M. Becker). New York, NY: Monthly Review.

Walker, T (ed.) 1982. *Nicaragua in Revolution*. New York, NY: Praeger.

_____ (ed.) 1986. *Nicaragua: The First Five Years*. New York, NY: Praeger.

Waksman Schinca, D. 1979. Entrevista con Tomás Borge. *Combate* (Stockhom), 21-22.

_____ 1986. *The FSLN: Background and Internal Structure*. Managua: Centro de Communicacion Internacional.

Chapter 8

THE POLITICS OF PRODUCTION, FRELIMO AND SOCIALIST AGRARIAN STRATEGY IN MOZAMBIQUE

Bridget O'Laughlin

Abstract *Socialist revolution is not just a single moment when power is defied and defeated; it must be a continuing process of class struggle to change both the forces and relations of production. In Mozambique, Frelimo rejected any strategic redistribution of land to the peasantry from settler farms, estates and plantations and steered both investment and consumer goods towards industry, urban areas and state-farms. Its management of the farms – patterns of cropping, the organisation of work, labour recruitment and stratified wage-forms – and its gendered assumptions about the subsistence orientation of the peasantry mirrored those of the class relations typical of the colonial period. The farms were a failure in economic terms and undercut the political legitimacy of Frelimo in the countryside. They also contributed to private accumulation of capital in parallel commercial networks and to patterns of debt that opened Mozambique to the liberalisation policies of the IFIs.*

Introduction: Revolution and Millenarianism

> The social revolution of the nineteenth century
> cannot take its poetry from the past but only from
> the future. It cannot begin with itself before it has
> stripped away all superstition about the past. The
> former revolutions required recollections of past
> world history in order to smother their own content.
> The revolution of the nineteenth century must let
> the dead bury their dead in order to arrive at its
> own content. There the phrase went beyond the
> content – here the content goes beyond the phrase
> (Marx 1852).

This much cited passage from Marx's analysis of the
fall of the French Republic in 1851 (*The 18ᵗʰ Brumaire of
Louis Bonaparte*) captures the millenarian expectations
arising from Marx's theory of socialist revolution. All
should change; all is possible; the past is past. There is
much here to encourage revolutionaries to think that
socialist revolution is that moment when they have seized
state power and can set out to build a new and better
world.

There was a millenarian cast to everyday life in
Mozambique in the late 1970s. The Mozambique
Liberation Front (FRELIMO, from Frente de Libertação
de Moçambique) formed the first independent
government in 1975 after a prolonged armed struggle
and declared itself a vanguard Marxist-Leninist party in
1977. Many felt that they were living in revolutionary
times, a moment when people could do, say and imagine
things that had been impossible only a few years before.
Dockers changed out of their work clothes to attend
primary school classes in the middle of the day. Young
students went to the countryside for literacy or
vaccination campaigns. Manual workers, clerks and
managers, doctors, nurses and patients called each other
comrade. Neighbours got together to clean the rubbish
from the streets. Artists painted images of workers and
peasants on the walls of the city. Production councils kept

rural cotton gins and urban factories running even though the owners and managers had left. Women, rural and urban, stood up in meetings and criticised those in charge (mainly men) for not listening to them. Ideas, big and small, were borrowed from different socialist traditions: betterment campaigns (like killing flies) from Mao, dynamising groups from Cuban neighbourhood committees, choreographed May Days from North Koreans, women driving buses and tractors from the Soviets. The president, Samora Machel, would announce a new political slogan (*palavra de ordem*) in a broadcast speech, and all over the country people would offer different interpretations of what it meant, and act upon them in sometimes contradictory ways.

Yet a teleological vision that reduces socialist revolution to such transcendent moments would belie the importance that Marx himself assigned to the primacy of production and thus to socialism as a process of transforming both the forces and relations of production. This can only be a process, not a single moment, and it is a process that is contested and contingent, its course and outcome unknown. Because forces and relations of production are a contradictory and mutually constitutive unity, neither the seizure of state-power nor the physical flight and elimination of the bourgeoisie, nor state-ownership of enterprises silence class struggle. Relations of class remain embedded in the ways we work, in how distribution and consumption are organised and in how we understand and organise the politics of emancipatory change.

As Feuchtwang and Shah point out in their introduction to this book, socialist strategies are defined by the emancipatory ends envisioned by revolutionaries. In that sense, Marx wrote that social revolutions must take their poetry not from the past but from the future. But socialist strategies also depend on conceptions of beginning points; they must trace the ways we move from where we are to where we want to go. For socialist revolutionary movements, these beginning points have been historically quite variable, though each was embedded in a world dominated by the dynamics of capitalism as a mode of production. The historical forms of the relation between capital and labour have been diverse and shifting in ways that mattered deeply in the everyday experience of people. They have thus also mattered deeply to the revolutionary movements that navigate in their midst, forging alliances, defining the opposition, broadening the basis of support for revolutionary change. And sometimes revolutionary movements have erred in their analysis of their beginning points, in ways that profoundly and tragically shaped their strategies of socialist transformation.

This chapter deals with one such movement, the Frelimo Party of the 1970s, its analysis of Mozambican class structure, and the consequences of this analysis for how it conceived a socialist strategy for the countryside,[1] a strategy that concentrated resources, not just investment but also consumer goods, in state-farms. The chapter reconsiders the question that Frelimo could never satisfactorily answer – why were these state-farms not able to recruit the workers they needed when they were needed? It uses this very specific focus to interrogate both how Frelimo's emancipatory strategy envisioned its specific beginning points and the underlying assumptions it shared with many other socialist revolutionary movements.

There are few arguments to be made for dissecting the experience of Mozambican state-farms on economic grounds: they accumulated huge debts, both to the state financial institutions that extended almost endless credit and to their workers, who in the last few years seldom received their wages. But state-farms have figured in the strategies of agrarian transformation for many socialist movements. Their version of worker ownership should thus be interrogated as part of the critique that revolutionary movements must make of past strategies. If socialist revolution is a contingent process, not something to be simply read off the right recipe, what can we now say about the class politics of agricultural enterprises in the post-independence period? For

Mozambique this means reviewing rural political economy at the end of the colonial period, discussing Frelimo's socialist vision of the countryside, how it framed conceptions of what was to be done, and considering how class relations and struggles shaped the outcomes of its strategy.

The Theorisation of Strategies of Socialist Transition

Much of the classic theorisation of socialist strategy posits a linear series of steps that takes as a universal beginning point 19th century experiences of rapid industrialisation, wide proletarianisation and the emergence of well-organised urban working-class movements. Post-socialist critics are right to point out that this is also the basis of modernisation theories of development and that a kind of teleological vision of historical inevitability often infuses both traditions. There are, however, major differences between them. Marx insisted that the rapid pace of economic expansion and commodification that has characterised the capitalist world is not the product of inexorable adaptive efficiency or universal human progress. What drives change is capital's life or death competition for profit and labour's unending struggle against exploitation. Underlying the seemingly balanced terms of market expansion are violent historical processes of dispossession and proletarianisation.

Marx's theory describes the general tendencies of capitalism, but these are dynamic structural possibilities, contingent moments, not predictable outcomes. The exercise of collective agency, embedded in particular histories, but more than the summation of individual conceptions and desires, shapes these outcomes. Revolutionary moments will always be constructed though understanding particular cultural and historical experiences and lived through local struggles, but they also transform these experiences in collective action.

There is nothing in Marxist theory that precludes

recognising that capital may rely on non-free or non-commodified labour. The first was frequent in the late 19th and the first half of the 20th century when colonial power underlay forced cropping and labour regimes that were deliberately embraced to drive down the cost of labour and to discourage labour militancy. The second continues to be embedded in the notion of a sphere of 'domestic labour,' tasks that are necessary but labelled as unproductive because what is not bought and sold cannot directly produce profit. Some Marxist analysis has universalised the conceptual distinction between productive and unproductive labour whereas it actually applies only from the point of view of capital. This naturalises a historically constructed and hierarchical division of labour in which women have done much of this 'unproductive' work.

Mechanical developmentalism has characterised some Marxist approaches to socialist strategy, illustrated in an extreme form by manuals on socialising production with formulaic recipes such as 'the law of mechanisation.' It has also established a causal relationship between property and efficiency reminiscent of neo-liberal argumentation, though in an inverted form: suppression of private property and the market allows productivity to be increased through planning of material balances that replaces market signals with norms of efficiency and the setting of quantitative production targets. Protest against low wages, the intensification of work and monopoly pricing, defined as anti-capitalist struggle in the pre-revolutionary period, was redefined as a manifestation of counter-revolutionary attitudes when property belonged to the socialist state.

The central role assigned to state-farms in classic socialist strategies of agrarian transition reflected a focus on the immediate suppression of commodity production, the leading role of the proletariat and the suspension of class struggle. The lacunae in this strategy made it particularly inappropriate in Mozambique, but arguably it would also confront difficulties in the contemporary world of precarious employment and uneven commodification of work.

There has, however, always been a Marxist alternative to linear developmentalism. Just as the development of capitalism is contingent and historically variable so is socialist revolution a contingent process rather than a moment in which all is irrevocably transformed. Class struggle continues and workers' collective agency is as important as the efficiency of planning in the socialisation of production. This is the 'immanent critique' within Marxism itself discussed by Burawoy (2009: 47). It is present in classic debates about theorisation of the experiences of socialist transition, which suggest that the politics of socialist production are much more complex than the suppression of capitalist ownership and the development of the productive forces. These reflections include extended work by scholars such as Bettelheim (1976), but also the writings of critical 'participant scholars' like Bukharin and Chayanov, and texts of Lenin himself on 'socialist emulation' and cooperativisation. This body of work forces one to look at the class struggles embedded in the discourses and practices of management, in how labour processes are organised and different groups of producers, both within and between work-places, relate to each other.

Class and the Politics of Rural Production at the End of the Colonial Period

In the political narrative of colonial history written by Frelimo during the years of armed struggle and the first years of independence (Mondlane 1995), it was customary to speak of 500 years of Portuguese colonialism. Though the dynamics of coastal trade, and particularly the slave trade, had enormous impact on the history of eastern and southern Africa during those 500 years, the Portuguese political presence beyond coastal trade settlements was minimal until after the 1878 Congress of Berlin and even then only selectively evident. Direct colonial rule and settlement was most firmly established in southern Mozambique and financed by the export of labour to the mines of South Africa. In central

Mozambique, administration and plantation economies were at first organised by concessionary companies. Colonial revenue in northern Mozambique drew principally on taxes on companies trading in commodities produced by peasants, particularly the cheap cotton that provisioned the growth of the Portuguese textile industry from the 1930s through the 1950s.

Colonial Mozambique was divided between two interdependent social spaces. First were the 'native reserve' areas where peasants maintained their rights to land, organised smallholder production (sometimes subject to forced cropping) and lived (and struggled) within selectively adapted pre-colonial political institutions. Second were the urban, industrial and plantation areas where they went as temporary alien workers, subject to forced labour regimes and controls on their movement, and excluded from the rights of citizenship extended to settlers. In this first period of effective colonial rule, race – or nation – was almost perfectly congruent with class, though differences in the forms of exploitation established clear regional differences in the dynamics of households.

Gradual economic and political changes in the post-World War II period led, however, to much greater complexity of rural class structure and to a blurring of sharp regional differences. The reasons for these changes were partly due to the restructuring of capital in Mozambique, Portugal and the southern African region, which itself reflected growing and changing forms of opposition to the terms of colonial rule in Africa generally and in Mozambique and the southern African region in particular. Tanzania, Malawi, Zambia, Botswana, Swaziland, and Lesotho all gained political independence in the 1960s and national liberation movements of different historical depth were active in Mozambique, Angola, Namibia, Zimbabwe and South Africa. Attempts to stabilise the basis of white rule included a series of economic and political reforms: incentives for white settlement, including in areas once classified as native reserves, modernisation of productive capacity, including reinforcing industrialisation, freer regimes of labour recruitment, and schemes to develop a class of small specialised black commercial farmers.

In Mozambican rural areas these reforms included the formal abolition of forced labour and forced cropping in 1961 and 1962, administrative experiments with marketing cooperatives for small groups of black farmers in the 1950s and 1960s (Adam 1987), state funding for smallholder Portuguese settler schemes in new areas, with limited participation of black peasant families in the 1960s and 1970s (Hermele 1986), and experimentation with extension of crop credit to black farmers by the cotton and cereal authorities in the 1970s (CEA research Baixo Limpopo, Angonia, Manica). By the 1950s, the Zambezia plantations relied almost entirely on contract labour rather than forced labour (Vail and White 1980). State investment in expansion of the rural transport system facilitated labour movement and flexible recruitment.

Shifts in the nature of urban employment and use of labour controls also had an impact in rural areas. Economic growth in both Rhodesia under UDI and South Africa increased traffic and thus jobs in the ports of Beira and Maputo. With the expansion of fixed employment in urban centres there was a corresponding expansion of informal service jobs. In the 1950s women began to move from the countryside into domestic labour in the cities (Penvenne 1995: 152), despite the fact that this required the authorisation of their chief as well as the male head of household. The loosening of influx controls and diversification of urban employment drew young people from the countryside. Shortage of casual wage-labour in rural areas thus co-existed with urban unemployment, particularly in Maputo. Attempts to recruit agricultural workers from among the urban unemployed were not successful, however (Schaedel 1984).

The construction of the Cahora Bassa dam on the Zambezi and the expansion of coal production in Moatize increased off-farm non-agricultural employment in central Mozambique. Off-farm employment also increased in northern Mozambique with the development of the Nacala port and construction of the rail-line from Malawi. Ironically, the formation of FRELIMO and, in 1964, the launching of armed struggle in the north of the country, also increased off-farm wage-employment in the Pemba port and in construction with the expansion of the internal road-system and the building of military installations. Increased urbanisation and off-farm employment boosted the demand for staple food crops, particularly maize, rice and cassava, the latter almost exclusively a commercial crop of black farmers. At the same time, small and medium Portuguese settler farms continued to expand in areas of prime commercial potential, sometimes with government support for credit and even the provision of labour. In cotton growing areas, some new settler farmers were allowed to subvert the monopsony of the cotton companies by purchasing cotton from surrounding peasant producers and selling it with their own production, paying the company only a ginning fee (CEA research Nampula 1979). Other settlers provided inputs and marketing crops such as potatoes from peasant farmers (CEA research Angonia 1982).

The reshaping of rural life at the end of the colonial period thus reflected competition between different forms of capital and the formal political struggles of liberation movements in Mozambique and more broadly in Africa. At the same time, it reveals the struggles of working people within production and exchange. We know quite a lot about forms of individual resistance to forced labour or cropping – absenteeism or desertion on the plantations, for example, or sabotaging one's own cotton crop (Isaacman et al. 1980). Forms of resistance propelled proletarianisation and differentiation of the peasantry – embedding livelihoods more tightly in the world of commodities. Escaping the monopsony power of a concessionary cotton company in Nampula often meant cultivating an alternative cash-crop such as sunflowers, or planting more cashew-trees. Resistance to the terms of forced labour often meant signing up for a contract on the mines or plantations. Collective resistance was more limited, given high levels of repression and the exclusion of most black workers from trade unions.[2]

In the last decade of colonial rule, therefore, Mozambican class structure was much more complexly related to the dynamics of the market than the narrative of forced cropping and forced labour torn from rural native reserves might lead one to think. There were greater numbers of permanent and contract workers on farms, mines, and construction, and a larger and more stable black urban population. Incentives were given in terms of credit, differential pricing and labour recruitment to settler farmers that no black commercial farmer received, but there were enclaves of specialised black farmers scattered across all areas of Mozambique, many of them related to chiefs but also using the regular wage income of a household member as a basis for investment and working capital.

Yet movement between rural and urban areas was still controlled by administrative documents – the identity card, tax-receipt and pass. Local administrators and chiefs continued to be involved in forcible recruitment of workers both for settler farmers' seasonal labour demands and local infrastructural maintenance. Colonial agricultural statistics continued to distinguish on the basis of colour: yellows, whites, Indians, blacks, mixed. Only black workers were distinguished by gender, allowing one to trace the substantial importance of women wage-workers for agriculture in southern Mozambique. The casual labour of boys under 18 years was important in agricultural enterprises across all provinces. Extension workers pursued and beat farmers, particularly women, who were not giving priority to timely weeding of their cotton fields. If we asked in our rural fieldwork when forced labour and cropping ended in the region, the answer was almost invariably 'with Frelimo.'

The administrative institutions of a bifurcated colonial state created a dualistic political order, as Mamdani (1996) and others have emphasised. But they also promoted an evolutionary ideology and vision that explained the need for continuing oppressive state intervention in labour and agricultural markets as being rooted in the supposed subsistence orientation of the peasantry. For colonial planners, the poverty of the people of rural areas, including their deprivation of schools and health facilities, reflected their primitive backwardness, a condition to be slowly addressed, according to the development plans of the 1950s and 1960s (*Planos de Fomento*) through economic modernisation. This dualist vision did not fit well with the complex interdependence of rural and urban issues in Mozambique by the 1970s, but it continued to inform the vision that many Mozambican intellectuals had of their own society (O'Laughlin 1996).

Frelimo Strategy for the Socialisation of the Countryside

When in 1974 there was a left-wing coup in Portugal, FRELIMO was internally organised as a coherent party rather than as a front, crucial in its unified approach to the war. It was ready to push for independence, its rhetoric was firmly anti-imperialist, and settlers expected to lose property and privilege. FRELIMO had experience in administrating liberated zones in northern Mozambique, but it had no real experience in collectivising production from which to work (Adam 2006). Land was nationalised at independence.[3] This was closely followed by legal practices (including notaries), medicine, education and rental property, though banks and productive enterprises were not nationalised. As settlers fled, however, the state gradually took on administrative control of a wider range of different kinds of property.

Plantation capital and some settler farmers hung on after Independence, but most settlers, particularly the smaller farmers in the irrigation schemes and new settlements, rapidly abandoned their holdings.[4] Administrative commissions integrating farm workers and Frelimo commanders were formed to keep some of the farms going. Still much of the infrastructures, stock, crops and equipment were lost, some sold off or sabotaged by the departing settlers, sometimes appropriated by local people of influence. Administrative commissions could bring the crops in, but they had neither the capital nor experience to organise a new agricultural campaign.

Although the formation of the state-farms was initially a defensive response to the problems of managing these abandoned farms, settlers deserting their farms and jobs were responding to the angry tone in Frelimo's criticisms of colonial exploitation and to the popular support, sometimes menacing, they generated. Samora Machel's speeches and Frelimo documents made it clear that the old bourgeoisie were to go and would not be replaced. A Ministry of Agriculture document characterises the first phase of its activity as one where they knew what they did not want the abandoned farms to become: 'We wanted to avoid and combat the formation of a national bourgeoisie substituting the former land-owners, and, on the other side we did not want self-management appearing.'[5]

Thus the abandoned farms were first managed directly by the ministry as a series of holdings. Provincial planning offices were then formed to coordinate management of the farms and link with centralised planning of crops, inputs, marketing and investment. The largest units and clusters of settler-farms were consolidated into state-farms. Cooperatives were formed on some of the smaller or isolated settler farms, sometimes by a group of workers who stayed on, sometimes by a group of local residents, and very occasionally by a combination of the two. Some private farmers, often of Indian, Chinese, Portuguese or mixed origin, continued farming in peri-urban areas and in other regions with good market access or infrastructures for commercial agriculture. A few small-scale black Mozambican private farmers managed to appropriate abandoned marginal settler lands which were neither integrated into state-farms nor farmed cooperatively.

Frelimo's strategic directives on agricultural enterprises were not adopted until the Third Congress in 1977 when FRELIMO the front became Frelimo, the Marxist-Leninist party. Frelimo's strategy of rural socialisation was formalised in the theses for the Third Party Congress in 1977 and widely debated in the period of preparation for the Congress (Frelimo 1977). The basic lines of policy were, however, clear before that: all land belonged to the state but could be held by individuals or enterprises as long as they used it well. There was to be no general nationalisation of settler-owned farms, but where farms had been abandoned or were being badly run, they were to be taken over by the state. Abandoned or seized settler and plantation holdings would not be handed over to individual farmers but kept together to be cultivated either as cooperatives or state-farms. Collectivisation of the countryside was to be based on residential regrouping of the population in communal villages that would have as their productive base either cooperatives or a state-farm. Family farms were to be gradually reduced to one hectare of rain-fed land or half a hectare of irrigated land.

State-farms were to be the focus of investment because their large area, rational organisation of resources and access to mechanised means of production would allow them both to feed the nation and to be centres of agricultural science and teaching. The priority given to food production was intended to address the problem of feeding the cities and industrial centres in a strategy of rapid industrial accumulation. Agriculture would be the base and industry was defined as the dynamising element, i.e. surpluses for investment in industry would come by improving productivity in agriculture and establishing mechanisms for mobilising the resulting agricultural surplus.

Frelimo also used evolutionist Marxist-Leninist language to describe as 'semi-feudal' many of the institutions of the rural world, distinguishing those that it thought were bad – particularly traditional chiefs, beliefs in sorcery and witchcraft and bridewealth payments from those that were good – such as music, dance, herbalists and midwives. Such a view of rural people did not really depend on the texts of Marxism-Leninism, however, since it so permeated colonial thought. In the absence of a clear class enemy, underdevelopment became the principal enemy of the revolution; the word itself conjured up the hoe and hut of rural life.

Commercial profit was a potential source of accumulation, but Frelimo sought immediately to restrict the autonomy of the market as much as possible. Pan-territorial prices were declared, effective only if the state subsidised transport costs. Initially the network of rural shops, crucial for distribution of consumer goods and inputs and in marketing of peasant surpluses, was taken over by state-run 'people's shops' (*lojas do povo*) and seasonal government crop-buying brigades, pre-empting private trade, though by 1979-80, the latter had been reinstituted, giving selected rural traders quotas of consumer goods at official prices. Rural services, many of which had been provided by private farmers and traders, were also taken over by the state. Tractors left behind were either absorbed by state-farms or centralised in state-operated machine-posts that were to privilege provisioning of farm machinery and fuel to cooperatives.

The size of peasant farms was normatively restricted though in most areas this was difficult for Frelimo to enforce. In the Zambezi and Limpopo valleys the floods of 1976 and 1977 facilitated both the obligatory movement of people into nucleated settlements on higher ground, the communal villages, and limiting the size of peasant holdings of irrigable valley land (though not to the declared ½ ha.). Similarly the Rhodesian attacks in Manica facilitated regrouping of people into protected communal villages and effectively restricted easy access to land. Across the country, with the consolidation of scattered settler farms into large-scale state-farms, former settlement scheme farmers and small specialised commercial farmers lost their land.

Restrictions placed on market agents and the extension of prices controls and subsidies (neither alien to the previous colonial regime) meant that the state took over coordination between different groups of producers. Planning began as an effort to coordinate the use of resources controlled by the state, but in the period between 1977 and 1981 the institutional and legal framework was established to subject markets to the planning process (Wuyts 1989). A national planning commission was set up and all economic ministries subordinated to it. Advisors from socialist countries introduced material balances planning to replace monetary accounting. State enterprises were legally required to produce according to the plan, given annual production targets, to exchange with other state enterprises also subject to the plan and had to transfer financial surpluses to the state-budget.

In 1979, it was announced that the country would be preparing a ten-year plan, the PPI. Production councils were formalised in all state enterprises, but their principal tasks were not defined in the directives of the Third Congress as giving workers input into the planning process or assuring that the plan protected workers' interests. Class struggle was redefined as maintaining worker discipline, striving for higher productivity and transforming production (Wuyts 1989). Nonetheless, in practice the councils and party cells often disputed management's interpretation of how targets should be reached and explanations for why they were not.

Frelimo was particularly concerned about the potential resurgence of petty bourgeois political power in collective organisations that extended beyond workplaces. In the theory of Marxist-Leninist parties, mass organisations (women, youth, teachers, workers...) play an important political role in building alliances between working classes. Frelimo instituted many of these, but despite debate over the question within the party, did not permit the organisation of a national peasants' organisation. The National Union of Peasants (UNAC) was not organised until 1987 and then as an autonomous organisation not linked to Frelimo. Even the central trade union organisation (OTM), which was subordinated to Frelimo until 1990, was not formed until 1983. The orthodox wing within the party thought the production councils were not sufficiently 'mature' and feared that the clout of a national union led by a labour aristocracy might lead to an escalation of wage demands.

With control over the state apparatus, the flight of most settlers and the scope of private property limited, Frelimo treated both national liberation and the dissolution of capitalist relations of production as accomplished.[6] They spoke of racial inequalities in the past but not in the present; the worker-peasant alliance (aliança operário-camponesa) was declared the order of the day; almost everyone was considered to be either a peasant or a worker.[7] Behaviour, such as ambition or corruption, were defined as capitalist, not ownership of property. Gradually the definition of the political struggle shifted; by 1980 the class enemy had become very abstract – under-development with an analysis of causality vague enough to bridge capitalism, colonialism and semi-feudalism. In the large amphitheatre in the Medical Faculty in Maputo where political lectures and debates were often held, the national director of planning instructed everyone to pull in their belts, for the next decade was to be decade of the victory over under-development.

Retrospectively this linear view of socialist revolution – a march through history set at the moment when revolutionaries seize state power and impeded mainly by the actions of external and internal enemies – may now seem naïve. Yet in the late 1970s it did not appear to be so, either to revolutionaries or to western intelligence agencies, both of whom in the wake of the United States defeat in Vietnam saw generalised socialist revolution in southern Africa as a real possibility. In this context a materialist analysis of failure, such as that of the state-farms was extraordinarily difficult.

The State Farms as a Locus of Contradictory Relations of Production[8]

Marx's analysis of capitalism showed that commodities are not just things circulating in the space of markets but fundamentally the expression of underlying social relationships. Challenging the logic of markets thus means much more than outlawing or regulating them; it means transforming relations of production: not only the relations of exploitation between capital and labour, but also the frequently gendered relation between commodified and non-commodified production. Frelimo's strategy for displacing the logic of the market in rural areas was to concentrate resources in the hands of the state and then to plan how they would be used to fuel investment in state-farms and cooperatives.

It was initially expected that planning agrarian production would be relatively easy since most of the settler agrarian bourgeoisie had fled and the rural population was thought to be made up of a semi-feudal subsistence-oriented peasantry mainly living outside the market and employing rudimentary techniques of production. Instead very few peasants joined the cooperatives and when they did, their productivity, at least as measured by what was sold, appeared to be much less than what they achieved on their family plots.[9] As for the state-farms, planning failed miserably at finding a socialist answer to what has been arguably the central problem of capitalist agriculture: how to have enough workers when you need them and not have them when you do not.[10] It also failed to transform capitalist relations of production in the rural economy and consequently fuelled parallel processes of accumulation and class dynamics that undercut its emancipatory objectives. The reasons for this failure have to do with the inaccuracy of Frelimo's understanding of its strategic beginning point, class structure at the end of the colonial period, but they also reflect more general theoretical problems entailed in linear millenarian views of revolutionary transition.

Though each state-farm had its own particular history and distinctive management and cropping patterns, there was a common contradiction between the planning of labour use and real labour used and paid on most farms. Figure 1 below illustrates this with data from 1982 for one block of CAIA, an agro-industrial complex specialising in the production of maize and potatoes in Tete province.

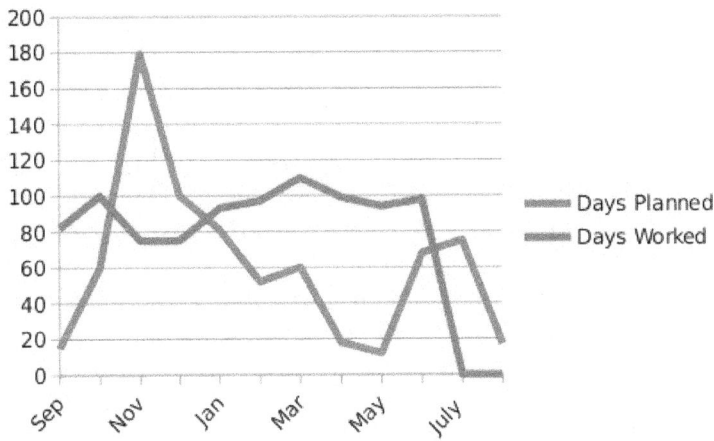

Figure 1 Days planned and worked, CAIA 1981-2 (000 days)

Source CEA (1983: 11) field research July 1982

The number of workers required in the peak labour month, November, the first weeding period for maize on both peasant and state farms, was around 7200. Yet November and December were the months when the fewest casual days were worked. On the other hand the most casual days were worked in March, when according to the plan there should not have been so much field labour required. Despite persistent shortages of field workers at appointed times, the overall wage-bill for casual labour was actually much higher than planned: around 39.2 million *meticais* vs. 27.4 million allocated. Crop yields were not surprisingly much below the plan and labour costs per unit of production much higher. Behind this technical question of productivity lay three inter-related lacunae in Frelimo's strategic vision of how state-farms would socialise relations of production.

The first failure in Frelimo's state-farm strategy was that it did not address the transformation of rural labour markets, which were assumed not to exist. It was presumed that underemployed labour was available in the pre-feudal subsistence-oriented family sector and could be politically mobilised to provide it. Implicitly women were expected to cover the loss of labour by intensifying their own work with no impact on levels of food production, nutrition or health.

The cropping patterns planned for the state-farms exacerbated the seasonal labour demands of former settler-farms. In Frelimo's strategic vision, economies of scale were key for state–farms. Large contiguous units could be worked by heavy machinery and even sprayed aerially. Frelimo policy was therefore to group scattered settler farms together in large units, reinforcing the mono-cropping patterns of conventional plantations. In 1981, a planner in the Ministry of Agriculture calculated the possible number of permanent workers on state-farms on the basis of current cropping patterns (Quental-Mendes 1981). Except for a horticultural farm all showed one or more sharp peaks in planned labour demand. Many of the state-farms shared the same agricultural calendar as the surrounding peasant households that were asked to furnish seasonal labour, inevitably leading to conflicts in weeding and harvesting periods.

Planning procedures minimised the implications of seasonality for recruitment, procurement and investment in housing by projecting a virtual stable labour-force. For budgeting purposes, the plan calculated that CAIA needed on average about 3000 workers a month. In discussing the problems of labour shortage, the director of CAIA repeated this estimate to us, dropping the key phrase 'on average.' Recruiting 7000 workers during some months and providing food and accommodation for them is quite different from recruiting 3000. Some of the casual workers we met at CAIA were sleeping in abandoned pigsties using potato sacks for blankets. Short rations were a complaint on almost all farms.

Shortfalls in seasonal labour supply were attributed to a political failure of consciousness on the part of the peasantry and thus addressed through political mobilisation. In theory 'mobilisation' was supposed to persuade people to do voluntary labour. Conscription was contrary to Frelimo's critique of colonialism and its celebration of emancipation. In practice it was often otherwise. In the case of the Lugela plantations in Zambezia, in 1980 workers were recruited in two ways. For immediate and small-scale problems, the director of the plantation informed the secretary of the party on the plantation who, accompanied by militia, would call on village secretaries in areas near the plantation to ask for workers, including women and school-children. Larger and longer-term requests for young men were channelled through the District Administrator who then allocated these requests to administrators at the local level. One administrator sent out militias to run document checks on young men to see whether or not they had paid their taxes. Generally they had not, so their documents were seized and they were sent off to a plantation until they had earned enough to pay their taxes.

Labour shortages at particular times of the year were so pressing that niceties broke down. A state cotton farm in Nampula in 1979 negotiated directly with local officials for seasonal weeding labour, sending trucks to distant areas to pick up women and children. On the large state-farms, one block might even steal workers from another block, just as the settler farmers had sometimes stolen each other's workers. At CAIA, there was a low-lying swamp block where it was unpleasant to work. The block-chief would send some militia and a truck to pick up workers from other blocks of CAIA. In accord with military idioms, this practice was euphemistically called 'going on patrol.'

When all else failed, a major Frelimo political figure might step in. Samora Machel, citing the Cuban sugar harvest, mobilised factory workers and students from Maputo for the rice harvest at CAIL. In 1982, an important minister visited Angonia just as the new agricultural year was about to begin. In a public speech, she called upon the party and the government to mobilise the population to provide workers for CAIA, people's property, when needed. After all, she argued, such a populous district as Angonia should have been able to provide 3000 workers (note the recurrence of the planner's average).

Criticism of the supposedly underemployed peasantry for failing to recognise the needs of the nation hardened with the continuing decline of state-farm production. In 1986, the governor of Nampula announced in a widely reported speech that the local administrators would have to recruit workers for all the state and private firms (by 1986 capitalism was renascent). Moreover, 'producing cotton and cashew nuts is not a favour; it is an order of the state.'[11]

Diversification of rural livelihoods by the end of the colonial period meant that many were willing to take on wage-work in agriculture, but they expected decent conditions of work and housing and a wage that would allow them and their families to buy the inputs and some of the same commodities people in cities wanted – staples like oil and sugar, clothing, soap, fuel, notebooks. Here they were stymied by the goods famine in the countryside, which undercut the value of the money-wage.

Here lies the second failure of state-farm strategy – not recognising the importance of local commodity markets for both state-farms and the peasantry. Given the scarcity of consumer goods, priority went to urban areas and selected sectors in rural areas: state-farms, cooperatives, schools and the army. The state farms were supposed to trade with each other, a sugar plantation exchanging with a nearby fruit and vegetable farm

(Cardoso 1991). But not only did the peasantry need consumer goods, state-farms needed staples to feed their workers, which in many areas meant buying peasant surpluses. These were not forthcoming, not because the peasantry were subsistence producers but because the state-farms offered no commodities in return. In the end, the state-farms and the army turned to private traders and became important agents fuelling the rise of parallel markets and thus accumulation of commercial capital (Mackintosh 1985).

The third strategic failure was the absence of new forms of management to deconstruct the extreme alienation of manual workers characteristic of colonial capitalist agriculture. Planning did not dislodge capitalist relations of production from the organisation of work or forms of payment or the relations between management and workers. There were three different layers in the labour force. First were the educated technicians and managers, a few foreigners but mainly Mozambicans, who were capable of understanding and responding to communications from the ministry, but did not always know much about local agriculture and even less about the livelihoods of people in the surrounding communities. Then there were the experienced permanent workers. When settlers left, their foremen and tractor drivers often stayed on. They came with ideas about which crops would grow on which fields, about how workers should be supervised and paid, about which machinery was good. There was tension between these two groups but also collusion. Both were paid a monthly wage, had privileged access to consumer goods and often had housing provided by the company. They also had access to the unused inputs and water rights of the state-farms, some of which were employed in their own fields and some they sold to local private farmers.

The third layer of the labour force were the casual workers, identified as peasants on the payroll sheets of some farms, paid by the day on a task- or piece-wage. Women and children were usually the truly casual workers, recruited from day to day, not knowing whether they would be hired, working only in periods of peak labour demand. A substantial part of the male day-workers on most farms became, however, effectively fixed. There was an informal system, organised at the field level, in which foremen recruited permanent teams, setting shifts and marking pay-cards to assure that their (mainly male) workers got a consistent monthly wage and to give them time-off for home-visits. This is why the second line in Figure 1, days really worked (or paid), is almost flat.

This team system was outside the plan and formally unrecognised by the director and the administrative staff. The permanent workers who dominated the production councils and party-cells knew of these informal arrangements of course, but pointed out that they were fulfilling Frelimo's mandate to protect and advance the rights of workers. Cardoso (1991) noted with some irritation that Frelimo members at the base meddled in management tasks, blocking the reforms he as director proposed and that higher-level party officials had approved. The administrative workers who controlled the time-cards also saw how the informal system worked, but regarded planning and control as formal exercises, intended 'for the Englishman to see.' So here again the 'rural proletariat,' the permanent skilled workers, were embedded in class relations of both conflict and collusion.

Conclusion: The Poetry of the Future

By 1983, it was apparent that the state farms could not sustain the recovery in yields made in the first few years of independence. Production was falling, debt was sky-rocketing, some land was not even being cropped, and there was not enough foreign exchange to sustain the country's dependence on imported inputs (Wuyts 1989). Results in the cooperatives were equally disastrous. The fourth party congress in May 1983 decided to privatise part of the state-farm land, to allow cooperatives to transform themselves into associations of small-holders and generally to provide more support for family and commercial private farming.

Some within Frelimo characterised this as a change in socialist tactics, a Mozambican version of Lenin's New Economic Policy, but others saw it as a shift towards capitalism. The key political slogan for the period was 'Land should belong to those with the capacity to work it.' Some interpreted this as meaning that the land should be in the hands of the peasants, but others took it to imply that it should belong to those with the capital needed to purchase inputs and hire labour. These were the years when USAID appeared, extending credit for vehicles and machinery in urban Green Zones. One would not say that a socialist revolutionary process was out of the question, but the words *'a luta continua'* (the struggle continues), took on an increasingly hollow ring. The areas in the countryside contested and then occupied by Renamo, the armed opposition movement, expanded rapidly and Frelimo's policies towards the peasantry grew increasingly authoritarian. In 1986, Frelimo began serious negotiations with the IMF and the World Bank concerning the terms of a structural adjustment package.

Some attributed the failings of the Mozambican revolution in rural areas to external support from imperialist powers for internal resistance. Contemporary academic analysts and now many within Frelimo itself focus on its attempts to marginalise 'traditional' authority politically.[12] This chapter suggests that the answer should begin where Marxist analysis – historical and materialist – always suggests, with the politics of production. This account of the failures of state-farm strategy has made some points that apply to Frelimo's agrarian strategy but that mirror questions raised by other histories of socialist revolution as well.

First, Frelimo's class analysis of its strategic beginning point placed most of the Mozambican population outside capitalist relations of production. There was only a small urban working-class, which Frelimo distrusted as a labour aristocracy; almost everyone in rural areas was viewed as part of a semi-feudal subsistence-oriented peasantry for whom the market was not a necessity. Failure to see the broad range of relations of production that subordinate labour to capital has not been just an issue for Frelimo. It underlies the difficulties confronted by Marxists in understanding the politics of the diverse forms of exploitation, oppression and resistance in nationalist struggles. It also surfaces in tensions between Marxism and feminism over concepts such as unproductive labour. In the case of Mozambique, where colonial patterns of labour recruitment and forced cropping intensified women's already substantial responsibility for agricultural production, calls to work harder in the context of severe goods shortage fell particularly flat.

Second, Frelimo took from the history of Marxist-Leninist movements a millenarian tendency to see socialist revolution as that moment when revolutionaries seize state-power, neutralise the bourgeoisie and then follow a fixed path towards an emancipatory future (unless perturbed or displaced by the need to confront enemy action). Its main strategic concern was with economic development; it had no strategy for addressing the ways that capitalist relations of production were embedded in the organisation of work, including non-commodified work. Its strategy for markets was to limit their functioning, not to reorganise how they continued to matter both for the state-farms and for the livelihood of rural people. Frelimo could not recognise ongoing class struggle in its planning processes and resistance to them as something other than 'enemy action.' The irony is that in the interstices of these lacunae there was room for private accumulation of capital.

So Frelimo's failures are not exceptional. In moments when power has been defied and defeated, other socialist revolutionary movements have also been tempted to envision the future as the suspension of the past, a new world with possibilities not yet experienced. But revolution is more than such millenarian moments and class struggle is not so easily suspended; socialist revolutions are long-term contingent processes of confronting the contradictions of the past embodied in the ways that people produce and reproduce their conditions of existence and in the theoretical images (poetry if you will) they construct to understand them.

Notes

1. This paper draws heavily on my experience as a teacher and researcher at Eduardo Mondlane University in Maputo from 1979 to 1992 and particularly on collective research done at the Centro de Estudos Africanos (CEA) under the direction of Aquino de Bragança and Ruth First.

2. The one important exception, the stevedores union, was limited only to those contracted by private shipping agencies for work in the boats and acted as a recruiting agency.

3. Some of Frelimo's critics have treated this as the dispossession of the peasantry by the state, but at the time this was simply a way of asserting that the land belonged to the Mozambican nation and not to those who claimed it through colonial dispensation.

4. These departures were often clandestine and quick, reflected in the use of Cuban terminology to describe leaving as a kind of betrayal, a flight (*fugiu*).

5. Photocopy, DINAPROC, Maputo, 1978.

6. Though one high-ranking Frelimo cadre, no longer socialist at all, was once heard to say in reference to his ultimate objective of bringing all rural production into state farms, that the cooperatives with irrigated land on the Limpopo were 'not our principal enemy.'

7. We were very reluctant to suggest in our CEA reports that they were not, lest that be taken as justification for the appropriation of more land for state-farms.

8. This section draws on various sources. The CEA studied a

range of state-owned or intervened farms and plantations with students from the Development Course: the UPBL rice farm on the Limpopo, a horticultural farm close to Maputo, tea plantations in Zambezia, a maize and potato complex in highland Tete and cotton and sisal plantations in Zambezia and Nampula. In these cases we also studied family farming and cooperatives in surrounding areas. There are also in-depth studies of two important state farms done by their former Mozambican directors as doctoral theses, the CAIL complex on the Limpopo (rice, wheat, vegetables, some livestock) (see Mosca 1988) and the Maragra sugar estate (see Cardoso 1991).

9. Various CEA research projects across Mozambique 1979-1983. There is not space to discuss why cooperatives failed here, but the approach – treating them as a space of class struggle – would be the same.

10. Sidney Mintz's formulation.

11. Moyana (1986: 14-15).

12. As Dinerman (2006) emphasises, Frelimo's self-critique here is significantly partial, obviating the need for any critical analysis of its economic policies.

References

Adam, Y. 1987. *Cooperativização agrícola e modificação das relações de produção no período colonial em Moçambique*. Maputo: Universidade Eduardo Mondlane.

_____ 2006. *Escapar os Dentes do Crocodilo e Cair na Poca do Leopardo, Trajectório de Moçambique Pos-Colonial (1975-1990)*. Maputo: Promédia.

Bettelheim, C. & B. Pearce 1976. *Class Struggles in the USSR. First period: 1917-1923*. New York, NY: Monthly Review Press.

Burawoy, M. 2009. Working in the tracks of state

socialism. *Capital & Class* 33: 2, 33-64.

Cardoso, F. J. 1991. *Estratégias, economias locais e empresas agrárias: o desenvolvimento rural em Moçambique*. Lisboa: Instituto Superior de Economia e Gestão, Universidade Técnica de Lisboa.

Dinerman, A. 2006. *Revolution, counter-revolution and revisionism in post-colonial Africa: the case of Mozambique, 1975-1994*. London: Routledge.

Frelimo. 1977. *Explicação das teses do III Congresso*. Maputo: Frelimo.

Hermele, K. 1986. *Contemporary land struggles on the Limpopo: A case study of Chokwe, Mozambique, 1950-1985*. Uppsala: Department of Development Studies, University of Uppsala.

Isaacman, A. et al. 1980. Cotton is the Mother of Poverty: Peasant Resistance to Forced Cotton Production in Mozambique, 1938-1961. *The International Journal of African Historical Studies* 13: 4, 581-615.

Mackintosh, M. 1985. Economic tactics: Commercial policy and the socialization of African agriculture. *World Development* 13: 1, 77-96.

Mamdani, M. 1996. *Citizen and Subject: Contemporary Africa and the Legacy of Late Colonialism*. Oxford: James Currey Publishers.

Marx, K. 1852. *The 18th Brumaire of Louis Bonaparte* (available on-line at: http://www.marxists.org/archive/marx/works/, accessed 4 August 2015).

Mondlane, E. 1995. *Lutar por Moçambique*. Maputo: Centro de Estudos Africanos, Universidade Eduardo

Mondlane.

Mosca, J. 1988. *Contribuição para o estudo do sector agrário do Chókwè*. Maputo: Ministério da Agricultura.

Moyana, S. 1986. Produzir algodão e castanha decaju não é favor é ordem do Estado. *Tempo* 836, 12-15.

O'Laughlin, B. 1996. Through a divided glass: dualism, class and the agrarian question in Mozambique. *Journal of Peasant Studies* 23: 4, 1-39.

Penvenne, J. 1995. *African workers and colonial racism: Mozambican strategies and struggles in Lourenco Marques, 1877-1962*. Portsmouth, NH: Heinemann.

Schaedel, M. 1984. *Eingenborenen-Arbeit: Formen der Ausbeutung under der portuguiesichen Kolonialherrschaft in Mozambique*. Koln: Pahl-Rugenstein Verlag.

Vail, L. & L. White 1980. *Capitalism and colonialism in Mozambique: a study of Quelimane district*. Minneapolis, MN: University of Minnesota Press.

Wuyts, M. E. 1989. *Money and planning for socialist transition: the Mozambican experience*. London: Gower.

Epilogue

Chapter 9

FURTHER THEORETICAL REFLECTIONS ON EMANCIPATORY POLITICS

Stephan Feuchtwang and Alpa Shah

Until now, we have left out of this book one of the key terms for an emancipatory project: humanity. Whether it is the Enlightenment project or the Communist project of international solidarity, the creation of humanity out of the potential that exists in all conceptions of humanity for a universal, differentiated but mutually acknowledging humanity has been, and still is, a political project that may or may not require armed struggle. Imperialism, chattel slavery, colonial settlement and the racism that they engendered made this project urgent, realistic, and violent.

Franz Fanon (1961) is one theorist of liberation and human emancipation who took into close account the details of local culture and the violence of colonial occupation suffered and felt. Although his ideal was human liberation free of violence, for him this could only be realized locally and through violence. Writing at the height of the Algerian war for independence, Fanon laid bare the economic and psychological degradation of colonial bondage as a form of violence against which a counter-violence can, and must, be waged. This was, for Fanon, embodied and libidinal and could – when it recognized itself as the source of a new world – become a politics of liberation through which fighters learn by action. For those who valorised Fanon, such as Sartre (1961) who wrote the preface to his book, this violence becomes a crucial condition through which the 'wretched of the earth' could recreate themselves and become human. The question raised by the case studies in this book is whether politicisation can take place through such counter-violence and whether it can become a politics of liberation. But the crucial and inescapable truth Fanon drew attention to is the experiential and cultural condition of armed struggle and emancipatory politics. Let us elaborate this truth.

In her biography of Fanon who was her senior colleague, Alice Cherki (2006) establishes a number of crucial elements of his politics. First, his psychiatric work emphasised the alienation suffered by the mentally ill, which could only be overcome by a new 'socio-therapeutic' activity of mutual work and mutual respect between patients, staff and each other – a mini-politics of combating alienation in the hospital. Second, Fanon's experience of racism in his Second World War service and in much of his medical and psychiatric education had done two things to him. It formed a long-standing and impassioned, uncompromising humanism, and the conclusion that the traditions of the colonised had been completely transformed, along with the so-called 'civilisation' of the colonisers by the politics of colonial oppression. A culture of racism, enforced by state powers, encapsulated and trapped the traditions of the colonised and the projective fantasies of both colonised and colonisers. The experience of this culture of racism is of course both somatic as well as psychic as is all illness mental and physical; but in this case it is the embodiment of violence on a cultural scale. Fanon set out on a politics of liberation to search for 'paths out of the alienation and oppression of all humankind' (2001: 77). In his work as a leading psychiatrist in the main mental hospital in Algeria between 1955 and 1957 he helped the newly formed National Liberation Front and its combatants, medically and psychiatrically, in sheltering them from the occupying French state and its torturers, and in his publications, resigning and moving to Tunisia, to carry on open psychiatric, editorial and writing support of the liberation of encapsulated northern and sub-Saharan African peoples. He had been dismayed by the French Communist Party's pro-Soviet stance in 1956 and its siding with the French Socialist colonial power in Algeria and later by the dictatorial stance of many of the military, as distinct from the political leaders, of the Algerian liberation movement. In short, Fanon's position was beyond formulaic class struggle; it emphasised the battle against racism and for a democratic and participatory liberation through counter-violence, an armed struggle such as those discussed in this book.

One of the first to criticise Fanon's conception of the necessity for counter-violence was Hannah Arendt (1969). Arendt mounted a political and philosophical critique based on her conception of armed force as instrumental for other ends, including ideological ends, but with the danger of becoming its own end. For Arendt, as for Fanon, the political use of violence is a means to end violence. However, the danger that Arendt draws attention to is that the means (violence) used to achieve this political goal (ending violence) becomes more often than not of greater relevance to the future than the intended goal; the means overwhelms the ends.

To Fight for Politics

In her earlier work, Arendt (1951) identified the forces of totalitarianism as a form of governance that eliminated the very possibility of political action. She therefore advocated a fight for politics. Forces of totalitarian regimes preventing political action could in principle generate a legitimate case for armed violence as defence. Arendt took her own experience, as a stateless and displaced person against fascism during and after the end of the Second World War, to compel us to look beyond nationalism and its states toward a politics of humanisation, of recognizing humanity as a capacity for action. What Heidegger called 'mass-man' was for her the result of a new kind of state power, which dehumanised, that is to say depoliticised people through the atomisation of individuals into masses manipulable by demagogues and the organisations of commerce.

For Arendt this kind of rule, totalitarianism, is characterised by three elements. One, ideology becomes a substitute for the reality of having to take into account the existence of others, acting rather to make the world into the image produced by that ideology (this includes racism and supra-nationalism). Second, bureaucracy is rule by technical efficiency and administrative regulation, rule without people (or rule by nobody), which is clearly the most tyrannical form of domination since no one can be asked to answer for what is being done (see also Arendt 1969: 38).[1] Third, terror is the use of violence to enforce ideology and bureaucracy.[2]

These elements exist in every contemporary state jurisdiction, particularly in zones of extreme restriction where state-sanctioned organisations of policing are permitted to use *extra* force, beyond what is authorised and considered legitimate on the normative side of the line, which is the citizens. Such situations include refugee camps and immigration detention centres. They also include institutional racism, resulting in a racialised population harassed by police and a criminal justice system that imprisons a hugely disproportionate number of black citizens in Britain and the USA. On another scale, beyond the confines of any particular state, they include the often large areas of fragmented states where rival gang-masters seek the spoils of armed exploitation and trade, including trade in arms – situations of endemic violence.

People trapped in these situations of extra violence have their own capacities for action in the performance of their daily lives and their networks of self-help. Their own resources include grim irony at the expense of the normative order, so violent and humourless. They include an extraordinary inventiveness for survival and the possibility of maturing and having children in dire circumstances. On a greater scale of encompassment, they include the preservation and reinvention in changed circumstances of traditions of ritual and story-telling that include imagining a transcendental possibility of justice and righteousness, an ideal state. But in many instances, they do not include the conditions for organising armed counter-violence.

We cannot ignore the extreme restrictions and violence that traps these people, often killing them and stunting their lives, crippling and scarring them psychically, and creating an internalised violence of humiliated rage. This was Fanon's main point. Such destructive brutality is perpetrated by legitimised police and armed forces acting as gangs but also by the gangs that they license to capture and destroy. There may indeed be collusion between the two. Such situations include entrapment in enclaves of discrimination and super-exploitation, humiliation exerted at checkpoints, humiliation of the casual and undocumented worker, and extreme violence exerted on female bodies, the gang violence of enforced prostitution, an economy of shame and anger, externalised as paranoia and internalised as self-harm. Only in some circumstances is there the space for armed self-defence to be organised as a release. In other circumstances, we must ask, what forms of action can relieve such crippling internalisation of violence.

In the forests and hills of central and eastern India, wherever there is adequate space for counter-violence, as in much of the Amazon, the tribal inhabitants have been glorified as noble savages and treated with extreme brutality and barbarism by the dominant states. These areas have remained at the extreme margins of their states, without provision of decent health care or education and left to the mercy of extractive multinational companies mining their rich mineral reserves, clearing their forests for timber or for planting soya beans, dispossessing them of the few means they have to sustain themselves. It is hardly surprising then to find societies against the state (Clastres 1974) or that have sought to keep the state away (Shah 2010).

Yet one need not go to such remote regions to find similar brutality against human beings. A quick observation of the daily queues of construction labourers in any large city brings into focus the number of people living a hand-to-mouth existence. Mike Davis (2006) argues that this – the informal working class – is the fastest growing social class on earth, standing currently at about a billion people. They live in slum wastelands often without clean water or a chance of education, where medical crises leave families in life crushing debt.

Defence against these dehumanising states is also a fight for the possibilities of action, which for Arendt is at once human and political; it is the capacity to bring about change, to make something new. The fight for politics is a fight against all the totalitarian processes that dehumanise us and banish thought, but in particular it is a release from extreme situations of violence.

Arendt, Fanon, and Mao

So, if violence sometimes may be the only way to achieve a better world and is a realistic possibility, let us consider more carefully what Arendt means by politics in her critique of violence. It carries with it a due warning to any armed struggle for emancipation. Arendt wrote 'On Violence' in the context of the ongoing student and workers' movement against universities and governments and the global anti-Vietnam war movement. These movements supported a sense of revolutionary, socialist possibilities as well as serious contemplation of armed struggles for emancipation from imperialist capitalism – a continuation of armed struggles to rid colonies of their occupying states. These were times when the example of Maoist politics, against both US imperialism and Soviet 'revisionism,' brought about splits in virtually every Communist Party in the world. There were advocates of anti-imperialist armed struggle and of urban-based organisation and participation through electoral politics.

Quite independently from Maoists' advocacy of armed

struggle, but indicating a similar split, Franz Fanon's theory of counter-violence, based on his personal involvement as a psychiatrist and as a political activist, had picked up an earlier theory by George Sorel on the necessity of violence to enhance the productive power of the working class, for whom the general strike and its defensive militia were crucial weapons.

Arendt's essay 'On Violence' pays particular attention to Fanon and Sorel as theorists of the necessity of violence for emancipatory revolution. At the same time her essay is a critique of the statement by Mao that power grows out of the barrel of a gun. Arendt's criticism is based on an important distinction between violence and power, which we must heed. Violence, for Arendt, is always instrumental and should never be conflated with politics itself: 'it can always destroy power; out of the barrel of the gun grows the most effective command, resulting in the most instant and perfect obedience. What can never grow out of it is power' (1969: 53). Though she was not a pacifist, and recognised that violence is sometimes necessary as a short-term solution, Arendt sees violence as always giving rise to unintended as well as unpredictable outcomes beyond the immediate ends pursued. Among these unintended outcomes, sustained violence becomes a politics of terror that simply maintains the status quo instead of opening up the capacity to make changes, to be creative politically.

Power on the other hand, for Arendt, is action in concert through a collective will, eventually supporting laws by enacting active consent to them. Power is then 'an end in itself,' (1969: 51) a human ability to empower each other. Unlike violence, power cannot be thought of instrumentally. The greater the scale of agreement to act in concert, the greater the power. Its negation, closing down such action, leads either to terror and the atomisation on which it relies, or to the bureaucratisation of rule and of politics (these were of course the very forces against which the student movement of the time was acting).

Arendt does not acknowledge in the colonial situation the daily humiliation, backed by arms, of an occupied population. In other words, she does not take into account a situation of long-term embedded violence. Nor does she address how collective, not individual, self-defence might be organised. She does not recognise that this collective self-defence is qualitatively different from the naturally and legally justified violence of individual self-defence against being violated. Collective self-defence would in her terms have to be concerted – combining the power to act and in the first instance to act violently.

Fanon's theory of counter-violence is that it is not psychological in the biological sense of instinctual drives, including those of individual self-defence and survival. To take up arms to defeat destructive violence is to seek and find a liberating violence, one that liberates both the tortured and the torturers from dreams in which the tortured would merely replace the torturers and the torturers' fear precisely the same. It is to substitute for these un-political dreams, the vision of a national liberation. In 1954, Ben Bella and eight other Algerian revolutionary leaders created the National Liberation Front (FLN). They maintained that 'the only negotiation is war' (Joffe 2012). Under Ben Bella, the first President of independent Algeria from 1963 to 1965, the national liberation government of Algeria seemed to match these generous politics, but his increasing autocracy eventually led to a military coup by his former comrades in arms and subsequently to an exclusive Arab nationalism and religious sectarian opposition, both appealing to a supranational and exclusive totality.

For Arendt such supra-nationalism becomes linked to the violent means to command and to bureaucratic administration, which was the character of imperialism and racism. It spells the end of power and politics. This supra-nationalism is to be distinguished from what Jürgen Habermas (1994) has called 'constitutional patriotism,'[3] loyalty to the institutions of plurality, as in a federation or a treaty between entities or parties of acknowledged difference, and to institutions that increase and encourage the possibility of politics.

It is possible to agree with Arendt's critique of violence, while aspiring to a politics of armed, concerted self-defence: how can this lead, or rather cede to a politics that continues to be emancipatory? How can it avoid becoming anti-political? Fanon envisioned an organisation of armed warfare that did more than what all wars do, which is to create comradeship in the face of death, a collective that will survive the death of the individual who is prepared to sacrifice his/her life. It would in addition politicise and inform the isolated and politically uninformed. This is surely not automatic. It depends on the politics of the organisation of violence. It is a matter of an open leadership being held to account by those it leads, and of all being vigilant against the propensity of the organisation of violence to turn into mere command and to an organisation of warlords and gangs.

The organisation of armed insurrection is the main subject of this book. But it is not the only possible form of countering dehumanising, brutal, atomising violence. The urban organisation of self-defence militias, and even the shielding needed for militant non-violent protests would be both necessary and part of a liberating process.

Concerted action against the violence and anti-politics of corporate bureaucracy, of states and large multi-national firms, has to be re-thought from this point. In the context of a far greater integration of places into bureaucratically organised and sub-contracted rule, we have to ask what difference urban and rural situations, the city and remote or marginal locations make to the organisation of concerted counter-violence. We must also ask what a socialist social movement might be that can hold its leadership to account. And what kind of state power would be wielded by such a movement, whatever self-defence is organised by it.

Notes

1. And bureaucratized unions, administrative organs of a working class that provide a purely defensive organisation, of income and conditions of work, were to a large but not complete extent to maintain the purchasing power of their members and a deflection from their potential as a basis for a new, emancipatory politics.

2. This summary relies on our own reading, but also on the one provided by Young-Bruehl (2006).

3. See Habermas (1994).

References

Arendt, H. 1970. *On Violence*. New York, NY: Harcourt Brace and World.

_____ 1985. *The Origins of Totalitarianism*. San Diego, CA: Harcourt.

Cherki, A. 2006. *Franz Fanon: A Portrait*. Ithaca, NY and London: Cornell University Press.

Clastres, P. 1987 [1974]. *Society Against the State: essays in political anthropology*. New York, NY: Zone Books.

Davis, M. 2006. *Planet of Slums*. London: Verso.

Fanon, F. 2001 [1961]. *The Wretched of the Earth*. London: Penguin.

Feuchtwang, S. 1985. Fanon's politics of culture; the colonial situation and its extension. *Economy and Society* 14: 4, 450-473.

Habermas, J. 1994. Citizenship and national identity. In *The Condition of Citizenship* (ed.) B. van Steenbergen, 20-55. London: Sage Publications.

Joffe, L. 2012. Obituary of Ben Bella. *The Guardian,* 11 April (available on-line at: http://www.theguardian.com/world/2012/apr/11/ahmed-ben-bella, accessed 10 July 2015).

Sartre, J.P. 2001 [1961]. Preface to *The Wretched of the Earth*. London: Penguin.

Young-Bruehl, E. 2006. *Why Arendt Matters.* New Haven, CT and London: Yale University Press.

ABOUT THE AUTHORS

James J. Brittain

James J. Brittain is an Associate Professor within the Department of Sociology at Acadia University in Wolfville, Nova Scotia, Canada. For much of the past fifteen years, Brittain's work was heavily devoted to the study of Colombia's political economy and the praxis of social change in Latin America, the relevance of classical social theory in contemporary geopolitics, and alternative forms of international development. He is the author of *Revolutionary Social Change in Colombia: The origin and direction of the FARC-EP* (Pluto Press 2010). While his current academic research has deviated in scope to evaluating class-consciousness and escape within North American societies,Brittain remains enamoured with the struggles for social justice and emancipation within the majority world. His e-mail address is james.brittain@acadiau.ca.

Dominique Caouette

Dominique Caouette is an Associate Professor with the Department of Political Science and Coordinator of the research network on transnational dynamics and collective action (REDTAC) at Université de Montréal where he teaches international relations and Southeast Asian politics. Before joining the University, he worked for five years with Inter Pares a global social justice organization where he was part of the Asia Team. His current research interests include food sovereignty, transnational advocacy networks, global social movements, and armed resistance in Southeast Asia. He has co-edited with Pascale Dufour and Dominique Masson, *Solidarities Beyond Borders: Transnationalizing Women's Movement* (UBC Press 2010), with Sarah Turner, *Agrarian Angst and Rural Resistance in Contemporary Southeast Asia* (Routledge 2009), and with

Dip Kapoor, *Beyond Colonialism, Development and Globalization: Social Movement and Critical Perspectives* (Zed Books forthcoming). His e-mail address is dominique.caouette@umontreal.ca.

Bernard D'Mello

Bernard D'Mello is deputy editor of *Economic & Political Weekly* and a member of the Committee for the Protection of Democratic Rights, Mumbai. He has edited and introduced *What is Maoism and Other Essays* (Cornerstone Publications 2010), and is the author of its lead essay. His e-mail address is bernard@epw.in.

Stephan Feuchtwang

Stephan Feuchtwang is Emeritus Professor in the Department of Anthropology, London School of Economics. His main area of research has been China. But recently he extended it to the comparative study of the transmission of great events of state violence, in China, Taiwan and Germany. This research was published in 2011 in *After the Event* (Berghahn Books 2011). Other recent publications include (with Wang Mingming) *Grassroots Charisma: Four local leaders in China* (Routledge 2001). Other related publications include 'Remnants of revolution in China' in Chris Hann (ed.), *Postsocialism: Ideals, Ideologies and Practices in Eurasia* (Routledge 2002: 196-213); 'History and the transmission of shared loss: The Great Leap famine in China and the Luku Incident in Taiwan' in Eric Sautede (ed.) *History and Memory* (Matteo Ricci Institute 2008: 163-189); 'Recalling the Great Leap Famine and recourse to irony' in Everett Zhang, Arthur Kleinman and Tu Weiming (eds) *Governance of Life in Chinese Moral Experience; the quest for an adequate life* (Routledge 2011: 47-61). His e-mail address is S.Feuchtwang@lse.ac.uk.

Gautam Navlakha

Gautam Navlakha was associated with the academic journal *Economic and Political Weekly* for more than three decades and is currently active with the non-funded democratic rights organisation, People's Union for Democratic Rights. Navlakha writes about India's military sector, armed conflicts and Rules of War, with a particular interest in Kashmir's Freedom Movement and the Maoist Movement in India. He is the author of *Days and Nights in the Heartland of Rebellion* (Penguin 2012). His e-mail address is gnavlakha@gmail.com.

Bridget O'Laughlin

After leaving Mozambique in 1992, Bridget O'Laughlin taught at the ISS (Institute of Social Studies) in The Hague. Now retired, she is a research associate of IESE (Institute of Social and Economic Studies) in Maputo. Her current research deals with the political economy of rural health in Southern Africa. Her e-mail address is brolaughlin@iss.nl.

Anne de Sales

Dr Anne de Sales is an anthropologist who holds the position of Senior Researcher in the French National Centre for Scientific Research (CNRS). Her publications on Nepal include a monograph on an ethnic minority, the Kham-Magar, and numerous articles on shamanic practices and oral literature. Since 1999 her publications have addressed a range of anthropological issues concerning the impact of the Maoist insurrection on rural Nepal. Her e-mail address is anne.desales@gmail.com.

Alpa Shah

Alpa Shah is Associate Professor-Reader in Anthropology at the London School of Economics and Political Science. She is the author of *In the Shadows of the State: Indigenous Politics, Environmentalism and Insurgency in India* (Duke University Press 2010. Also republished in India by Delhi: Oxford University Press). She has researched and written extensively on the Maoist movement in India and has made radio documentaries and presented for BBC Radio 4 and the World Service on the movement. Her recent co-edited publications include: with Stuart Corbridge, 'The Underbelly of the Indian Boom,' *Economy and Society,* 42:3 2013; with Crispin Bates, *Savage Attack: Adivasi Insurgency in India* (Social Science Press 2013 forthcoming); with Sara Shneiderman, 'Towards and Anthropology of Affirmative Action: the practices, policies and politics of transforming inequality in South Asia,' *Focaal,* 65:3 *2013,* with Jens Lerche and Barbara Harriss-White, 'Agrarian Transitions and Left Politics in India,' *Journal of Agrarian Change,* 13, 2013; and with Judith Pettigrew, 'Windows into a Revolution: Ethnographies of Maoism in India and Nepal' (*Dialectical Anthropology* Special Issue 2009. Also republished in India with Delhi: Social Science Press, 2012). Her e-mail address is A.M.Shah@lse.ac.uk.

Harry E. Vanden

Harry E. Vanden is Professor in Government and International Affairs and the Institute for the Study of Latin America and the Caribbean at the University of South Florida, Tampa. He received his PhD in political science from the New School for Social Research and also holds a graduate Certificate in Latin American Studies from the Maxwell School of Syracuse University. He has lived in several Latin American countries, including Peru, where he was a Fulbright Scholar and later worked in the revolutionary Velasco Alvarado government's National Institute of Public Administration, and Brazil where he held a second Fulbright grant and taught at the State University of São Paulo. His scholarly publications include numerous articles and book chapters and some fourteen books including: *Democracy and Socialism in Sandinista Nicaragua* coauthored with Gary Prevost; *The Undermining of the Sandinista Revolution*, coedited with Gary Prevost; *Inter-American Relations in an Era of Globalization: Beyond Unilateralism?* coedited with Jorge Nef; *Latin American Social Movements in the Twenty-First Century*, co-edited with Richard Stahler-Sholk and Glen Kuecker; *Latin America: An Introduction*, co-authored with Gary Prevost; *José Carlos Mariátegui: An Anthology of His Writings*, translated and edited with Marc Becker (US and Indian editions); *Social Movements and Leftists Governments in Latin America*, co-edited with Gary Prevost and Carlos Oliva; *U.S. National Security Concerns in Latin America and the Caribbean: the Concept of Ungoverned Spaces and Sovereignty*, co-edited with Gary Prevost, Luis Fernando Ayerbe, and Carlos Oliva; and *Rethinking Latin American Social Movements, Radical Action from Below*, co-edited with Richard Stahler-Sholk and Marc Becker. His e-mail address is vanden@usf.edu.

www.ingramcontent.com/pod-product-compliance
Lightning Source LLC
Chambersburg PA
CBHW072039280526
45788CB00006B/2111